Working Towards

Inclusive

Education

SOCIAL CONTEXTS

Peter Mittler

David Fulton Publishers

This edition reprinted 2008 by Routledge
2 Park Square, Milton Park, Abingdon, Oxon, OX14 4RN
Simultaneously published in the USA and Canada
By Routledge
270 Madison Avenue, New York, NY 10016

First published in Great Britain by David Fulton Publishers 2000
10 9 8 7
Reprinted 2001 (twice), 2003, 2004, 2005, 2008

British Library Cataloguing in Publication Data
A catalogue record for this book is available from the British Library.

ISBN 1 85346 698 0

Typeset by Kate Williams, Abergavenny
Printed and bound in Great Britain

Contents

To my granddaughters, Ellie, Anna, Freya and Marlie.
May they live in a more inclusive society

Acknowledgements

I owe a debt of gratitude to many people who have helped to change and develop my ideas over the years. High on the list are young people with difficulties and disabilities who have succeeded 'against all odds' and who made me wonder how many others might also follow their example, if only they were given the opportunity. Early in my career, Jack Tizard showed me by his example how research could be harnessed to influence public policy and I learned from Gunnar Dybwad how scholarship and advocacy could be integrated. I have learned much from my students and from parents in many countries. Of the many colleagues with whom I have had the privilege to work, I want to single out Mel Ainscow for special thanks, not least for his perceptive comments on the first draft of this book.

My greatest debt is to my wife Penny who has helped me at every turn not only by sharing her professional knowledge and experience but by sharpening my vision of what is possible and what has to be.

Introduction

Explanations

I owe the reader a word of explanation about where this book has come from and what position it is taking. At a time when inclusion is on everyone's lips and laptops, this is the least I can do.

Having spent the past 40 years working in and around universities, I should perhaps begin by saying it is not a 'review of the literature' about inclusion and makes no attempt to balance the evidence for and against ordinary and special schools. This task has challenged generations of scholars and researchers but has not given us clear messages to send to policy makers. This is not the fault of the researchers but is a reflection of the immense complexity of the subject and the impossibility of unravelling its many strands in ways that make sense to those who have to make decisions. In any case, many of these studies were about integration, not inclusion, and are therefore now of largely historical interest.

Policies change not because politicians are waiting for researchers to say the word but because society demands change. Researchers no longer need to weigh the evidence for and against something most countries have decided to do anyway. Their task is to evaluate the process as well as the outcomes of change and to address the question 'What works in inclusive education?' (Sebba with Sachdev 1997). How can we interpret and apply the knowledge that is already there? How can we best learn from experience?

It is time to move on. The endless debates and the streams of publications about 'integration *versus* segregation' for a minority of children have been overtaken by a new agenda, which is about human rights and about the kind of society and the kind of schools we want for all our children. Because inclusion is not only about schools but about society, the book has a lot to say about the social contexts of the inclusion debate and in particular about poverty and its effect on learning and development.

Inclusion is not about placing children in mainstream schools. It is about changing schools to make them more responsive to the needs of all children. It is about helping all teachers to accept responsibility for the learning of all children in their school and preparing them to teach those children who are currently excluded from their school, for whatever reason. It concerns all children who are not benefiting from schooling, not just those who are labelled as having 'special educational needs'.

When I began my professional career, some 30,000 children were still regarded as ineducable; many were living very isolated and unstimulating lives in long stay hospitals with very little to do all day. Conditions for adults with what we now call learning disabilities were even worse. Today, there are no children left in such hospitals and the number of adults is a fraction of what it was.

If anyone had told me then that the day would come when children with severe intellectual impairments would not only attend ordinary schools but succeed in passing the ordinary school leaving examinations, I would not have believed them. By the same token, I would not have expected to meet adults with intellectual disabilities living in ordinary houses, holding down a job, having a family, lobbying members of parliament or addressing the United Nations. All these things, and many more, have happened to some and could have happened to many more if the opportunities had been made available and if there were enough people to turn the vision into a reality.

I have learned a great deal from research but I have learned more from the achievements of people of whom little or nothing was expected by anyone, myself included. I have come to believe that the main obstacles to change lie in ourselves, in our attitudes and fears, in our tendency to underestimate people and to exaggerate the difficulties and disappointments they might encounter if they 'failed'. But this is to slip into the language of 'we' and 'them': hardly the words that build an inclusive society or an inclusive school.

Inclusion is about everyone being able to have opportunities for choice and self-determination. In education it means listening to and valuing what children have to say, regardless of age or labels. But as a society, we have not distinguished ourselves in listening to children, despite legislation such as the Children Act 1989 and the Education Act 1981. When it comes to choice of school, it is always others who know what is 'in the child's best interest'. Children in residential care who have tried to report persistent abuse have been ignored or punished and some have had to wait 20 years for their stories to be accepted by a public inquiry. Despite help lines and clearer procedures, children are afraid to disclose abuse because they know the consequences to themselves and to their families. A great deal has been done to improve the quality of provision but professionals do not always appreciate how powerful they are.

A guide to the book

The underlying theme of the book as a whole is the pervasive influence of poverty and social disadvantage as forces of exclusion. Every teacher working in areas of poverty has firsthand experience of their effects on the learning and development of children but we know very little about the processes involved. If we did, we might by now have made more progress in weakening the link between poverty and underachievement.

In search of definitions, Chapter 1 summarises the growing consensus about the essential differences between inclusion and integration. It makes a link between inclusion as a process of school reform and the human rights argument based on the social model of disability, which stresses that it is society and its institutions that create barriers to participation. Exclusion from school and outmoded, exclusionary terminology are prime examples of this.

Because inclusion is not just about what happens in schools, this book aims to set issues around inclusion in a series of wider social and international contexts. Chapter 2 provides an overview of the impact of various United Nations (UN) initiatives which aim to promote Education for All (EFA) and to ensure that children with learning difficulties and disabilities are fully included in these initiatives. It concludes with brief vignettes from Lesotho and Italy.

Chapter 3 summarises the radical changes to the planning and delivery of early years provision, including support for families and young children living in areas of poverty, building on earlier work such as Portage and Headstart, and asks whether and how these services will reach all families in need. Chapter 4 looks in greater detail at social and health as well as educational inequalities in British society and their impact on vulnerable children, such as those who are in the care of local authorities and those who are the victims of physical, sexual and emotional abuse.

Chapter 5 considers the impact of new government initiatives designed to reduce exclusions and truancy, such as Education Action Zones and Excellence in Cities which are aimed at areas of disadvantage, as well as more general reforms aimed at all children such as the Literacy and Numeracy Strategies. It also raises questions about the relationship between inclusion and the school effectiveness and improvement movement and the impact of these developments on children who are underachieving or failing.

Chapter 6 looks more closely at the government's policies for inclusion as set out in the *Programme of Action*, and questions whether the proposed revisions to the *Code of Practice on the Identification and Assessment of Special Educational Needs* (Department for Education (DfE) 1994) are consistent with inclusive policies. Chapter 7 welcomes the revised National Curriculum as potentially more inclusive than its predecessors on the strength of its clear statements both on values and on inclusion, the relevance of the citizenship curriculum and the emphasis on promoting curriculum access within each subject area. On the other hand, it suggests that the government should consider more radical alternatives to the present system of assessment and reporting, and particularly league tables in their present form.

Chapter 8 considers what inclusive schools and classrooms might look like and summarises some examples of inclusive practice as described by its practitioners. It introduces the Index for Inclusion, which has now been sent to all schools and local education authorities (LEAs) in England as a vehicle for schools to consider where they are and where they would like to be. This chapter provides brief summaries of some of the ways in which schools have developed inclusive practice. These include differentiation, assessment and record keeping, collaborative learning, collaborative teaching, peer teaching and the role of special educational needs coordinators (SENCOs), learning support assistants (LSAs) and external support staff such as educational psychologists and LEA advisory services. The chapter ends with a discussion of the importance to inclusion of teachers' attitudes and perceptions.

Taking up the theme of teacher attitudes, Chapter 9 reviews the new opportunities for professional development that are becoming available to teachers and discusses ways in which the knowledge, skills and attitudes that may be needed by teachers at different stages of their career can be permeated by principles and practice necessary to work in inclusive settings. It suggests that staff development programmes should build on the skills that teachers already have to teach inclusively and aim to demystify the aura of expertise around special educators. The chapter reviews the work of the Teacher Training Agency (TTA) in developing standards for newly qualified teachers, head teachers, SENCOs and specialist teachers and considers how these can be related to the government's new proposals for professional development for all teachers.

Chapter 10 returns to the social and community contexts of inclusion and suggests that the time has come for all schools to explore ways of working in closer partnership with parents and the local community and to renew their efforts to overcome the obstacles to doing so. This would benefit all children but particularly those experiencing difficulties. The chapter reviews examples of good practice such as shared reading and considers how relationships between parents and teachers have changed over the years and the potential for further developments in this area as a result of the Code of Practice and the Parent Partnership schemes. As against this, the work of the SEN Tribunal has highlighted deep-rooted tensions between parents and local authorities in coming to an agreed decision about the needs of children. These go beyond the work of the tribunal itself and are system-wide and difficult to resolve.

The final chapter looks to the future and highlights both the strengths and the tensions involved in embarking on the journey towards inclusion. The policy is based on political will and leadership from the centre and is reflected in a comprehensive and multifaceted programme of action, matched by resources that have not previously been available. But in the last analysis, inclusion depends on the day-to-day work of teachers in the classroom and their success in ensuring that all children can participate in each lesson and in the life of the school as a whole. They in turn need to work in schools that are planned and managed along inclusive lines and supported in doing so by their governors, by the local community, the LEA and above all by parents.

As things stand now, many tensions remain and many issues remain unresolved. Is inclusion compatible with the government's wider standards agenda and with a divisive ideology that singles out some schools from others and promotes partial segregation of children from one another as a route to learning?

This last tension is expressed most fully in the government's unwillingness to get to grips with the place of segregated special schools in an inclusive system. At present, special schools will be retained in an education system that also includes independent schools, grammar schools and the whole raft of secondary schools with new labels denoting superiority to neighbouring schools. Is this diversity or divisiveness? Major decisions also need to be made about the future of LEAs, whether 'statements' will be retained in their present form and whether newer and fairer funding mechanisms can be devised for all schools and pupils.

The chapter concludes with a more optimistic look at new plans for post-16 education and improved prospects for all students under the proposed Learning and Skills Councils and the adoption of the recommendations of the Tomlinson report, aptly entitled *Inclusive Learning*. Both the vision and the concrete recommendations of this report are relevant to inclusion in all sectors of education and society. The Tomlinson report sees young people's self-determination and self-advocacy as central to all planning and provision. In the field of education, the voices of children and their parents have been drowned by those of politicians and journalists. A major challenge for the future is to empower all young people to think and speak for themselves.

If so much has happened in the past 50 years, how much more can be achieved in the next 50 years? What changes will today's newly qualified teachers see in society and in our education system before they retire? How will they themselves contribute to those changes? Will they retain a vision of what is possible or will they become demoralised and disillusioned?

Inclusion is a vision, a road to be travelled, but a road without ending and a road with all kinds of barriers and obstacles, some of them invisible and some of them in our own heads and hearts. This book is about some of these obstacles and how they might be overcome and the kind of partnerships that are needed to do so.

Peter Mittler
Manchester, March 2000

Chapter 1

From Exclusion To Inclusion

Children of below average ability are badly served by our education system. The less academically able continue to suffer disproportionately from whatever acute or chronic problems affect the education service.
                    (Department of Education and Science (DES) 1991: 2).

The challenge of social and educational inequality

These words from Her Majesty's Chief Inspector of Schools for 1989 and 1990 highlight the failure of the education system to meet the needs of children whose attainments and abilities are below average. Although this analysis still has the ring of truth a decade later, it makes no reference to the fact that most children who are underachieving or academically less able are also living in areas of social and economic disadvantage.

We are far from understanding why and how children from poorer backgrounds so often underachieve in school, far less what can be done to reduce or eliminate such disparities. There is no single or simple explanation. Some blame the children for being less intelligent or less ready to learn. Others criticise parents for failing to take an interest in their children's development and for not providing an environment conducive to development and learning. Schools are blamed for having low expectations and too easily accepting that poor children are more likely to do badly in school than others. Nearly everyone blames the government for not spending enough money on children or for spending it in the wrong way.

One thing is clear: schools and the education system do not function in isolation. What happens in schools is a reflection of the society in which schools function. A society's values, beliefs and priorities will permeate the life and work of schools and do not stop at the school gates. Those who work in schools are citizens of their society and local community, with the same range of beliefs and attitudes as any other group of people; so are those who administer the wider education system, including appointed and elected members of local government, school governors or professional administrators.

In the past few years, there have been encouraging signs that politicians are beginning to think in wider terms about the social context in which schools find themselves but the process has barely begun (Dyson 1997; Mittler 1999). Families living in poverty, whose children are more likely to experience educational failure or exclusion, are also at risk of poorer health, more frequent hospitalisation and higher mortality rates, inferior housing, family breakdown and long-term unemployment (Acheson 1999). Moreover, children from Afro-Caribbean families are much more likely to be excluded from school than other children from the same community.

There is now strong encouragement – and money to back it – for a joint approach to the alleviation of poverty, involving not only schools and LEAs but also the National Health Service (NHS), social services and social security and job centres, as well as the voluntary and private sector and business and industry. This is an example of the new 'joined up planning' at both central and local level.

The government has expressed a strong commitment to a more inclusive society and a more inclusive school system. Can this be reconciled with the unequal and divisive education system that they have inherited, and that in some measure they themselves support? Can this tension be resolved? Is it even being faced? For example, is it possible to work towards a more inclusive school system when thousands of pupils are excluded from school each year because of unacceptable behaviour?

Inclusion and school reform

The aim of 'inclusion' is now at the heart of both education and social policy. Although official definitions are hard to find, there are some useful points of departure.

In the field of education, inclusion involves a process of reform and restructuring of the school as a whole, with the aim of ensuring that all pupils can have access to the whole range of educational and social opportunities offered by the school. This includes the curriculum on offer, the assessment, recording and reporting of pupils' achievements, the decisions that are taken on the grouping of pupils within schools or classrooms, pedagogy and classroom practice, sport and leisure and recreational opportunities.

The aim of such reform is to ensure access to and participation in the whole range of opportunities provided by a school to all its pupils and to avoid segregation and isolation. Such a policy is designed to benefit all pupils, including those from ethnic or linguistic minorities, those with disabilities or learning difficulties and children who are frequently absent or those at risk of exclusion.

Shifting paradigms: from defect to social model

This concept of inclusion involves a radical rethink of policy and practice and reflects a fundamentally different way of thinking about the origins of learning and behaviour difficulties. In formal terms, we are talking about a shift from a 'defect' to a 'social model'. These models have been widely discussed by writers and activists in the field of adult disability for many years but have rarely been directly applied to education, despite the close similarities in the two fields.

It is important to avoid polarising these models as though they are mutually incompatible, because we need to think of them in a state of constant and complex interaction. There is no reason why a within-child model must necessarily be incompatible with a social and environmental model. Indeed, their cooperation and co-existence may be in the interests of the child.

A defect or 'within-child model' is based on the assumption that the origins of learning difficulties lie largely within the child. According to this view, it follows that in order to help the child we need to find out as much as possible about the nature of these difficulties by means of a thorough assessment of the child's strengths and weaknesses, to make a 'diagnosis' where possible and to plan a programme of intervention and support based on such an analysis. The aim is to help the child to fit the system and to benefit from what the school has to offer. There is no assumption that the school needs to change in any way to accommodate any particular child or to respond to a greater range of diversity in its student population.

The social model of disability is based on the proposition that it is society and its institutions that are oppressive, discriminatory and disabling and that attention therefore needs to be focused on the removal of obstacles to the participation of disabled people in the life of society, and in changing institutions, regulations and attitudes that create and maintain exclusion (Campbell and Oliver 1996). In the context of education, the restructuring of schools along inclusive lines is a reflection of the social model in action.

Although the defect model *per se* is rejected as a single explanation, it remains highly influential and profoundly affects policy, practice and attitudes. It has deeply influenced generations of teachers, parents and legislators and is still part of the general consciousness of almost everyone who works in education. It is not going to 'go away' merely because academics and activists argue that it is obsolete and discriminatory.

Some aspects of the 'within-child' view are clearly relevant, particularly for children whose difficulties arise in large measure from major impairments of sensory organs or the central nervous system. But these impairments, however severe, in no way explain all their difficulties, and there is plenty of scope for environmental interventions at a variety of levels: teaching, parenting, peer supports and friendships, positive attitudes from neighbours, removal of barriers of all kinds.

In addition to children with clear evidence of specific impairments, the past decade has seen a spate of 'new' diagnostic categories where an organic aetiology has not been clearly established, even though research might in due course identify such a link. Obvious examples include dyslexia, attention deficit disorder (with or without hyperkinetic behaviour), autism and Asperger's syndrome. So far, there is little convincing evidence that accurate diagnosis of these or similar conditions necessarily calls for syndrome-specific types of educational interventions. By the same token, although we now have a great deal more information about the characteristic learning styles of children with Down's Syndrome, fragile X or tuberous sclerosis, these are again not unique to such children. What is agreed is that they all need good teaching, which takes account of their individual patterns of learning.

The very title of the *Code of Practice on the Identification and Assessment of Special Educational Needs* (DfE 1994) reflects a within-child model. The individual education plan (IEP) programme that it prescribes is based on a similar assumption and has been criticised as a device that could isolate and segregate (Ainscow 1999), and that in practice has been found to be problematic (Tod 1999). Furthermore, despite the official abandonment of categories, the Code of Practice provides advice on pupils with moderate learning difficulties, specific learning difficulties, emotional and behavioural difficulties and sensory impairments, although the advice given within these sections reflects more overlap than specificity. It will be interesting to see whether this categorical advice survives the revision of the Code, which will come into operation in 2001. The possibility of removing these headings was not even considered in the consultation document, possibly because schools still feel the need for advice along categorical lines.

Despite this categorical element, the essence of the Code of Practice also reflects a social model because it proposes major environmental modifications and changes of professional role with the aim of enabling children with special educational needs to remain in ordinary schools. The Code outlines a range of ways in which the organisation and structure of schools and the work of teachers should change to accommodate a greater diversity of pupil need. The appointment of a SENCO to every school is designed to support mainstream teachers in carrying out their responsibilities. SENCOs are catalysts, facilitators and managers. They are not appointed to carry out additional one-to-one remedial teaching.

The head teacher, governors and SENCO are, in different ways, responsible for ensuring that all pupils have access to the whole curriculum and the whole range of experiences provided by the school. But, as we have seen, inclusion demands more than this. It is not enough for pupils to be supported in having access to what is available. The essence of inclusion is that there must be scrutiny of what is available to ensure that it is relevant and accessible to the whole range of pupils in the school. Sooner or later, this range will include many or all of the pupils who are now in special schools or special classes.

Although there is a great deal that schools can do to work for inclusion, there are limits to what any one school can achieve on its own. There has to be systemic change and a national policy. The creation of a National Curriculum in 1988 could have offered such an opportunity in England and Wales. Unfortunately, it was introduced in such a hurry that children with special educational needs were initially overlooked in an avalanche of demands for a ten subject curriculum, each with its programmes of study, attainment targets (ATs) and multiple assessment procedures tied to key stages.

The Dearing review (Dearing 1993) provided some relief for all teachers in beginning the process of slimming down the National Curriculum but was particularly welcomed by teachers working with pupils with special educational needs because it provided a special needs presence on every working party and listened to special needs interests during a genuine consultation process. The Dearing report also reflected a degree of understanding of the resourcefulness and sheer inventiveness shown by teachers in both mainstream and special schools in working more flexibly within the framework provided by the National Curriculum. This was complemented by a series of guidelines and 'worked examples' provided by teacher working parties (e.g. Fagg et al. 1990) and by the National Curriculum Council (NCC), some of these discussing the whole range of pupils with special educational needs (e.g. NCC 1989a) but many focusing on children with severe learning difficulties (e.g. NCC 1992; School Curriculum and Assessment Authority (SCAA) 1996a).

The new National Curriculum, which is to be implemented in September 2000, has incorporated the concept of inclusion as a fundamental principle from the outset and this was reflected in the work of every subject committee. If this new version of the curriculum is genuinely more accessible to a wider range of pupils than its predecessors, a major step will have been taken in working towards inclusive education (see Chapter 7).

Influences from the adult disability movement

It is significant that the disability movement, which has traditionally concerned itself with the rights of adults, is now turning its attention to children and, more specifically, joining forces with organisations campaigning for inclusive education. In some countries (e.g. Lesotho) it was the disability movement that initiated a demand for inclusive schools and joined forces with organisations of parents to put pressure on government to launch a pilot project, which has since been extended (Khatleli et al. 1995). In the UK, the British Council of Organisations of Disabled People (BCODP) is also working with other organisations to advocate the phasing out of special schools – a more radical model of inclusion than that favoured by the government (Campbell and Oliver 1996).

In common with world-wide groups such as Disabled Persons International (DPI), BCODP are tireless in their fight to achieve full civil rights and to outlaw discriminatory practices at every level. For example, DPI has played a key role in UN organisations and in the development and monitoring of the *Standard Rules on the Equalisation of Opportunities for Disabled Persons* (UN 1993). Another major concern at present is the rapid growth of biotechnology and genetic research, which raises issues about 'designer babies' and the elimination of 'imperfect' foetuses (Rioux and Bach 1994).

> The disability movement has a comprehensive agenda, including:
> * the passing and enforcement of anti-discrimination legislation;
> * the abolition of laws and regulations that permit segregation and restrict access to goods, services and ordinary entitlements available to other citizens;
> * campaigns to increase public awareness of the rights and responsibilities of disabled persons; and
> * involvement of disabled persons and their chosen representatives in all decisions relevant to their full and equal participation in society.

In the UK, the struggle to achieve anti-discriminatory legislation has been long and painful. Successive governments have consistently blocked attempts to pass anti-discrimination legislation, despite all-party agreement and determined advocacy in both Houses of Parliament. The Disability Discrimination Act was finally passed in 1995, amid much controversy between those who wanted to reject it because it lacked teeth and those who argued that it should be used as a spring-board for further advocacy. Since then, the Labour government elected in 1997 has set up the Disability Rights Commission, which began work in April 2000. The commission will work for the enforcement of the legislation and also seek to enlarge its scope to include most employers and all sectors of education, starting with higher and further education.

Human rights

The advocacy of disabled people themselves has transformed the debate about inclusion and localised it firmly as a fundamental issue of human rights. These rights derive from a range of UN Declarations and Conventions, the latter embodying a legally binding commitment to implement and an agreement to international monitoring (see Chapter 2 for a fuller discussion).

The disability movement has transformed what was becoming a rather tired debate about the relative advantages and disadvantages of mainstream and special schools. Many scholars have painstakingly combed the enormous research literature on integration and valiantly sought to summarise the 'evidence' on both sides. Starting with Kirk (1964) in the USA, through to the much more voluminous current literature summarised by Hegarty (1993a), Jenkinson (1997) and Farrell (1997), the results of such meta-analyses have been largely inconclusive, partly because of the difficulty of finding convincing evidence that satisfies criteria for rigorous research. Although some general trends were discernible to those bold enough to come to conclusions, these are mostly about integration, rather than inclusion. Time has moved on and this research is now mainly of methodological and historical interest.

Human rights and research

Those who insist on mainstream education as a human rights issue take the view that research validation is irrelevant (Hall 1997). Furthermore, since research evidence is not generally a pre-condition for a change of policy in most countries, why should an exception be made for inclusion? How many innovations have proved their worth in scientifically controlled studies before being introduced? The field of education, and special needs education in particular, includes many practices that have either not been evaluated or have actually been found to be ineffective. After reviewing the evidence for a wide range of educational interventions, including conductive education, instrumental enrichment, peer tutoring, coloured lenses, facilitated communication and reading recovery, Hornby *et al.* (1997) come to few definite conclusions about effectiveness that would provide hard evidence for a policy change.

The conclusions of the same authors concerning inclusion are not primarily based on an exhaustive examination of the research evidence for effectiveness but rest largely on doubts about whether mainstream schools are able, in the current climate, to meet the whole range of needs. Like others, their verdict on the research evidence might be 'not proven' (see Hornby (1999) for a more recent discussion).

An example of a different approach to summarising research is reflected in the title *What Works in Inclusive Education?* (Sebba with Sachdev (1997)). This review was commissioned by Barnardo's as part of a What Works? series, which aims to 'make information on *effective* good practice on working with children and young people available to practitioners' (Sebba with Sachdev 1997: 5). At this stage, it is worth quoting one passage from the conclusions to this review:

> The factor which emerges from this review as having the greatest impact on the effective inclusive education of pupils with learning difficulties or disabilities is the expectations of staff, parents and pupils themselves. Staff in both mainstream and special schools can set the example in their own behaviour through their expectations, use of language (positive rather than disabling, patronising or infantilising) and apparent flexibility and adaptability to

overcome barriers as they arise. The message from all involved must be that difference is valued.   (Sebba with Sachdev 1997: 75)

This passage suggests that the main barrier to inclusion lies in teachers' perceptions that special children are different and that the task of educating them requires special expertise, special equipment, special training and special schools (e.g. Forlin 1995). Fortunately, the research evidence also suggests that such attitudes often change once teachers have had direct experience of including such children in their classrooms. Nevertheless, teacher perceptions and attitudes present the most formidable single obstacle to inclusion and cannot be ignored.

Changing terminologies

The reference to our use of language in the above review is highly pertinent at the present time. Can we really work for a more inclusive system and continue to talk about 'special educational needs'? What alternatives would be acceptable?

Many people are now uncomfortable with the continued use of language that is becoming offensively inappropriate. Their discomfort would be greatly increased by reading Corbett's *Bad-Mouthing: The Language of Special Needs* (Corbett 1996), which makes its readers confront their own attitudes, prejudices and use of language. The continued use of such terminology can be considered to be as unacceptable as sexist or racist language, which create stereotypes based on the assumption of common characteristics attached to a label.

Special?

Eleven years ago, Peter Pumfrey and I wrote a short article in the *Times Educational Supplement* in which we suggested that 'the concept of SEN has now outgrown its usefulness and should be laid to rest' (Pumfrey and Mittler, 1989; see also Mittler (2000) for a paper revisiting this issue). Even if it were abolished by ministerial fiat tomorrow, the damage done by the use of such language will take a long time to heal.

This is more than an issue of 'politically correct' language. It is about the constant use of words that create or maintain mind-sets that perpetuate segregation at the very time when we are talking about moving towards a more inclusive educational system and a more inclusive society. In this context, the continued use of 'special' is not only anachronistic but discriminatory.

If we are now to reconceptualise our field from the 20 per cent envisaged by Warnock to an even larger constituency embracing all children living in poverty and therefore at risk of significant educational underachievement, we have to ask ourselves whether the language we use serves or undermines our aims. The children concerned are 'special' only because so far the education system has not been able to meet their needs. The challenge of inclusion is that it aims to restructure the system to cater for the whole range of individual needs. We should therefore find a form of words that avoids labelling children and that instead emphasises the challenge to the system.

Needs?

The introduction of the concept of needs in the early 1970s (Gulliford 1971) and its subsequent adoption in the Warnock report was certainly useful at the time. It helped to change the emphasis from defects and deficits to an identification of the unique needs of individuals, regardless of categorical labels.

Unfortunately, the definition of needs was increasingly limited by the resources available and was guarded by warring professionals and agencies, leaving parents and the pupils themselves on the sidelines. Some notable legal judgments encouraged authorities to believe that they did not have to provide a service if they could not afford to do so.

Corbett (1996) suggests that the use of needs sends out signals of dependency, inadequacy and unworthiness. Finally, legislative definitions of need assume that some children require provision that is different from that which is 'generally available'. The aim of inclusion is precisely to change what is generally available by reforming the organisation and curriculum of schools and the education system as a whole to meet a wider range of needs. Diversity and difference are regarded as normal.

In search of a new terminology

Special educational needs (SEN) terminology has survived so long because it is not easy to find an acceptable substitute and also because it is embodied in legislation. There are areas where dispensing with 'special' may not be too difficult. At a personal and professional level, we could all try to use it as little as possible in speaking and writing. Some journals have been renamed; for example, from *Remedial Education* to *Support for Learning*. Most secondary schools changed the names of their SEN (or even Remedial) Departments to Learning (or Curriculum) Support. It is a pity that SENCOs could not have been given another name, such as learning support coordinator. In the meantime, the use of 'additional' or 'individual needs' is becoming more common. No doubt these terms too will also become discredited with time. In the adult field, the term learning difficulties and disabilities is widely used.

> Norwich (1996) has drawn an interesting distinction between individual
> needs, exceptional needs and common needs:
> * individual needs arising from characteristics which are unique to the child
>   and different from all others;
> * exceptional needs arising from characteristics shared by some (visual
>   impairment, high musical abilities); and
> * common needs arising from characteristics shared by all (e.g. the
>   emotional need to belong and to feel related).

Accordingly, I will try to avoid SEN terminology except where it is historically
or legally necessary and experiment with the use of 'exceptional', conscious that
this too has limitations and will probably be short-lived. We have learned to avoid
sexist language. It will take time to develop a language that avoids labelling and
segregation and that promotes inclusion. But we need to make a start.

From integration to inclusion

The change from integration to inclusion is much more than a fashionable change in
politically correct semantics. Even though the terms are often used as though they
are interchangeable, there are real differences of values and practice between them.

Differences between integration and inclusion cannot be authoritatively
summarised because there is, at this stage, not enough consensus to justify this.
Nevertheless, even at the risk of oversimplification, we can identify some
signposts in the fog with the help of recent publications and return to the concept
and practice of inclusion in later chapters.

Integration involves preparing pupils for placement in ordinary schools. It
implies a concept of educational or social 'readiness' for transfer from special to
ordinary school (Blamires 1999). The pupil must adapt to the school and there is
no necessary assumption that the school will change to accommodate a greater
diversity of pupils. Integration is about making ordinary schools special by trans-
planting the best special school practices, teachers or equipment into regular
settings, even when these may not be necessary. Some argue that the IEP originally
developed to good effect in special schools has been oversold as a requirement for
children in mainstream school.

Inclusion implies a radical reform of the school in terms of curriculum, assessment, pedagogy and grouping of pupils. It is based on a value system that
welcomes and celebrates diversity arising from gender, nationality, race, language
of origin, social background, level of educational achievement or disability.
Schools can do a great deal to reform their practice along these lines but national
legislation concerning curriculum and assessment, recording and reporting set
limits to how far they can go.

Booth argues that inclusion cannot be considered in isolation from exclusion: 'I define inclusion in terms of two linked processes. It is the process of increasing participation of learners in and reducing their exclusion from the curricula, cultures and communities of neighbourhood mainstream centres of learning' (Booth 1999a: 78). Similarly, Ainscow characterises inclusion as follows:

> The agenda of inclusive education has to be concerned with overcoming barriers to participation that may be experienced by any pupils. The tendency is still to think of 'inclusion policy' or 'inclusive education' as being concerned with pupils with disabilities and others characterised as having 'special educational needs'. Furthermore, inclusion is often seen simply as involving the movement of pupils from special to mainstream contexts, with the implication that they are 'included' once they are there. In contrast, I see inclusion as a never ending process, rather than a simple change of state, and as dependent on continuous pedagogical and organisational development within the mainstream.   (Ainscow 1999: 218)

Inclusion normally implies attending the school that the pupil would have attended in the absence of a significant special need. Going to the neighbourhood school is important for social reasons, both to pupils and parents. However, as Booth points out, this is not necessarily the nearest school, since government policy encourages parents to go further afield, in the light of league table results. Moreover, the neighbourhood school may not necessarily be the most accessible. Over and above any problems of physical access, it may be anything but inclusive in its practice or in the attitudes of its staff. In this case, parents may well want to look at a different mainstream school.

Inclusive education is provided in the regular classroom but is not incompatible with the notion of support. This may be planned and delivered with an LSA or another teacher in the class. An alternative takes the form of planning between the class teacher and SENCO outside the classroom to vary the approach used by the class teacher with the class as a whole or with the individual. The nature and intensity of the support will vary from pupil to pupil and will differ for a single pupil throughout the day. However, there is now much greater awareness of the many ways in which the very presence of a support worker can unwittingly segregate a pupil in the regular classroom (see Chapter 8).

Inclusion implies that all teachers are responsible for the education of all children. In this task they are entitled to expect and to receive appropriate preparation in initial teacher education (ITE) and continuing professional development (CPD) throughout their careers (see Chapter 9). They also deserve support from their head teacher and from governors, as well as from the school SENCO and the staff of support services external to the school. This should be clearly expressed in the school's development plan and special needs policy.

Definitions along these lines suggest that inclusion is incompatible with special classes in ordinary schools because of the degree of segregation of pupils from one another. Some LEAs have opted for several specially resourced mainstream schools over a wide area that take children with significant disabilities in the ordinary classroom but that may be some distance from the child's home. Most special schools have active, weekly links with nearby mainstream schools in which pupils have opportunities to join in regular lessons (Fletcher-Campbell 1994). Few of these approaches meet strict criteria for inclusion because the schools are not in the child's neighbourhood and because there is no evidence of curriculum reform to accommodate a wider group of pupils.

On a strict interpretation, inclusion is also incompatible with the long-term maintenance of a separate system of special schools, for the same reason that comprehensive education is often held to be incompatible with the continuation of grammar schools. However, this is clearly not the view of the government, which refers to a spectrum or continuum of provision in which special schools will continue to provide an option, albeit with a changed role that has still to be debated (Department for Education and Employment (DfEE) 1998a).

Conclusions

This chapter has painted a broad-brush picture of some of the key challenges that we face in moving towards a more inclusive system of education. The road to inclusion has no ending because it is essentially a process rather than a destination. It does represent a change in mind-set and values for schools and for society as a whole because the underlying philosophy is one of catering for and celebrating diversity. Although we use the language of diversity, social justice and equal opportunity, the society in which we live is still riddled with inequalities, which are in turn reflected in the education system. How can we change a divided system into one that is more inclusive? Can this paradox be resolved? Can schools show the way? We therefore need to see special needs in the broader context of social inequality and marginalisation. It is also part of part of the challenge of reducing poverty and achieving social justice.

The process of working for inclusive education can also be seen as one expression of the struggle to achieve universal human rights. Because this is a global priority, and one in which the UN has provided leadership, Chapter 2 provides an international context against which we can then consider developments in the UK.

Chapter 2

Global Dimensions

Amid so many other pressing concerns, it is difficult to find time on the world's agenda for problems, which, it may be argued, have always been with us and cannot be regarded as exceptional or urgent. But for the children who will unnecessarily fall to malnutrition, disease, disability and an early death in the decade ahead, and for families of those children, such an argument carries very little weight. If the 21st century is to be a better one for mankind than the twentieth has been, then it is essential that the principle of first call for children becomes part of the new political intellect.

(James Grant, Director of UNICEF, 1991)

We are guilty of many errors and many faults.
But our worst crime is abandoning the children,
neglecting the fountain of life.
Many things we need can wait:
The child cannot.
Right now is the time his bones are being formed,
His blood is being made
And his senses are being developed.
To him we cannot answer 'tomorrow'.
His name is Today.

(Gabrielle Mistral, Chilean Nobel prize winning poet)

Introduction

Because inclusion is now a world-wide movement, with exemplary leadership and support provided by UN agencies, this chapter will highlight some of the major developments and initiatives around the world. This will provide a comparative context for later chapters, which will be largely concerned with developments in the UK.

The UN Education for All initiative

Ten years ago, the world's heads of state and education ministers made a public commitment to the goal of 'Education for All by 2000' (EFA 2000) by providing free education to 200 million children world-wide who were not getting access to schooling. This commitment was made at a high-level conference held in Jomtien, Thailand, which was organised by UNICEF, UNESCO, the UN Development Programme and the World Bank. It was attended by ministers of education and officials from 155 governments and 1500 delegates from non-governmental agencies, as well as observers and press representatives. A few months later, the world's heads of state renewed this commitment at a one day Summit on Children in New York.

Each country was asked to set national targets for the coming decade in five domains:
- expansion of early childhood care and development activities, including family and community intervention, especially for poor, disadvantaged and disabled children;
- universal access to, and completion of, primary education (or whatever higher level of education is considered as 'basic') by the year 2000;
- improvement in learning achievement such that an agreed percentage of an appropriate age cohort (e.g. 80 per cent of 14-year-olds) attains or surpasses a defined level of necessary learning achievement;
- reduction of the adult illiteracy rate to say one half its 1990 level by 2000, with sufficient emphasis on female literacy to reduce the current disparities between male and female literacy rates; and
- expansion of provisions of basic education and training in other essential skills required by youth and adults, with programme effectiveness assessed in terms of behavioural changes and impacts on health, employment and productivity.

Jomtien ten years on

Ten years on, there is little cause for global celebration. A few countries have achieved a great deal and there are some encouraging trends. For example, the decline in school enrolments that took place in the 1980s has been reversed in all areas except sub-Saharan Africa and there has been a significant fall in adult illiteracy, such that there are now 300 million fewer illiterates than there would have been if previous trends had continued.

Up-to-date figures published by Oxfam International (1999a) speak for themselves.

- 125 million children never attend school; two-thirds of them are girls. This total is equivalent to all children aged 6–14 in Europe and North America combined.
- Another 150 million start school but drop out before they can read and write.
- In 16 countries in sub-Saharan Africa, accounting for almost half of all children in Africa between 6 and 11, school enrolment rates have actually fallen. This region accounts for one-third of the world's children who are out of school. On current trends, the proportion will rise to three-quarters by 2015.
- The proportion of girls attending schools has fallen in some countries – e.g. Pakistan and Afghanistan – but has risen in Bangladesh and in some Arab countries.
- One in four adults in the developing world – 872 million people – cannot read or write; two-thirds of them are women.
- Some Asian countries with high enrolment rates experienced major drop-out problems associated with the recession that began in that region in 1997.
- Poverty is not the sole explanation. Some poor countries do invest in education: e.g. Cuba, Sri Lanka, Vietnam, China, Indonesia, Zimbabwe.
- The Ugandan government is implementing a policy of four children in every family having free access to primary schools. Disabled children get first priority. The number of children attending school has doubled in two years.

Understandably, EFA 2000 has now been pushed back to 2015 but the Director of Oxfam argues that on present trends even this target is unattainable, and that 75 million children will be deprived of basic education in 2015. He sees this as an infringement of their basic human rights and of the Convention on the Rights of the Child.

Can the world afford not to educate its children?

According to these figures it is impossible to escape the conclusion that children are not a high priority for most governments and that other areas of spending take precedence. This is a short-sighted as well as inhuman policy, since we now know that investing in education, particularly that of girls, is the single most effective means of raising the standard of living and improving the health of the nation.

Twelve million children die each year as a result of avoidable infectious diseases associated with poverty. But all the evidence now available points to the same conclusion: 'the more educated the mother, the more healthy the mother and child. In Niger, which has the world's highest infant mortality rate, maternal primary education would improve survival prospects by 60 per cent' (Oxfam 1999b: 11).

Priorities, priorities, priorities

It has been estimated that $8 billion (US) a year would be needed overall to meet the EFA targets.

According to Oxfam, $8 billion is:
- four days' worth of global military spending;
- half of what is spent on toys in the USA every year;
- less than Europeans spend on computer games or mineral water; and
- less than 0.1 per cent of gross national product.

The total amount spent internationally to deal with the millennium bug scare was roughly twice the debt owed by the world's poorest countries. Africa is spending $13 billion on debt repayment. The cost of achieving universal primary education in Africa is estimated at $3 billion. Pakistan spends six times more on defence than on education and India twice as much. The President of Ecuador, speaking at the Jomtien conference, said that 'The cost of a single nuclear submarine would finance the annual educational budget of 23 developing countries and meet the needs of 160 million school age children'.

Many governments are faced with huge debt repayments to the World Bank or the International Monetary Fund and some countries spend more on repaying their debts than they do on education. In Zambia the government spends four times more on debt servicing than on education. Each man, woman and child in Zambia owes $700 to debtors in rich countries. A mere 10 per cent reduction in the country's debt repayments would make it possible to eliminate school fees and, as in Uganda, enable many children to go to school.

Oxfam has proposed a strategic solution to this impasse. Donor countries and organisations should offer partial or full debt relief to countries that guarantee to put 80 per cent of the money thus saved into social programmes, particularly education and health. In addition they calculate that the proportion of aid from donor countries that goes to education should be increased from 2 per cent to 8 per cent. This would cost every taxpayer in the richest donor countries a total of $4 a head.

This suggestion has met with a good response from the UK, the Chancellor of the Exchequer taking the lead in offering to cancel debt repayments to countries that undertook to invest 80 per cent of the money saved into social development, including health and education. It is not clear how many other countries are following this example.

From Jomtien to Salamanca

Although the Jomtien documents make explicit references to disabled children, very few governments have reported new initiatives to enable disabled children to go to school. It was therefore necessary to take some positive steps to ensure that governments committed to EFA did not 'forget' disabled children or deliberately give them a low priority.

The Salamanca conference marked a major milestone on this road. It was organised by UNESCO and the government of Spain and was attended by 94 senior government representatives, as well as by representatives of many non-governmental organisations (NGOs) (UNESCO 1994).

Salamanca was significant for a number of reasons:

- It succeeded in reminding governments that children with difficulties and disabilities must be included within EFA and it provided a forum for discussion and exchange of ideas and experiences on how this challenge was being met across the world.
- Children with learning difficulties and disabilities were now seen as part of a much larger group of the world's children who were being denied their right to education. This wider group includes:
  - children living on the street or forced to work, often in appalling conditions
  - children who are the victims of war, disease or abuse
  - children from remote and nomadic communities
  - other disadvantaged and marginalised groups
  - disabled and gifted children.
- It clarified the philosophy and practice of inclusion and resulted in a commitment to work for inclusive education by most governments. What follows are extracts from the Salamanca Declaration and Framework for Action, which are part of the main congress report (UNESCO 1994).

Philosophy, values and principles

- Inclusion and participation are essential to human dignity and to the enjoyment and exercise of human rights.
- Human differences are normal.
- Learning differences must be adapted to the needs of the child.
- Ordinary schools must recognise and respond to the diverse needs of their students.

- Regular schools with an inclusive orientation are the most effective means of combating discriminatory attitudes, creating welcoming communities, building an inclusive society and achieving education for all.
- Moreover, they provide an effective education to the majority of children and improve the efficiency and ultimately the cost effectiveness of the entire education system.
- Governments should adopt as a matter of law or policy the principle of inclusive education, enrolling all children in regular schools, unless there are compelling reasons for doing otherwise.   (UNESCO 1994)

The Standard Rules on the Equalisation of Opportunities for Disabled Persons (UN 1993)

A second major UN initiative is specifically concerned with disabled persons. Its origins go back to the UN International Year of Disabled Persons in 1981, which was remarkably successful in many countries in leading to lasting improvements, including mechanisms to ensure that disabled people were involved in consultation and policy making. The subsequent Decade of Disabled Persons (1983–92) was underpinned by the *World Programme of Action Concerning Disabled Persons* (UN 1983), which is still accepted in principle today.

Organisations of (and sometimes for) disabled people took the lead in the preparation of these instruments and enjoyed special status in the UN system. Understandably, they expressed their dissatisfaction with the lack of progress at national level in enabling disabled people to enjoy equal opportunities and to contribute to public life. This dissatisfaction led to an attempt to get support for an international legally binding convention on the elimination of all forms of discrimination against disabled people. Italy and Sweden presented draft outlines for such a convention to the UN General Assembly but it became clear that there was not enough support for the proposal from national governments or their representatives at the UN in New York. Ironically, it was felt that existing human rights documents should provide sufficient guarantee for disabled people and that a separate convention would be discriminatory.

As an alternative, the UN agreed to the development of a set of standards or quality indicators. These were drafted by an *ad hoc* group consisting both of national policy makers and organisations of disabled persons working under the auspices of UN offices in Vienna, and were finally adopted unanimously by the UN General Assembly in December 1993.

The 22 Standard Rules cover a wide range of needs including education, accessibility, employment, income maintenance and social security, family life and personal integrity, culture, recreation and sports and religion. Some rules are concerned with preconditions for equal participation and others with monitoring and implementation.

Rule 6 is concerned with education and is followed by nine specific points of principle and guidance: 'States should recognise the principle of equal primary, secondary and tertiary education for children, youth and adults with disabilities, in integrated settings. They should ensure that the education of persons with disabilities is an integral part of the education system' (UN 1993: 23).

For the past six years the impact of the Standard Rules has been monitored by Mr Bengt Lindqvist (a former minister and himself blind), who is special *Rapporteur* to the UN Secretary General, supported by a working group that consists of representatives from the main international NGOs. It would seem from his reports that the widespread dissemination of the Standard Rules, and in particular Rule 6, has had an impact in raising awareness, in encouraging national self-advocacy groups to lobby their governments and in hastening action, but no hard evidence on the implementation of this or other rules is available up to now.

Lindqvist has succeeded in integrating the Standard Rules into the work of key international agencies, including the World Bank's Human Development Department, the UN Statistics Division and the UN Development Programme. He has also worked closely with the World Health Organisation (WHO) in the development of a comprehensive disability policy across all areas of its work and on a global survey covering medical care, rehabilitation and support services and personnel training. In his final report to the UN, he argues for a reconsideration of a new proposal for a Convention on the Rights of Disabled People, based on a revision of the Standard Rules in the light of six years' experience.

World Summit on Social Development, Copenhagen, 1995

The Social Summit, which was attended by world leaders, as well as by NGOs, made a triple commitment to the eradication of poverty, unemployment and marginalisation. Representatives of disabled persons, who formed a strong advocacy group in Copenhagen, argued strongly that because all three of these were priorities for disabled people, their interests should feature prominently in Summit resolutions. The final report included the following commitment:

> 6f) Ensure equal educational opportunities at all levels for children, youth and adults with disabilities in integrated settings, taking full account of individual differences and situations.

It remains to be seen whether the five-year review of the World Social Summit, and also of the World Summit on Women held in Beijing, will be able to provide evidence of progress in implementing this resolution.

UN Convention on the Rights of the Child

The UN Convention on the Rights of the Child was finally signed in 1989, after 18 years of negotiation. Governments that ratify the convention are under a legal obligation to implement and to report on progress to the UN. Nearly all governments have signed and ratified the convention, with the exception of the USA (UN 1989).

Article 2 specifically mentions disability in calling for the implementation of the convention without discrimination of any kind. Article 23 is directly concerned with disabled children: 'States Parties recognise that the mentally and physically disabled child should enjoy a full and decent life, in conditions which ensure dignity, promote self-reliance and facilitate the child's active participation in the community. States Parties recognise the right of the disabled child to special care'.

It is a pity that the language of Article 23 is not stronger or more explicit in relation to the right to education: 'care' is not a substitute and carries outdated overtones. However, the reference to 'the child's active participation in the community' can be interpreted as including a right to education in the regular education system. Article 28 also states that 'primary education should be compulsory and freely available to all, while Article 29 adds that 'the education of the child shall be directed to the development of the child's personality, talents and mental and physical abilities to their fullest potential'.

United Nations Educational, Scientific and Cultural Organisation (UNESCO)*

UNESCO is undoubtedly the key UN agency that has stimulated global awareness and actively promoted national development in the field of special needs and inclusive education. For the past 20 years this work has been energetically led by Lena Saleh, who retired in 1999. Although the UK pulled out of UNESCO for political reasons in the early 1980s, this did not prevent British subjects from working on UNESCO projects and activities. Fortunately, the newly elected government resumed membership of UNESCO on its first day of office, thanks to the initiative of Clare Short, Secretary of State for International Development.

UNESCO's work can be summarised under the headings information dissemination, consultancies and teacher education.

---

* 7 place Fontenoy, Paris VII, France. Fax 33 1 40 65 94 05. URL: http://www.unesco.org

Information dissemination

UNESCO has published a large number of reports on developments in particular countries or regions or in specific areas of provision, such as early childhood. These provide examples of good practice but often include a frank account of obstacles and ways in which they are being tackled. From time to time it publishes summative overviews of provision and practice, or guidelines on planning for development along inclusive lines. Recent publications include: *Review of the Present Situation in Special Needs Education* (1995); *Legislation Pertaining to Special Needs Education* (1996); *First Steps: Stories on Inclusion in Special Needs* (1997); *International Consultation on Early Childhood and Special Educational Needs* (1997); *Making it Happen: Examples of Special Needs Education and Community-Based Programmes* (undated).

Consultancies

UNESCO can provide consultancies and field visits to governments requesting advice on the development of policy and practice in their countries. Although, by definition, this has to be at government and specifically Ministry of Education level, terms of reference can be modified to involve other ministries, as well as NGOs, such as parent associations. In Ghana, for example, UNESCO worked as partners with the International Labour Organisation and the WHO and the corresponding ministries at national level, with the aim of working for community based rehabilitation.

Teacher education

UNESCO has developed a resource pack designed to prepare mainstream teachers to restructure their schools and classrooms along inclusive lines with the aim of reaching out to all learners (Ainscow 1994). After piloting in eight countries, the pack has now been used in over 50 countries, at both pre-service and inservice levels, and has been translated into 15 languages.

The aim of the UNESCO resource pack is not so much to support schools in integrating pupils with disabilities from special schools but to build on existing strengths to enable teachers to reach out more successfully to all pupils. Particular emphasis is given to collaborative teaching and learning and to the use of other pupils as peer tutors and the development of support teams within the school to work for continuity and 'local ownership'. A particular strength of this project is that it seems to have succeeded in crossing cultural as well as political frontiers and has been found useful in many different settings across the world, including the UK (see Ainscow 1999 for an up-to-date discussion of this programme; also Chapter 9 of this book for a general discussion of teacher preparation and support).

Organisation for Economic Cooperation and Development (OECD)*

The OECD has been described as a policy think tank and sometimes as the 'rich man's club' because its members are drawn predominantly from Europe and North America and include Australia, New Zealand, Mexico, Japan and Korea. The work of OECD in the field of inclusive education is not as well known as that of UNESCO but has undoubtedly been influential at government and national level. Since the end of the 1970s, the OECD has been working in two related areas: the education of disabled students in mainstream schools and transition from school to the world of work. Their interests also include 'children at risk' and ways in which different ministries can work together to promote social goals.

In a paper that provides the most accessible summary so far of how the programme works and what it has achieved, Peter Evans, who has headed the inclusive education programme for some years, characterises the work of the OECD as 'speaking truth to power' (Evans 1999). The work is requested by governments who want to advance policy and practice and at the same time work collaboratively and learn from other countries within the wider framework of debate and discussion provided by the OECD, which can draw on over 20 years of experience of developments in its member states.

In the past the OECD produced reports on changing practice in particular countries: for example, the first report in English on the Italian experience of integration prepared by Yvonne Posternak (1979) stimulated a lively debate because of its radical approach to the closure of special schools. These national reports are written in close collaboration with governments and official bodies but often include the perspectives of voluntary organisations such as parent groups.

More recently the OECD has worked with groups of countries with the aim of distilling common themes. For example, Evans (1999) refers to a recent study involving eight countries (Australia, Canada, Denmark, Germany, Iceland, Italy, UK and USA), each of which prepared case studies of progress towards inclusive practice under a number of agreed headings. Lessons learned from this collaborative exercise are then shared with the other OECD member states and with the wider international community.

A number of key issues have emerged from this study so far (OECD 1999).
- It is important to have a single legislative framework to guide policy making. This was provided for the first time in the Education Acts 1993 and 1996 in England and Wales, where legislation for special needs was clearly included in a wider framework.

---

* 2 rue Andre Pascal, 75775 Cedex 16, Paris, France. Fax 33 1 45 24 8500.
URL: http://www.oecd.org/els

- Funding arrangements must be equitable and must not, for example, provide disincentives for inclusion.
- The training of teachers and other professionals must prepare them for the task of working in inclusive systems.
- Support systems must be carefully designed and delivered to enable schools and the education system to work more inclusively and should therefore support schools and teachers rather than students themselves.

Other key issues include:
- involvement of parents and community agencies
- pupil assessment
- curriculum development
- adult–pupil ratios
- the role of classroom assistants.

European initiatives

Although the European Union (EU) was originally concerned only with work and transition to work, rather than with education, it has taken a number of initiatives to develop exchange of people and ideas between its member states in the field of inclusive education, particularly in the Handicapped Europeans Living in an Open Society (HELIOS) programmes. Early developments are vividly described by Patrick Daunt, who was the first head of the EC's Bureau of Action in Favour of Disabled People (Daunt 1991; see also 1993a and 1993b). More recently, this programme has been badly affected by funding restrictions and by lack of dynamic leadership.

SOCRATES is a recent EU action programme for cooperation in the field of education; there is also a link to Part-Base, which enables schools and other education institutions to find partners and develop twinning arrangements (http://www.european-agency.org).[*]

European Agency for Special Needs Education[†]

Outside the official EU framework, the European Agency for Special Needs Education has recently been established with the initial support of the Danish government. It provides a forum for government representatives from 17 countries, including some not in the EU (such as Iceland and Sweden) and a key lead agency from each country (such as the National Foundation for Educational

---

[*] More information from the European Commission, DGXX11, 5 rue Belliard, B 1000, Brussels, Belgium . Fax 32 2 296 42 58. URL: http://www.europa.eu.int/en/comm/ dg22.html

[†] http://www.european-agency.org

Research (NFER) in the UK). The agency publishes 'state of the art' reports, as well as regular bulletins about developments and key issues, and also organises occasional conferences. The DfEE, having been rather isolated until its recent commitment to the Salamanca declaration, is well placed to contribute and to become a partner in European developments.

The agency has already published the following reports: *Integration in Europe: Provision for Pupils in 14 European Countries* (1998); *Early Intervention for Children with Special Educational Needs: Trends in 17 European Countries* (1998); *Teacher Support in Relation to Special Needs Education* (1999); and *Financing of Special Needs Education* (1999).

It is now much easier for people in the UK to obtain information on progress and problems in other countries. In addition to the internet, the regular series of country reports in the *European Journal of Special Needs Education,* and occasional reports in the *International Journal of Inclusive Education*, more reports of provision are now being published in book form (e.g. Mittler *et al.* 1993; Meijer *et al.* 1994; O'Hanlon 1995; O'Toole and McConkey 1995; Pijl *et al.* 1997; Armstrong and Barton 1999; Daniels and Garner 1999; Armstrong *et al.* 2000). Booth and Ainscow (1998) have published a particularly interesting comparative study of provision in which they, as editors, have provided a critical and analytical commentary to accounts of developments in eight developed countries in process of change.

Case studies

Because UN declarations and resolutions are a far cry from national and local practice, this chapter will conclude with a brief sketch of two countries that could hardly be more different – Italy and Lesotho – partly because they are of interest in themselves and partly because their approach to inclusion offers a striking contrast to the UK.

Italy

Italy is generally credited as being the first country to legislate for and introduce a radically new system. Surprisingly few detailed accounts, far less attempts at evaluation, are available in English. The original legislation, which was introduced in 1971 and implemented in 1975, was radical even by today's standards because it involved the closure of most special schools and the transfer of all their pupils to their local neighbourhood schools.

Buzzi (1995) sees the integration movement as an expression of wider reforms involving the abolition of segregation through academic selection, both being based on articles in the Italian Constitution that refer to the rights of all citizens to education. Her paper summarises the changes that needed to be made to the organisation of schools and classrooms, including the recruitment and training of very large numbers of support teachers (*sostegni*), the statutory involvement of local health professionals and a reduction in class sizes. It will be apparent that the last two programmes have hardly begun in the UK (where there is difficulty in securing adequate speech and language services and reduction in class sizes is not being tied to special needs indicators).

The impetus for school integration came from a parallel revolutionary movement known as *psychiatrica democratica*, inspired by Professor Franco Basaglia in Trieste. This involved the closure of large psychiatric hospitals and a wholesale transfer of mental health services to the community. The groundswell of popular opposition to institutions of any kind was due in part to revelations of poor conditions and lack of treatment, but was also a reflection of anti-clericalism, since many of these institutions were run by religious orders.

The legal basis for integration was laid down in law 118/1971, which stated that compulsory education should take place in the regular class 'except for those children who suffer from severe mental or physical impairments that make regular education impossible or very difficult'. No criteria were offered to identify such children, with the result that many were included in regular classes from an early stage (Abbring and Meijer 1994).

Later laws and regulations made further provision for support. Free transport had to be provided and school buildings had to be made accessible. Not more than two children with special needs were to be placed in any class and the total number of pupils in such classes was not to exceed 20. A school is entitled to one support teacher for two children with severe disabilities or four children with mild disabilities. External support teams are made available, consisting of psychologists, speech therapists and education officers.

Although 99 per cent of children with special needs are in regular schools, and there is still strong support for the principle of integration, Abbring and Meijer (1994) conclude that many serious problems remain. These include:

- major regional and local variations, with implementation much greater in the north than in the south;
- very little coordination by central government and large variations in the amount and quality of support given to pupils and teachers;
- an increase in the number of severely disabled children attending private special schools;
- teacher training not changing to meet the needs of the new system, with content being more theoretical rather than practical;
- support teachers not being well trained and often performing poorly in the classroom;
- poor collaboration between class teachers and support teachers; and
- disappointing implementation at upper secondary level.

All this was not without controversy, either inside or outside Italy. Even active supporters of inclusion refer to this early period as '*integrazione salvaggio*' (wild integration) because it was not carefully planned and because it was carried out as a matter of ideology. Despite these problems, Italy seems committed to the principle of integration and is taking steps to develop a more effective system. As a strongly child-centred society, there is every chance of success.

There is an apocryphal story of a northern city where the town band paraded through the streets at the head of a procession of civic and educational dignitaries, followed by children from special schools, each of whom was taken to the entrance to their local school where they were given a warm reception by staff and pupils and a welcoming speech by the head teacher. It is hard to imagine the counterpart of such a scene in any school in the UK, but then there are many ways of welcoming a new pupil.

A personal anecdote illustrates another facet of the Italian approach to innovation. In response to the interest generated in the UK by what became known as 'the Italian experiment', a group of young professionals who were closely involved in these local developments visited Britain to talk about their experiences and answer questions from generally favourably disposed audiences. At the end of their tour they were asked to give their impressions about the prospects of England following the Italian example. They seemed embarrassed by the question but after some consultation among themselves answered that the main difference that they could discern was that the 'British way' was to delay such reforms until the country was 'ready' and the time was 'ripe' (shades of the euro). Italians were not prepared to wait indefinitely but preferred to launch the experiment in order to create the foundations for change, even though they could not be sure that what they were doing would necessarily meet the needs of all the children involved. They emphasised that their aims were not only educational but social in so far as they wanted to ensure that the next generation of Italian adults would have had the experience of going to school with children who would previously have been excluded from mainstream schools. They hoped to build a society that celebrated difference and diversity.

A number of authors, both Italian and foreign, who have written about the Italian experience of integration, have freely recognised that neither schools nor services were anywhere near 'ready' to meet the needs of their new pupils. Despite this, there is widespread acknowledgement that intensive efforts were made at all levels to ensure the success of these reforms and to extend them first to preschool children and then to the selective high schools (Posternak 1979).

At around the same time a distinguished Scandinavian visitor who had evaluated the Italian integration movement concluded a similar visit to the UK by stating that Britain would never achieve integration because both the structure of society and the organisation of schools were too deeply divided by barriers of wealth and privilege (Vislie 1981, personal communication). Her comment anticipates the central theme of this book.

Lesotho

Lesotho is a small, independent, land-locked, mountainous kingdom in the middle of South Africa, with a population of just under two million people. It is one of the poorest countries in the world, particularly since the liberation of South Africa, which has led to emigration in search of employment across the border.

Despite major economic and social problems the government of Lesotho sees education as a priority, which in turn reflects a national commitment to education by the population at large. Compared to other countries in sub-Saharan Africa, this is reflected in a relatively high level of primary school enrolment, especially for girls, and in above average rates of adult literacy. Although there is a high drop-out rate from primary education, many young people return to school when their herding duties are taken over by other members of the family.

The government had already commissioned a report on the possibilities of integration in 1987, but as part of its commitment to EFA it launched a pilot programme in 1993 in which ten rural primary schools included all local disabled children in the regular classroom (Khatleli et al. 1995). About 300 disabled children took part in the pilot programme, out of a total enrolment of over 9000 pupils.

As a first step, nearly all the teachers in the selected schools were given an intensive three-weeks' training. A subsequent evaluation suggested that this training had resulted not only in full commitment to the programme, but in a feeling of confidence and empowerment in the teachers concerned. The summary of the evaluation report concluded:

> Our observations of teachers' lessons in the pilot schools indicated that they were for the most part highly successful in including disabled children in the ordinary classroom, despite class sizes of 50 to 100+ pupils. Disabled children appeared socially, as well as educationally integrated. We saw a range of teaching strategies, including differentiated curriculum, small group work, one to one teaching and peer tuition. We also observed a range of practical strategies to enable students with physical and sensory disabilities to have ready access to the teacher and the chalk board without being separated from other students. At all times, students with special needs remained fully on task, as did their peers.   (Mittler and Platt 1995: 10)

Interestingly enough, the pedagogic and classroom skills listed in this extract were not the product of the three-weeks' training but were clearly already part of the teachers' natural teaching skills. Teachers with 50–100 children in a class never lost track of the need to include all children in a lesson. The fact that the children seemed highly motivated to learn and were naturally supportive of one another provided strong natural foundations to a programme that extended the already wide range of pupils in the classrooms. We felt that these teachers were 'naturally inclusive' in their practice.

Our observations in Lesotho, reinforced by later experience in places as different as Hong Kong and Bangladesh, led to some doubts about the general insistence that intensive teacher preparation is necessary before inclusion is introduced. It led us to wonder whether those of us who have been pressing for more and better teacher training were not perhaps underestimating the skills and abilities already being used in regular classrooms. What teachers lacked was not competence in teaching inclusively, but confidence in their own ability to include a wider range of pupils. If this is true, then teacher training needs to build on the competencies already in place (see Chapter 9 and Mittler and Mittler 2000).

Conclusions

The brief sketches of developments in Italy and Lesotho show that progress towards inclusive education is possible in settings with fundamental differences in culture and resources. In fact one of the lessons of the past decade is that so-called developing countries have much to teach richer countries about inclusion. Reference has already been made to Uganda, which is implementing a radical plan to provide free primary education to four children in every family and to give priority to disabled children within that programme. Similarly, countries such as Ghana, Vietnam and the Peoples Democratic Republic of Laos, as well as India and China, are well on the way to developing more inclusive schools.

The leadership provided by UN initiatives and the commitment of nearly all governments to EFA and the Salamanca Declaration and Framework for Action have undoubtedly helped to strengthen these programmes, but very little would have been achieved without the initiative of local communities. Parent groups, associations of disabled persons, churches and business and community leaders have worked for the inclusion of disabled children into local schools and have demonstrated that partnership with government and with professionals can be a powerful instrument of change. There are lessons here for all countries, which we will explore in later chapters.

Chapter 3

Early Years

Early childhood should be conceived not in terms just of individual children needing certain health, education or welfare inputs but as a protected, special space that ought to receive the best of what society is able to offer. It is a special period in which children should experience happiness and well-being; in which they can develop autonomously, yet in relation to the needs and rights of other children and adults; in which they are allowed to come to terms at their own pace with the social, cultural and educational experiences of their societies. (Bennett 1999)

Right from the start

The importance of the first few years in the life of a child has been common knowledge for a very long time, but Britain has lagged far behind its neighbours in the quality of its provision for young children. Fortunately there is clear evidence that government is at last providing both leadership and resources to redress decades of neglect and underprovision in this field.

Since taking office in May 1997, the government has launched a range of new initiatives, all designed to improve the quality of provision, support families in bringing up their children and develop a more coordinated approach to planning and provision at local level. These include Early Years Development and Child Care Partnerships, Early Excellence Centres, Sure Start, Baseline Assessment and the Early Learning Goals. Indeed the scope and cost of these initiatives is almost overwhelming and it is difficult to keep track of so many developments and possibilities. Moylett and Abbott (1999) produced a useful summary chart up to 1998. The National Children's Bureau and government websites provide up-to-date information.

In reviewing these developments, my concern in this book must be the extent to which these initiatives will be truly inclusive in reaching all children and families. Although government policy statements reflect a strong commitment to the principle of inclusion, we know from recent history that there are always some children and families who are overlooked or difficult to reach and that sustained advocacy may be needed to ensure that all families are aware of new opportunities for them and for their children. Furthermore, inclusion is not only about access but about the need for planning and provision to be restructured to meet a much wider range of needs.

Setting the scene

I should begin with a few clarifications and definitions but this is anything but straightforward. Who are the children who are to benefit from improved provision? When does early intervention begin and end?

Traditionally, we have talked about 'preschool children' on the assumption that most of them are under 5 years old. But this is no longer valid since nearly all 4-year-olds are now attending some form of schooling and half of all 3-year-olds will be able to do so by 2002. More recently, we have begun to talk about 'early years', as beginning at birth and continuing to about the age of 7. When we take such a broad view, it soon becomes clear that we know much more about 3–5-year-olds than about meeting the needs of families of children between birth and 3 years old.

There is also some confusion about young children with 'special educational needs': a strange term for children who may not yet be at school and whose educational needs may not have been identified. As indicated in Chapter 1, I prefer to avoid the term unless it is strictly necessary and propose to use 'exceptional' or 'additional' needs whenever possible.

The Warnock report (DES 1978) identified under-fives with special educational needs as one of its three overriding priorities, but the report is in fact concerned with provision for children with significant disabilities rather than the much larger numbers of children living in poverty whose development is delayed and who are 'at risk' of educational underfunctioning once they reach school. This 'narrow focus' on children with disabilities is still evident today; for many people, reference to SEN in an early years context is construed as being about meeting the needs of disabled children. This mind-set is far too narrow and needs to be changed if we are to benefit from new developments at national and local level and to ensure that the needs of children with disabilities are fully included in a more comprehensive and broadly conceived service.

New policies for early years

There can be no doubt about the government's commitment to a fresh start to provision for young children. Numerous new initiatives have been launched and funded, all underpinned by a clear strategy involving priority for young children.

All children, regardless of background, are to be offered increased provision at local level but those living in areas characterised by poverty and deprivation are being given particular priority. At the same time, all the new programmes are required to demonstrate that children with special educational needs are being included at local level and within inclusive services. Of course, it remains to be seen whether government policies are translated into practice at local level. This in turn depends on public and professional vigilance, as well as on effective local monitoring and informed and sensitive inspection from the centre.

Historical context

The expansion of provision for preschool children with exceptional needs must be seen in the wider political and financial context of services for all young children. The time is long past for 'special' pleading for 'special' children, precisely because there is no longer a clear dividing line between children with and without special needs.

Margaret Thatcher's 1972 White Paper *Education: A Framework for Expansion* (DES 1972) heralded a vast expansion of nursery education but delivered disappointingly little. The overall participation rate of 3- and 4-year-olds attending all types of preschool facilities rose from 44.3 per cent to 52.8 per cent between 1981 and 1991: a far lower rate than our European partners. Indeed, the past 20 years are littered with disappointed hopes, including the shelving of a persuasive Parliamentary inquiry chaired by Angela Rumbold, then a serving Minister of State for Education (House of Commons 1990).

The Warnock committee identified early intervention as one of their three top priorities (DES 1978). This reflected the optimism of the 1960s and 1970s and the prevalent assumption that the earlier the intervention, the greater the benefit for the child, the family and society. Looking back with hindsight to Warnock's recommendations, we can see that they were naive and overly optimistic in assuming that preschool services would be made available for all children or that children with special educational needs would automatically be included in such expansion.

Preschool provision in general has always been exceptionally vulnerable to political change and financial exigencies. Both central and local government look first to non-statutory provision when they are forced to make cuts in services or to revise their more optimistic planning forecasts. The preschool lobby has always tried to make its voice heard but its impact has been weakened by the belief of certain politicians and sections of the public that young children should stay at home and be looked after by their mothers.

During the 1980s, publicly funded early years provision was not a high priority for central government, which preferred to encourage the growth of private and voluntary provision, resulting in the appearance of many preschool playgroups and a great increase in the number of registered and unregistered childminders. These developments favoured mothers who could find the time and money to attend the playgroups or pay childminders but did nothing for poor families with the greatest needs.

Some researchers were also expressing doubts about the long-term benefits of early intervention, particularly for children with disabilities (Guralnick 1991). For example, some children who received intensive, high-level interventions made relatively little progress, while others made excellent progress despite the absence of structured teaching or family support. On the other hand, most parents have reported benefits for the family as a whole as a result of the support that they received and because they felt involved in their child's growth and achievements.

The Children Act 1989 greatly encouraged the development of a framework for collaboration between social services, education, health and the whole range of relevant voluntary organisations. Although the focus was originally on child protection, the Act underpins all local developments concerned with children. It is highly relevant to the whole range of 'children in need', defined in very broad terms as 'children who are unlikely to achieve, or to maintain, a reasonable standard of health or development without the provision of services by a local authority . . . and whose health or development would be likely to be impaired without the provision of such services' (Children Act 1989).

The argument for the extension of preschool education to larger numbers of young children was greatly strengthened by the recommendations of the National Commission on Education (NCE) (1993) and by an influential report from the Royal Society of Arts (Ball 1994). They were also strongly supported in the report of the Commission on Social Justice (1994), set up by John Smith when he was Leader of the Opposition. These reports argued that the case for preschool provision was not only a matter of long-term gains for families and for society as a whole. Meeting the immediate needs of young children whose development might otherwise be adversely affected should be seen as a top government priority now.

Evidence from Headstart

These reports drew heavily on emerging evidence from the USA about the long-term benefits of the American Headstart programmes, which arose from the War on Poverty launched by President Johnson and on their smaller scale counterparts in the UK (Halsey 1972; Osborne and Millbank 1987; Ball 1994; Sylva 1999).

The longer term benefits of early intervention for young children from economically disadvantaged backgrounds have been well publicised for some 20 years but it is only recently that politicians have fully grasped their significance. They were first clearly demonstrated in a series of follow-up studies from the USA (Lazar and Darlington 1982). The American evaluations suggested that the most effective programme were those that were available for the whole year for five days a week and involved parents and other family members in the day-to-day running of the programmes. Children were selected by neighbourhood rather than individual need and were mostly black.

The best publicised example of Headstart is the High Scope Perry preschool study in Ypsilanti, Michigan. Fifty-eight children were given high quality learning programmes with the aim of enhancing social and cognitive skills. In addition to the centre based programmes, the teachers visited each family once a week and encouraged family members to follow through on games and activities. The progress of these children was compared every year with that of a comparison group from the same background. The results of this and similar studies showed that the Headstart children tended to remain at school longer, were less likely to be referred for special education, had higher employment rates, fewer children, lower rates of family breakdown and committed far fewer criminal offences.

Furthermore, cost-benefit analyses indicated that preschool education would yield a net financial benefit from increased taxes paid by working mothers and reductions in the need for welfare benefits. Ball (1999) quotes a major American review which concluded that 'Over the lifetime of participants, the pre-school programmes return to the public an estimated $7.16 for every dollar invested' (Schweinhart *et al.* 1993).

These long-term outcomes are all the more remarkable because the first results of the programmes were originally thought to be disappointing, largely because the early evaluations were (surprisingly) looking for gains in terms of IQ scores. The fact that these were not at first apparent led to Jensen's headline hitting paper, which stated that 'compensatory education has been tried and failed' and to his notorious conclusion of genetically determined differences between children from different ethnic backgrounds (Jensen 1969).

In reviewing these studies, Sylva (1999) emphasises that the long-term benefits of preschool education are reflected in social and emotional outcomes and not just in academic achievement. This comment is particularly pertinent in the context of the government's preoccupation with standards and measurement: 'The most lasting contribution of early education to children's development is the way it shapes motivations, self concept and social commitment – not formal "school" skills' (Sylva 1999: 165).

These gains were clearly due not only to the benefits of preschool programmes as such. Even the preliminary results clearly showed that children showed greater benefits when parents were involved in the programmes than when they were not (Bronfenbrenner 1974). In addition, most of the Headstart programmes not only provided a great deal of support to the families but involved them in the planning and delivery of the programme. In the Milwaukee programme, for example, support and intervention began even before the child was born, in the form of nutritional supplements to the mother, followed by suggestions from home visitors on games and activities that would provide a linguistically stimulating and cognitively challenging environment for the baby. In some cases, intensive efforts were made to ensure the economic and financial stability of the family, by helping them to find jobs. Such preschool programmes are particularly important in laying the foundations for learning and development and also for parental involvement for children from the poorest sections of society who are most at risk of underachievement and underfunctioning once they reach school (Silver and Silver 1991).

It would be naive to suggest that preschool early intervention programmes for children who are already showing signs of developmental delays could prevent the underfunctioning associated with poverty and disadvantage once children enter full-time education. On the other hand, there is insufficient recognition of the strong association between social background and educational underachievement and a certain pessimism reflected in the over-quoted aphorism 'Education cannot compensate for society'. Results of early intervention programmes suggest that such pessimism is not justified and that investment in high quality, properly staffed early intervention and family support and involvement is likely to be worthwhile for the children, their families and for society as a whole.

Recent initiatives

In the following section, I will briefly summarise the most important of the many new early years initiatives taken by the government since May 1997. The sheer number and complexity of these schemes is bewildering, especially as they overlap at significant points. The guidelines provided generally make it clear that local schemes are expected to show what steps have been taken to ensure that children with special educational needs are fully included and able to benefit. This is also built into the mechanisms for funding, review and inspection. Time will tell whether these guidelines are being implemented at local level.

Meeting the childcare challenge

Most of the initiatives summarised in this chapter can be related to *Meeting the Childcare Challenge* (DfEE 1999a). This consultation document represents a new attempt to place early years developments into a wider childcare framework that covers all children aged 0 to 14. The overall aim is to 'ensure good quality affordable childcare for children aged 0–14 in every neighbourhood, including both formal childcare and support for informal arrangements' (DfEE 1999a). At all stages, the document reflects a policy of ensuring that children with:

> special educational needs and disabilities need:
> * opportunities to participate in activities with their peers;
> * close attention to all children's individual needs and development;
> * cooperation and good communication with parents, schools and other relevant services.   (DfEE 1999a)

Early years development and childcare partnerships

All local government areas will by now have set up Early Years Development and Childcare Partnerships (EYDCPs) in association with local voluntary agencies and the independent sector. These have the duty of planning and providing early years provision for all 4-year-olds and 66 per cent of 3-year-olds by 2002 and for an integrated childcare service up to the age of 14. A qualified teacher must be involved in all early years settings developed under the auspices of the partnership. Provision for children with disabilities and special needs 'should be inclusive where possible and where appropriate' (DfEE 1999a). At first sight this language seems disappointingly weak, especially since other references to equal opportunities make no further mention of special needs and refer only to cultural, ethnic and religious backgrounds. However, Annexe 8 of the guidelines leaves no doubt about what is expected (DfEE 1999b).

> Partnership plans must include:
> - details of the support which will be provided to ensure that all early years education providers are able to identify and address special educational needs;
> - information about the childcare and early education provision available locally for children with special educational needs or with disabilities (including any special support such as the LEA's support services);
> - the partnership's plans for making provision more inclusive;
> - details of any specialist training available locally for early years education and childcare staff working with children with special educational needs or with disabilities (including training shared between sectors); and
> - details of information and advice available to parents and other carers about childcare and early education for children with disabilities or special educational needs.

Sure Start

Sure Start is probably the most ambitious and expensive programme yet. It is aimed at children under the age of 4 and their families living in the poorest and most disadvantaged localities. Starting with 60 pilot areas, there will be at least 250 programmes by 2002. Funding of £540 million is being made available over this first three-year period in the UK as a whole. It has been described by one of the authors of the scheme as 'part of the government's policy to prevent social exclusion and aims to improve the life chances of younger children through better access to early education and play, health services for children and families, family support and advice on nurturing' (Glass 1999). Support for children with special needs is explicitly included.

The joint foreword to the launching document by David Blunkett, as Secretary of State for Education and Employment, and Tessa Jowell, as Minister of State for Public Health, says:

> All the evidence shows that early intervention and support can help to reduce family breakdown; strengthen children's readiness for school; and benefit society in the longer term by preventing social exclusion, regenerating communities and reducing crime. Inside the home, we want to offer support to enable parents to strengthen the bond with their children; outside it, we want to help families make the most of the local services on offer.
>
> (DfEE 1999c: 1)

In the light of experience of the first 60 'trailblazer areas', the government has tightened criteria for the second wave of applicants for the scheme. More detailed information is required on the range of provision and services that have been and will be made available to children with special needs and their families. Characteristically, the government has set a target of ensuring that 90 per cent of all children have 'normal speech and language development at 18 months and three years' and that 100 per cent of children in the area have access to good quality play and early learning goals when they get to school (Russell 2000; Khan and Russell 1999).

The essence of Sure Start is accessibility: the projects are in very small localities, within 'pram-pushing distance' of all the families in the local community. There is a strong commitment to support for parents of young children with special needs, for ensuring that full information is made available to them and that they are financially and personally supported in gaining access to all relevant services. Evaluation and monitoring of Sure Start will reveal whether these aims are being achieved and whether parents are satisfied with the outcomes.

Early learning goals

The early learning goals (DfEE and qualifications and Curriculum Authority (QCA) and DfEE 1999), which come into effect in September 2000, will replace the earlier 'desirable outcomes', published by the former SCAA (1996a), following a protracted debate about the right balance between the importance of play and discovery on the one hand and the need to enable young children to be better prepared for the demands of the National Curriculum at Key Stage 1 on the other. The Secretary of State for Education has expressed the view that a more structured approach at preschool level is essential if children from the poorest sections of society are to be given firmer foundations for their baseline assessment in the first weeks of infant school and for reaching higher standards for the rest of their primary education. He dismisses criticism as coming from middle-class educationalists whose children have not experienced the effects of deprivation and poverty. Be that as it may, the early learning goals appear to have been more warmly welcomed as at least making an effort to strike a better balance between play and structured learning.

The principles underlying the early learning goals include a clear commitment to children with special educational needs: 'No child should be excluded or disadvantaged because of his or her race, culture or religion, home language, family background, special educational needs, gender or disability' (QCA and DfEE 1999).

A section of the document provides clear and specific guidelines under the headings:
- providing for those who need help with communication, language and literacy skills (e.g. signs and symbols; large print; information technology (IT));
- planning to develop understanding through the use of all available senses (sight, touch, sound and smell; using word descriptors);
- planning for full participation in learning, physical and practical activity (e.g. additional adult support; using specialist aids and equipment); and
- helping children who have particular difficulties with behaviour (e.g. setting reasonable expectations; establishing clear boundaries; appreciating and praising children's efforts; fostering the ability to work with other children and to value their contribution).

Baseline assessment

Because baseline assessment has been a statutory requirement for all primary schools since September 1998, it is inevitable that the content of any preschool curriculum will be affected by the knowledge that its graduates will be assessed within the first seven weeks of starting infant school. This could be within a few weeks of a child's fourth birthday. Staff keep careful records of all children and make suggestions to parents on ways in which children as young as 2 can develop their skills and abilities in areas where they appear to be delayed in reaching particular skills and milestones; for example, colour discrimination.

Baseline assessments must cover aspects of language and literacy, mathematics and personal and social development, as specified in the early learning goals (SCAA 1997). The accredited schemes from which head teachers can choose an appropriate form of baseline assessment suitable for their school must include guidance on 'how the scheme links to more detailed assessments which identify children's special educational needs' and those of more able children. Head teachers also have the power to modify assessment where in their judgement this is inappropriate for particular children.

The educational justification for baseline assessments given by governments is that they provide information to help teachers make a quick initial assessment of a child's areas of strengths and needs and therefore enable them to plan effectively to meet the child's individual learning needs. But there is a second aim, namely 'measuring children's attainment, using one or more numerical outcomes which can be used in later value-added analyses of children's progress'.

Doubts have been expressed about the extent to which these two aims are compatible and also about the proliferation of assessment schemes and the absence of quality control or clear criteria for accreditation from the centre (Lindsay and Desforges 1998; National Association for Special Educational Needs (NASEN) 1998). Furthermore, there are concerns that results of baseline assessments are being used for purposes for which they were not designed. These include identification of children's special educational needs, resource allocation by LEAs, school improvement initiatives and identification of planning needs for all children.

Early excellence centres

These are early years centres that are distinctive by virtue of being run on a multi-agency basis; for example by education and social services. Children with special educational needs and their families must be assured intervention or support from all relevant agencies, who should be seen to offer a model service to children and families.

Education action zones (EAZs)

EAZs were announced soon after the government took office as part of its commitment to raising educational standards in areas of disadvantage and poverty (see Chapter 5). At the same time, health action zones were also established, with a brief to work closely with their education partners. An additional £2 million was provided at an early stage to raise standards of early years provision in the new EAZs and in particular to work closely with the early excellence centres.

The Code of Practice

The *Code of Practice on the Assessment and Identification of Special Educational Needs* (DfE 1994) (to be discussed in greater detail in Chapter 6) contains a chapter on assessments and statements for under-fives, which reviewed the then current legislation and regulations, as well as a range of consensus views on good practice. The Code acquired special significance for children under 5 years old when the previous government began to issue vouchers to parents of 4-year-olds. Although the scheme had to be abandoned in that form, it was made clear to all providers that they had to 'have regard to the Code'. This led to renewed interest in the Code from providers who were previously unaware of its existence.

Most children neither have nor need a statement at this age and assessments of children under 2 years old do not need to follow the statutory procedures. At this age, LEAs may issue a statement if parents agree and must do so if the parents request it. For children aged between 2 and 5 who are attending a maintained nursery school or class, the stages of assessment will be similar to those recommended for older children but the process of assessment and decision making will be more complicated when children are going to social services or voluntary or private provision or taking part in a Portage or other home visiting programme. Once a statement is issued, it should be reviewed every six months.

Following a period of consultation, the government proposes to issue a revised Code of Practice, which will come into effect in 2001, a year later than originally intended, in order to harmonise the new Code with other developments, particularly in relation to early years provision.

Parent partnership schemes

Parent partnership schemes have been available for school age children in some areas since 1994 but will now be required in all parts of the country. They will also be extended to parents of children below school age, who will in future have access to independent parent supporters (Chapter 10).

A new training agenda

A key feature of the spate of new initiatives in the early years sector is that the implications for staff development and training are being considered from the outset, rather than as an afterthought. All early years partnerships are expected to develop training initiatives and some leadership is being provided centrally. For example, the QCA is working on a national framework for accredited qualifications.

The development of a coherent and integrated training strategy presents some major challenges that could have implications beyond the early years sector. Training will need to be planned and delivered to early years practitioners along multidisciplinary lines and across traditional boundaries to match the integrated approach to early years provision. Practitioners are defined by the QCA as 'all adults who work with children . . . in early years settings'. 'Settings includes child minder networks, local authority nurseries, nursery centres, playgroups, pre-schools or schools in the independent, voluntary sectors, and maintained schools' (QCA and DfEE 1999).

Practitioners will therefore include teachers, LSAs, social workers, health professionals, childcare and playgroup staff, childminders and many others such as befrienders, volunteers, independent parent supporters and parents and family members themselves. In the past, these groups have trained in splendid isolation from one another because this is how training has traditionally been organised and funded. The new partnerships will need to develop more inclusive strategies in the future for children, families and practitioners. They apply equally to the whole range of young children, whether or not they have special needs or disabilities.

Provision for disabled children

Improved provision for children with significant disabilities needs to be seen in the context of the newly emerging services for all early years children.

In addition to the initiatives already listed, a new element is being introduced by the implementation of the Disability Discrimination Act 1995. This already applies to providers in the independent and voluntary sectors but will now be extended to schools and other educational provision before the end of 2000. All early years premises, including schools, will then need to be accessible or show plans for all necessary 'reasonable adjustments' to make them so. Staff will also need to be given access to disability equality training and develop policies that 'present positive images of disability' (DfEE 1999c).

Most children with disabilities are now identified early and many are in main-stream provision of one kind or another, such as playgroups, day nurseries, nursery schools and nursery classes attached to mainstream schools. DfEE statistics for 1999 indicate that of the 448 maintained nursery schools in England catering for a total of 47,492 pupils, 12 per cent (5684) were pupils with special educational needs, most of them without a statement. No national figures are available on the number of children with special educational needs under 5 years old attending special schools (DfEE 1999d).

Nevertheless, despite consensus at least among professionals about what constitutes a good service, there are enormous variations in the quality of provision across the country and many parents are anything but satisfied with the services or supports that they or their children receive (Carpenter 1997).

At birth

The way in which parents are told that their new baby has a disability remains with them for the whole of their lives and can affect all later relationships with other professionals and managers. Despite better awareness among health professionals, and fewer complaints by parents, the way in which such communications are handled is still far from satisfactory in many maternity units. In a review of 30 studies, Cunningham (1994) reports that up to 80 per cent of parents in some studies were dissatisfied with the way in which they were first informed about their child's impairment.

A recent publication by the Down's Syndrome Association contains quotations from parents of statements of health professionals at this stage (Rutter and Seyman

1999). Although some of the statements were made some years ago, others are very recent:

> Our paediatrician has never given us anything positive to look at. She has basically told us that he will not amount to anything and be a burden throughout our lives.   (mother of 18-month-old)

> The treatment, understanding and care we received when our son was born was disgusting. I will never forgive or forget the nightmare we had in hospital.
> (parent of 10-month-old)

> We were given the diagnosis 10 days after her birth. A paediatrician broke the news to us. No counselling was offered and he told us 'You have 15 minutes to pull yourselves together and I'll see you again in two months' time. He then sent us home with a handful of leaflets. I still have a gut feeling that the hospital knew that my daughter had Down's Syndrome but never said a word. A nurse kept coming 'to have a chat', she kept asking me what we would do if our baby had Down's Syndrome and would my husband leave me if she did.
> (mother of 19-month-old)

Much has been written by parents and professionals about the first discussion with parents and sensible guidelines on principles and practice are now available, based on interviews with parents and other research. The birth of a baby with Down's Syndrome is often taken as an example, since the indicators are not difficult to spot and a tentative diagnosis can be confirmed by genetic testing. Even so, the birth of a baby with Down's Syndrome only occurs in one out of 600 births and often finds doctors and nurses unprepared and themselves in a state of shock at having to communicate information to the new parents (Carr 1995). For this reason, the training of health professionals should include at least awareness of the issues and written guidelines should be available on every maternity unit.

Cunningham's suggestions are based on extensive research with parents and on a substantial literature (Cunningham 1994):
- Parents should in general be told together and as soon as possible by a consultant paediatrician and specialist health visitor, in conditions of privacy and without students or onlookers but in the presence of the baby.
- On no account should a mother be left to guess that 'something is wrong' from unguarded remarks by other staff.
- Parents should have more than one opportunity to ask questions and are entitled to written, up-to-date information on the condition and on local sources of support.
- Parents should be given the name of a relevant voluntary organisation and be offered an opportunity to meet another parent (Cunningham 1994; Rutter and Seyman 1999).

This last point has in fact been a statutory requirement since the Education Act 1981. The same Act required health authorities to communicate to the local authority the name of any child likely to need special educational provision by the age of 5 but a survey carried out in 1987 found that 82 per cent of health authorities had no written guidelines or policy in this area (Campaign for People with Mental Handicap 1987). In future, LEAs will also have a duty to inform parents of the names of appropriate voluntary organisations and also to give them the address of the local parent partnership service, which all LEAs will have to make available.

The first 12 months

New parents need to know that there are people in their local community who can provide support and to whom they can express their concerns. Although this can come from other parents, there is often reluctance to make contact at this early stage and parents have to rely on their general practitioner (GP), who may only have met one or two babies with Down's Syndrome over many years of practice. In some areas, health visitors are attached to GP practices and are well placed, through their wide experience with other children, to offer support and advice.

Child development centres

Most localities now have a child development centre attached to a local hospital and staffed by a multidisciplinary team, usually led by a paediatrician but including specialist nurses and sometimes a teacher with experience of young children with developmental delays and difficulties. Ideally, these centres can call on other specialists such as speech and language therapists, physiotherapists and clinical or educational psychologists. Some centres have good facilities for observation, so that assessment is not a 'one-off' series of tests but is based on studying the response of young children to a wide range of learning opportunities. Where these facilities exist, staff are well placed to make suggestions on the most suitable placement for individual children.

Although most young children are now placed in mainstream playgroups and nurseries, staff and parents are entitled to information and support in ensuring that the child's needs are met. Sometimes, it might be necessary that such support is given by someone with a great deal of experience in working with children whose development is severely delayed. It is not enough simply to place such children in ordinary settings in the hope that a lively environment and the company of normally developing children will promote learning and development.

In contrast to a centre based service, specialist community learning disability teams have been established at community level in some areas to work with families at home. They usually consist of a community nurse and a social worker but with access to clinical psychologists, therapists and physicians. Such teams should be also be familiar with preschool provision both in mainstream and in specialist settings.

The case for more effective screening and provision for preschool children with relatively mild developmental delays, or for those who are at risk of developing such difficulties, has received rather less attention from the special needs lobby, which is more concerned with the needs of children with significant impairments and which includes strong parent and professional advocacy groups. By way of contrast, the much larger group of children without identified disabilities but with significant special needs lacks powerful voices to speak on their behalf. This is the group that would benefit greatly from an increase in provision in nursery classes and schools. Private and voluntary provision, which has expanded greatly during the past decade, tends to be used by people with the time and resources to bring them into being, rather than families beset by poverty, unemployment, poor housing and ill health.

In some localities, particularly in economically and socially disadvantaged areas, health visitors have been trained to carry out screening surveys, using scales such as the Denver developmental scales (Frankenburg *et al.* 1971), which provide rough indices for intellectual and language development as well as physical and motor development (Mittler 1994).

The Portage programme

The Portage programme originated in the USA as a response to the difficulty of supporting parents living in rural areas who were worried about delayed development in their children. It was first introduced in one or two pilot areas in the UK in the mid-1970s. By 1996, there were 125 Portage services across the country, usually paid from public funds (see Cameron and White (1996) and White (1997) for recent accounts).

In essence, Portage is a home based service in which the parent is supported by a home visitor in helping the child to reach short-term goals over a period of one or two weeks. The teaching targets are agreed between parent and home visitor, following a period of joint observation of the child's strengths and needs in key areas of development, such as language and communication, play, social relationships, gross and fine motor development, as well as self-care skills such as eating, dressing and toileting. Parents are helped to select methods of teaching that match their child's preferences and styles of learning.

> In its early development, Portage was brilliantly innovative and stood traditional practice on its head in a number of ways (Mittler 1996a).
> - It took the service into the home, rather than assuming that families would always travel to meet professionals on their own ground.

- The detailed knowledge of their children that families possessed could be harnessed to assess the strengths and needs of the children and to decide on appropriate short-term teaching goals.
- Family members could be highly effective in teaching their children to reach these goals.
- It did not require years of study and training to become a skilled home visitor. Anyone with experience of young children, including parents of children with special needs themselves, could learn, within a very short time, to become a competent home visitor.

These conclusions seem self-evident today but they had to be demonstrated by experience, by the testimony of family members and the progress made by the children concerned, as well as by research and energetic advocacy.

An independent inspection of 13 Portage services by the Office for Standards in Education (OFSTED) (1998a) was broadly positive. The inspection report concluded that:

> provision at all the services inspected is acceptable in promoting the desirable learning outcomes; strengths shown included good relationships, good use of Makaton signing, good quality teaching and assessment, good range of equip-ment, close links with the QCA Desirable Learning Outcomes, the supervision system for all workers and the overall teamwork across the range of specialists involved with each child.   (OFSTED 1998a)

Criticisms of the Portage model
Despite the undoubted evidence of the success of the Portage movement, a number of reservations have been expressed (Mittler 1996a):
- Home based projects can deprive children of the opportunity to attend schools and other preschool facilities and therefore to learn with and from others.
- Portage does not lend itself easily to work with children with profound and multiple difficulties, to those with additional challenging behaviour and to those with severe communication impairments in comprehension or expression.
- The Portage model assumes that family members will have the time and energy to devote to the teaching of their child and the fact that so many families have successfully done so is a reflection of their commitment. But we cannot assume the same levels of participation from the wider group of families whose children come from impoverished backgrounds and who are at risk of educational failure.

- Some families are too exhausted by day-to-day domestic tasks and by the sheer need for survival to be able to teach their children.
- Not all families are comfortable in the role of teachers; they may dislike record keeping and may feel guilty if they or the child fail to meet targets, especially if they themselves have selected the targets.
- The needs of other family members are at risk of being neglected.
- Some less experienced home visitors may set goals that are too ambitious for a family.
- Developmental gains may last only as long as the intervention itself and can 'wash out'. There is little firm evidence about the superiority of any one form of early intervention and some doubt about whether very early intervention necessarily produces better outcomes (Guralnick 1991).

Looking ahead to the next 25 years, the Portage movement faces some major challenges:

- Should it widen its remit to work more with children from the poorest and most disadvantaged backgrounds?
- Does Portage have an advocacy role not only for individual children and families but for children in need in general? Should it be politically more proactive?
- How can Portage influence and support schools in becoming more inclusive?
- How can Portage collaborate more effectively with other organisations and agencies?
- How can Portage support the development of parent organisations and promote parent empowerment?
- Does Portage have a part in promoting more positive attitudes towards children with exceptional needs on the part of decision makers and the general public? Does the public need to know more about its work?

Conclusions

The process of working towards a more inclusive society has to start long before children first go to school. Its foundations lie in a society in which parents can feel supported, both economically and socially, in bringing up a family, a society in which children are valued and cherished and in which they can flourish.

The early years initiatives that we have summarised provide fresh opportunities for every community to rethink the aims and objectives of local provision and to examine some of the hallmarks of a good service.

The following questions are relevant:

- How inclusive is the service? Have existing services changed their organisation and methods of working to accommodate greater diversity?
- Is it jointly planned and delivered by all the relevant statutory and voluntary agencies and have parents and voluntary organisations been involved from the outset?
- What training courses are available to local practitioners and do parents provide any of this training?
- How will the effectiveness of an early intervention programme be assessed both for the child and the family?
- How does such a programme link with local preschool services for all children?
- How will it prepare the child for inclusive schooling?

Chapter 4

Social Exclusion

This Report addresses an issue which is fundamentally a matter of social justice; namely that although the last 20 years have brought marked increases in prosperity and substantial reductions in mortality to the people of this country as a whole, the gap between those at the bottom and those at the top of the social scale has widened. Yet there is convincing evidence that provided an appropriate agenda of policies can be defined and given priority, many of these inequalities are remediable. The same is true for those that exist between various ethnic groups and between the sexes.   (Acheson 1998: v)

Social exclusion starts very early, long before a child is born. It is rooted in poverty, inadequate housing, chronic ill health and long-term unemployment. Children born in poverty are denied the resources and opportunities available to other children. Some children face additional obstacles because of their gender, race, religion or disability. Although most grow up in loving families who care passionately about wanting a better life for their children, too many children living in poverty begin and end their childhood in a state of social exclusion and educational underfunctioning and continue to experience unemployment, poverty and ill health throughout their adult lives. The challenge to our society is to loosen and break the stranglehold of poverty on the development of our children.

Poverty and underachievement

The early years initiatives summarised in Chapter 3 and the work of the Cabinet Social Exclusion Unit represent a new attempt by government to reduce the impact of poverty and to support parents and community agencies in laying better foundations to enable young children to learn and to develop their skills and abilities. Can government deliver its commitment to social justice and equal opportunities? Can schools, parents and local communities build on these foundations to reduce the impact of poverty and disadvantage?

The challenge is formidable. Children from families living in poverty tend to benefit less from schooling than those coming from more advantaged backgrounds. There is no single or simple explanation for these differences, which widen rather than narrow as children go through schooling but will already be reflected in their first baseline assessments. At this stage, teachers will be working with children who have never held a pencil or turned the pages of a book, as well as others who will be reading, drawing, thinking and using language at a level well above expectations for their age.

> Over thirty years ago, I carried out a study of the language development of some 300 children who were all within two weeks of their fourth birthday. Of the 100 children who were attending state nursery schools at that time, the language skills of children from social class one and two averaged 53 months, in contrast to children from social class four and five who averaged 41 months and those from social class three whose scores were at a 48 month level.
>
> (Mittler and Ward 1970)

This is just one of many studies that document the achievement gap between children from different backgrounds before they even start compulsory schooling. Although we now have a much better understanding of the complex forces at work, we are still far from understanding the ways in which social and family background and the process of schooling itself affect learning and development and what can be done to support children from disadvantaged backgrounds (but see Cox (2000a) for an excellent compilation of articles).

Until very recently, the link between poverty and educational underachievement has been virtually a taboo subject in education or dismissed as 'barmy theories' by ministers. If standards are too low or falling, the fault must lie with schools: where else? Any attempt on the part of teachers to relate the achievements of pupils to their social and family background is dismissed as 'excuses', on the grounds that some schools in very poor areas are able to 'beat prediction' by helping their pupils to achieve well above expectation. Although such schools certainly exist (Smith and Tomlinson 1989; OFSTED 2000a), their success does not diminish the evidence for a powerful association between poverty and educational underachievement. By the same token, many children living in poverty and disadvantage also succeed against the odds both at school and in society, as we shall see later in this chapter.

Although most children from poor backgrounds are brought up by loving parents and do reasonably well at school, there can be no doubt from the evidence that, as a group, they are much more at risk of educational underachievement and failure. By the same token, there are children living in comfortably off families who also underachieve, even though as a group they are likely to be more successful. The fact that there are children and schools whose achievements go against the trend should lead us to ask what it is about these children and schools that make them different. Our knowledge here is limited but we can apply what we know and support what is likely to work (Mortimore and Whitty 2000; Cox 2000b).

Some facts about poverty

The gap between rich and poor has grown at a faster rate in Britain than in any other country in Europe and is second only to New Zealand in the whole world.

Here are a few facts and figures, taken from official statistics summarised in the National Children's Homes (NCH) annual Action for Children Factfile reports (e.g. NCH 2000).

- Twelve million people, nearly a quarter of the population, are living in poverty in the UK: three times as many as in 1979.
- The proportion of children living in households whose income was below half the average income increased from 8 per cent in 1979 to 32 per cent in 1993: an increase from 1.4 to 4.2 million children. Children and young people have now overtaken the elderly as the largest age group in poverty.
- Three million children live with only one parent. Over three-quarters of children being brought up by lone parents are living in poverty, compared with 18 per cent in two parent families.
- About 1.3 million school age children are living in overcrowded and 'officially declared unsuitable' housing.
- Over a million families living on benefits are struggling with debt and in arrears for gas and electricity bills. Two in three families on benefits sometimes miss meals and have to borrow for basic necessities. Twelve thousand children under 16 will go hungry because there is not enough money to buy food. Another 750,000 will not eat a good enough diet.
- Nine hundred thousand children live in families where there is a serious alcohol problem.

Having no money and living below the official poverty line affects every other aspect of living. It causes immense stress and worry to parents and carers, leaving them little time to enjoy their children, far less cooperate with schools in promoting their child's learning. It has a major effect on nutrition and general health and therefore heightens vulnerability to illness and accidents. It is nearly always linked to sub-standard housing and to overcrowding, which in turn makes it difficult for children to find a quiet corner.

The research evidence suggests that while many children can cope with one source of stress (e.g. divorce) their resilience decreases with each additional stress (e.g. poverty). Furthermore, just as some children can cope with a great deal of adversity, others are more vulnerable to similar or lesser challenges and circumstances (Little and Mount 1999).

Another way of bringing such statistics to life is to express them as 'A day in the life of Britain's children'. The following summaries are also taken from NCH annual summaries of official statistics. A few quick calculations will enable teachers, governors and local decision makers to estimate the number of children in their school or community who are likely to be experiencing disadvantage and who are therefore at risk of underachievement and social and educational exclusion.

Today and every day:
- parents of over 400 children will divorce: two children per hundred will have this experience each year and 25 per cent will have done so by the age of 16;
- 300 children will be accepted as homeless and be found accommodation;
- 81 children will be taken into care;
- 87 children will be added to child protection registers;
- 150 children will be born to teenage mothers;
- 1,500 children will truant from school: 1 million over a year;
- over 3,500 children will be victims of assault;
- 620,000 cigarettes will be smoked by young people aged 15 and 16;
- 3 million children will be in part-time work, 2.25 million of them illegally because they are too young or working the wrong hours.

Inequalities in health

We now know a lot more about gross inequalities in health and their social consequences than we do about inequalities in education but few attempts have been made to bring the two sets of data together, although they are obviously closely related.

Twenty years ago, the government of the day commissioned a major review of available knowledge from three distinguished academics from medicine and social sciences. This report (known as the 'Black report') was both rejected and suppressed by the then Secretary of State, although it was later reissued as a paperback by one of the authors (Townsend and Whitehead 1988).

The quotation at the head of this chapter is taken from the introduction to *Inequalities in Health,* which was commissioned by the government from its former Chief Medical Officer of Health (Acheson 1998). This report has been well publicised and has led, among other things, to the launching of Health Action Zones and to a joint approach to planning and provision reflected in initiatives discussed in Chapter 3, such as Sure Start and early excellence centres, as well as EAZs. Although focusing primarily on health, the report is equally relevant to education and to social policy generally.

The following are brief extracts from the report.

- The nutritional status of poor expectant and young mothers is a matter of grave concern and should receive priority attention.
- Out of every 10,000 babies born into social class five, 99 were stillborn or died within the first week of life, compared with 67 for social class one. Comparable figures for death in the first year of life were 83 and 46 respectively. Infant and childhood death rates have fallen steadily since 1986 but are still the highest in Europe.
- More than two-thirds of the babies born to women on a low income in one study were below the national average in birth weight. This in turn greatly raises the risk of heart disease, stroke and high blood pressure in later life and is also linked to delayed language development.
- Over half the households accepted by local authorities as homeless had dependent children and a further tenth had a pregnant household member.
- Of the 56,000 teenagers who gave birth in England, 3,700 were under 16. The UK teenage pregnancy rate is the highest in Europe: seven and a half times that of the Netherlands.
- Children in low income groups have twice as much long-standing illness as those in social class one. One in seven children (1.3 million) is affected by asthma, 155 being hospitalised every day.
- 2,700 children will have an accident and go to hospital. Children in social class five are four times more likely to die in an accident than those from social class one.
- 13 per cent of 11–15-year-olds in England are classified as regular smokers; 10 per cent of 14–15-year-olds considered themselves to be regular drug users; approximately a third have tried cannabis, the number rising to over a half at 18 and 19. Nearly all had drunk alcohol by the age of 16.
- Two million children will experience mental health problems, including 270,000 with a major depressive disorder.
- Suicide rates in young men are three times higher in poorer than in affluent areas.
- Studies of the health of ethnic minorities have concluded that the poorer health suffered in these communities (which varies from group to group) is a reflection of poverty.

An earlier survey of 120 young people living on a low income and mostly on benefits carried out in 1993 reported that, in the past 24 hours, 91 per cent had eaten no fresh fruit, 70 per cent no fresh meat or fish, 56 per cent no vegetables or salad and 30 per cent no bread or cereals. Many of these young people were or would soon become parents (NCH 1998).

These figures make it clear that the challenge of meeting health inequalities is not a matter for the NHS alone but affects all professions and services.

Poverty and educational attainment

Information on the association between social background and educational attainment has been available for a long time (Kumar 1993) but it is only now that government is beginning to address the challenges presented by such findings.

The National Child Development Study of some 17,000 children, all born in one week in 1958, has been documenting the educational and social development of cohorts of children from different backgrounds. Right from the beginning, the studies identified a group of children characterised as 'disadvantaged', using the then agreed objective criteria of low income and free school meals, severe overcrowding and lone parenting or coming from a large family (Davie *et al.* 1972; Wedge and Prosser 1973). The subsequent development of this group has been traced right through to their mid-thirties and beyond (Ferri 1993). Another group of children born in 1970 has also been followed to the present day, with similar results (Centre for Longitudinal Studies 1999; Feinstein and Symons 1999).

A few results from the National Child Development Study provide clear illustrations of the strength of the links between social background and educational outcomes:

- At the age of 7, five times as many children from social class five had reading difficulties as compared with those from social class one.
- At the age of 11, children with fathers in non-manual occupations were three years ahead in maths and reading compared with children in social class five.
- At the age of 16, 75 per cent of pupils from social class five had below average reading and maths scores and more showed behaviour problems.
- Half the pupils on free school meals had GCSE scores below 15 points, compared with one-sixth of those not on free school meals (Acheson 1998).
- Although a much higher proportion of the whole age group continue at school beyond 16 or proceed to higher education, only 14 per cent from an unskilled socioeconomic background enter higher education, compared with 80 per cent of young people from a professional background (NCH 2000).
- At the age of 33, women with low levels of literacy were five times more likely to be depressed, to feel excluded and to have difficulties in ordinary social life (Ferri 1993).

More recently, significant social class and postcode differences have been obtained from analyses of Standard Attainment Tasks (SATs) at Key Stage 1 (Shorrocks 1993) and Key Stage 2 (McCallum, 1997). The latter study suggested that 80 per cent of the differences between children's scores at this stage could be accounted for by home rather than school factors.

On the other hand, 11-year-olds in half the LEAs studied were performing better in the tests than would have been statistically expected from their socio-economic status. Similar though weaker relationships were found for GCSE results (McCallum 1996). It is findings such as these that have, justifiably, led to attempts to define and measure how schools 'add value' to the starting level of their intake, whether this is average, high or low, although the search for robust measures is proving elusive (Saunders 1996).

Vulnerable and looked after children

One of the first distress signals that children send out when they are under stress or unhappy for any reason, is that their school work or behaviour deteriorates, some-times quite dramatically. Although teachers become aware of this quite quickly, they often hope the problem is temporary and are reluctant to discuss their concerns with the child or the family or even with senior colleagues.

Although many children in our society have daily experience of family discord, stress and danger, teachers rarely have opportunities to become aware of the home lives of the children they teach. Unless children themselves or their parents or carers volunteer information either spontaneously or in response to teachers' questions, it is difficult for teachers to break through the barriers that traditionally separate home from school, even when both sides feel that the sharing of informa-tion would be in everyone's best interests. When children taken into care have talked about their experiences, they often speak very positively about individual teachers who have gone out of their way to listen to them and to meet their individual needs but without drawing attention to them unduly. In this respect, teachers are singled out rather more favourably than social workers (Jackson 2000).

Social services for children

Social work with children has changed out of all recognition in the past 10 years, since the implementation of the Children Act 1991 (NCH 1998, 2000; Jackson 2000).

- 90 per cent of children receive services while continuing to live at home (NCH 1998).
- There are about 53,300 'looked after children' in England, that is children who cannot live with their families or who are subject to a care order; this is perhaps two children per school on average, although numbers will be much higher in some areas.
- More than two-thirds of looked after children live with foster families. Less than 10 per cent of children in care are in local authority community homes.
- The most common reasons for social services starting to look after children are to give relief to parents (26 per cent), parents' health (12 per cent) and concern for the child's welfare (8 per cent). The figures for abuse and neglect reflect a rapid increase from 18 per cent in 1993–94 to 26 per cent in 1998 (NCH 2000).
- Many children are looked after for only short periods, about 30,000 entering and leaving this status every year.

Looked after children not attending school

Children who are looked after tend to drop out of the educational system for long periods because there is no clear allocation of responsibility for ensuring continuity of education. 'Once in care, an almost complete absence of educational support was a common experience' (Jackson 2000: 71). They are ten times more likely to be excluded and six to eight times more likely to have a statement of special educational needs than children living at home (NCH 2000).

A study of young people in or leaving care by Save the Children (quoted in NCH 1998) found that over a third said they had no support while at school, were heavily involved in fights and bullying and were punished a great deal by staff. They have an appalling record of school attendance and permanent exclusion. According to two recent surveys, 75 per cent leave school with no formal qualifications and only one in 300 goes on to higher education (NCH 1998; Little and Mount 1999). Studies of young people leaving care aged 18 show that between 50 and 80 per cent are unemployed and that many soon become homeless and are sleeping rough. Sonia Jackson has compared the experience of many looked after children with that of refugees or displaced persons. She quotes research that shows that 28 per cent had moved house more than six times and 9 per cent more than ten times in a single year.

Information about children in care not attending school has been in the public domain for many years but it is only now after a period of consultation on a draft circular, that the government has announced a series of measures designed to address the problem (*Times Educational Supplement* (*TES*) 24 December 1999).

The five new statutory requirements for looked after children are:
- the linking of education and care placements;
- a 20-day limit on finding a school place for the child;
- a personal education plan for every child in care;
- a designated teacher in each school to act as advocate and bring together support services; and
- a protocol within each local authority for sharing information.

Detailed action plans, based on work in pilot authorities and suggesting specific objectives for different agencies and for all of them acting jointly, have been published in a *Practice Guide*, published by the Who Cares? Trust (1999), a consortium comprising the Calouste Gulbenkian Foundation, the Department of Health (DoH) and the DfEE.

The government is making a strong effort to achieve much closer working relationships between social services and other agencies, particularly health and education. This arises from concern about the safety and standards of care available to the most vulnerable children, particularly those who are being 'looked after' by local authorities, whether they are living with their own families, with foster parents or in residential care. The work of the EYDCPs includes plans for collaboration on looked after and other vulnerable children up to the age of 14.

A new Children's Grant of £375 million has been established to fund improvements and new quality assurance and inspection mechanisms are being put in place. Each local authority will need to publish annual management action plans, which set out how each agency will strengthen and improve their services to meet new objectives. The first tranche of money focused on joint approach between education and social services but these were joined by health in the second round.

These reforms are overdue and badly needed but will they improve the life chances and educational opportunities for looked after children? Sonia Jackson sounds a positive note while criticising government for constantly failing to mention looked after children in the many new more broadly based initiatives that have been launched in the past three years, such as EAZs and Excellence in Cities. In this respect, the special needs lobby has been far more successful in ensuring that the interests of 'their' children are taken into account in all new government programmes. Unlike children with dyslexia or sensory impairment, looked after children have few advocates in parliament or in council chambers. This may go a long way to explaining the low priority that has characterised planning and provision and why they remain vulnerable.

Child protection and abuse

We now know that child abuse is much more common than was commonly assumed 10–15 years ago and that many children are abused by a member of the family or by someone they know well rather than by complete strangers. Unfortunately, despite much greater awareness and many initiatives at all levels, NCH Action for Children concludes that 'the abuses persist largely unaffected by such efforts as have been taken to prevent them' (NCH 1998).

There are 32,351 children under 18-years-old on child protection registers in England, 2,473 in Wales and 2,479 in Scotland. This is around one-third of 1 per cent: say three children in a school of 1,000 pupils at any one time. These figures reflect a sharp drop from a high of 45,000 in 1991, although they are now stable. It has to be remembered that the names on a local register will change frequently. As some children are taken off the list because they are no longer considered at risk, new children are entered for the first time.

Neglect accounts for 41 per cent of all children on registers, followed by physical injury (31 per cent), sexual abuse (21 per cent) and emotional abuse (16 per cent). (Some children are in more than one category.) Eight thousand children on protection registers are looked after by local authorities, around 5,000 of them living with foster families.

These figures greatly underestimate the true number of children being abused, partly because most cases of abuse are not disclosed or reported and partly because some cases are resolved before they go on a register.

Official definitions of neglect and abuse are as follows (but these are under review):

- *Neglect*: The persistent or severe neglect of a child or the failure to protect a child from exposure to any kind of danger, including cold or starvation, or extreme failure to carry out important aspects of care, resulting in significant impairment of the child's health or development, including non-organic failure to thrive.
- *Physical abuse*: Actual or likely physical injury to a child, or failure to prevent physical injury (or suffering) to a child, including deliberate poisoning, suffocation and Munchausen's syndrome by proxy.
- *Sexual abuse:* Actual or likely sexual exploitation of a child or adolescent. The child may be dependent and/or developmentally immature.
- *Emotional abuse*: Actual or likely severe adverse effect on the emotional and behavioural development of a child caused by persistent or severe emotional ill treatment or rejection. All abuse involves some emotional ill treatment. This category is used where it is the main or sole form of abuse.

There is now a substantial body of research on child sexual abuse summarised by the DoH (1995) (cited by NCH 2000).

- Child sexual abuse occurs across the whole spectrum of society but around half the families involved had a range of other problems related to severe poverty, such as chronic ill health, unemployment and poor housing.
- Effects on the victims are deep-seated and long term and may have a severely damaging effect on their own emotional and social development and ability to enter into adult sexual relationships. About half the children experienced post-traumatic stress disorder and 60 per cent of those removed from their own homes had suicidal thoughts or severe emotional or behavioural problems. Some become abusers in their turn and many remained vulnerable and unsafe even after extensive professional intervention. 42 per cent of child prostitutes in one study reported that their first sexual experience was one of abuse, sometimes occurring before the age of 10.
- Many children are not offered or do not receive therapeutic help, such as counselling, despite evidence that such help is often effective.
- The needs of family members, including non-abusing members, were often not met, resulting in significant psychological problems.
- Very few cases resulted in a successful conviction of alleged offenders. Many cases were not prosecuted because of lack of evidence that was thought likely to convince a court.

Escape from disadvantage

One of the most interesting areas of social science research concerns groups or individuals whose development 'beats prediction'. Despite all we know about the strong association between poverty and educational underachievement, these are after all only averages, trends and correlations and there will always be individuals whose achievements in school and in later life far exceed what might have been predicted from a knowledge of their early development. What is known about these individuals? What, if anything, do they have in common? What lessons can they teach us? A few studies have thrown some light on these questions.

The work of Kolvin in Newcastle upon Tyne is particularly interesting in this context (Kolvin et al. 1990). He and his associates traced a group of adults in their 30s who had been part of an exhaustive study of a group of children born in the city in May and June 1947. The study highlighted six aspects of deprivation: marital disruption, parental illness, poor care of the child and home, dependence on social services, overcrowding and poor parenting. Where three of these factors were present, 60 per cent of men and 10 per cent of women had committed criminal offences by the age of 33. Poor maternal and domestic care were the most powerful predictive factors, a finding addressed by the government's current Sure Start initiative, discussed in the previous chapter. The Newcastle study underlines the strong protection afforded by good maternal care and a warm supportive home life. Other protective factors included continuous engagement with school, family involvement in the school and the child's own temperament, particularly having a positive outlook on life.

Using the original National Child Development Study sample, Pilling (1990) looked in some detail at a group of young people who had 'escaped from disadvantage', with the aim of teasing out statistically and through structured interviews any special factors or circumstances that might distinguish this group from a less successful comparison group also characterised as socially disadvantaged. The results are complex but some trends did emerge.

- Boys seem to be particularly susceptible to social disadvantage in early childhood, whereas girls are more vulnerable at adolescence.
- Almost all the educational achievers were still living with both their parents at the age of 16, compared with only around half the comparison group. At the age of 23, only a quarter of the achievers gave 'problems at home' as the reason for leaving home, compared with half the comparison group.
- Differences in degree of parental interest in their child's educational progress were described as 'dramatic' by Pilling (1990: 196), this applying much more to fathers than to mothers.
- 'At least a third of the achievers had homes which combined parental involvement with the child in activities likely to be educationally stimulating, some interest in learning, an emphasis on the importance of school work and at least moderate ambition for the child' (Pilling 1990: 197). None of the comparison group appear to have had this kind of environment.
- Other differentiating factors included: shared practising religious belief and value system; self-employed status of father; the social composition of the school attended and encouragement from individual teachers, although this was ineffective without matching support from the home. The young people themselves saw determination and hard work as the main explanation of their success.

Building on the fact that the majority of looked after children are within the normal range of intelligence, Sonia Jackson (2000) identified a group of young people who had spent more than a year in care and obtained five or more General Certificate of Secondary Education (GCSE) examination passes at grade C or above. The subsequent career path of this group was strikingly more successful than that of other young people with similar experiences and care histories but who lacked educational qualifications. It seemed that education had enabled them to escape from adversity. They were also regarded as particularly resilient individuals, despite a whole series of damaging experiences: a third were the victims of serious physical, sexual or emotional abuse and neglect (Jackson 2003).

Jackson also draws an instructive parallel with the experience of 70,000 Bosnian children who arrived homeless and traumatised in Slovenia in a single month in 1992. The authorities gave top priority to the establishment of schools in the refugee camps and insisted on regular attendance and high standards of teaching and learning in the belief that normalisation of routine was the best approach to trauma. A follow-up study five years' later found that the children seemed to have adjusted both psychologically and educationally and were doing as well as their Slovenian peers (Jackson 2000: 68).

These studies show how education can provide an escape route from poverty, a finding that has at last penetrated political consciousness and is clearly reflected in David Blunkett's speech to the North of England conference (Blunkett 2000). Educational reform must be an integral component of social and humanitarian reform. The government now accepts in principle that school inclusion is only one facet of social inclusion.

A quotation from the final paragraph of Doria Pilling's book sets the agenda:

> The study re-emphasises the need for economic policies which will revive deprived and high unemployment areas, as well as a social security system that is more generous in its attitudes. Ways of giving more practical help and emotional support to families under stress also need to be sought. The study indicates that there should be continuing educational opportunities throughout the working life, including financial support, even for those with earlier failures and particularly for women. It suggests a need for schools, especially those in deprived areas, to have a more optimistic view of their pupils' abilities.   (Pilling 1990: 200)

Conclusions

This chapter has illustrated ways in which the forces of social exclusion affect the lives of children and families and summarised some of the available factual information about the number of children who are experiencing severe stress and living in conditions that we know to be unfavourable to learning. These include family breakdown, homelessness, separation from family and child abuse. These figures affect every school and impinge on the work of every teacher but there are few mechanisms for teachers to know about, far less support children who are vulnerable and under severe stress.

No school is an island, but discussions about educational reform often seem to be conducted in a social vacuum. Teachers are trained to teach their subjects in classrooms and now have to demonstrate several hundred competencies before they can be licensed. Their training makes little or no reference to the social contexts in which they will be teaching, nor does it prepare them to work with parents as equal partners. Once in school, there are few opportunities for them to become familiar with the community around them, to learn about the work of other agencies such as health, social services or voluntary agencies or to know about the range of provision that is available outside the school system. Most important of all, teachers often have little idea of how children live outside school and cannot know about the problems and crises being experienced by the families of the children they teach. They may be unaware of social work involvement in the lives of children and are not always informed even if a care or supervision order has been taken out for pupils with whom they are in daily contact.

The reasons for this will vary but no one can doubt that there are major barriers to the sharing of information between different agencies and among the professionals working in them, all claiming insight into 'the best interests of the child'. Although the Children Act 1989 tried to legislate for a 'whole authority' approach, there is still a huge gulf between teachers and social workers and between both of them and health professionals and voluntary agencies, with misconceptions and stereotypes on all sides.

Teachers are understandably reluctant to appear to be prying into the private lives of families, far less initiate any action that might be resented as interference by the family and particularly by the children themselves. By the same token, parents may assume that teachers are not interested in their family's problems. At the formal level, there are few channels of communication between schools and social work or voluntary agencies who may already be involved with a child. Teachers often say 'I'm not a social worker' and social workers in their turn have a duty to protect confidentiality until there is clear agreement on the part of those involved that it is in the interest of the child to share information. Child protection procedures are in a class of their own because there are clear, statutory guidelines as well as codes of professional practice that teachers and schools must follow if they suspect that a child is being abused physically, sexually or emotionally, or in a combination of all three.

A major task for the next decade, therefore, is to find new ways of breaking down the barriers between schools and families. Parents will need to feel that they can take schools into their confidence when there are problems at home: schools must organise themselves in such a way as to make this possible.

Chapter 5

Can Schools Prevent Learning Difficulties?

> Success for a few was an option in the past. Success for all is the challenge
> now.
> (Blunkett 2000: 8)

When the government first embarked on its whirlwind programme of educational reform, there seemed to be an implicit assumption that a determined drive to 'raise standards' would somehow reach all children. This was later seen to be naive and the government has now launched a number of new initiatives that focus directly on loosening the stranglehold of poverty on underachievement. This chapter will discuss major challenges confronting schools and summarise some of the measures proposed by government to address them. In reviewing these initiatives, we again need to scrutinise the extent to which they are likely to lead to a more inclusive society and educational system.

Challenges

Schools in areas of poverty are themselves working under multiple disadvantages, not least of which is a failure by politicians and media pundits to recognise the distinctive challenge that they face, namely that of helping their pupils to escape from the vicious cycle of underexpectation and to raise their motivation and self-esteem. Unlike their colleagues in more affluent areas, teachers cannot assume that parents will necessarily know about or be supportive of their work and cannot count on their cooperation. Many schools feel themselves to be in a state of siege, bombarded with criticism by politicians, the national and local media and at greater risk of being put into special measures or declared to be failing. The morale of staff is sometimes even lower than that of pupils and there is a high rate of sickness and stress. The main official yardstick of success – grade C or above GCSE examination results or level 4 at Key Stage 2 national tests – fails to capture much of what the schools are trying to achieve.

Low expectations: low achievement

A targeted programme of support seems justified by a whole series of earlier national Her Majesty's Inspectorate of School (HMI) and OFSTED reports that suggest that too many schools accept that underachievement in pupils and underestimation by staff are endemic.

Low expectations can be crippling because they result in self-fulfilling prophecies. If children are not expected to achieve above a certain level, it is only a few who 'buck the trend'. A long time ago, Douglas (1964) and Barker-Lunn (1970) first showed that teachers in English primary schools were heavily influenced by family background when making decisions about streaming, even for children within the same ability range, and that the subsequent development of the pupils could be interpreted as either confirming their predictions or locking the children into a self-fulfilling prophecy. At that time, children in top streams were expected to pass the 11+ exams while those in other streams were not expected to do so. At around the same time, the classic study (probably unethical) by Rosenthal and Jacobsen (1968) in New York showed that children's educational attainments rose rapidly after teachers were deliberately misinformed that special tests had shown them to be of superior intelligence.

The number of pupils leaving school with no qualifications has fallen from 50,00 to 35,000, while the percentage of pupils with five higher grade GCSE examination passes has continued to rise. But GCSE examination results show that only 33 per cent of 'inner city' pupils obtain five or more passes at grade C or above (or their vocational equivalent), compared with a national average of 46 per cent. Three out of four inner city schools fail to approach the national target of 50 per cent. The disparities remain even when the criterion is lowered to a single pass at grade G of GCSE/General National Vocational Qualification (GNVQ), although here there is a very wide variation between such schools, compared to metropolitan boroughs in general, outer London and unitary and shire authorities.

An OFSTED study of schools, support services and further and adult education provision in seven urban areas of social and economic disadvantage concluded that 'residents of disadvantaged urban areas were poorly served by the education system' (OFSTED 1993: 6).

The report highlighted a number of key findings that particularly disadvantaged children from economically deprived communities but also drew on examples of good practice to make suggestions for progress.
- Curricular planning does not address the needs of children from disadvantaged backgrounds and does not focus sufficiently on raising achievement.
- Underachievement is apparent at an early stage. Many pupils never recover from early failure in basic skills.

- Arrangements for learning support are poor. Schools lack expertise in initial assessment.
- Much teaching is superficial and lacks pace. The atmosphere in many classrooms is good natured but neither challenges the pupils nor secures their participation.

The report concluded that while the quality and standards of work revealed by their survey are inadequate and disturbing, there is enough work of good quality in each sector to mean that the situation is not irremediable. The report recommended that 'long term planning, improved dissemination of effective practice, carefully focused interventions and concerted efforts are required to bring about improvement' (OFSTED 1993: 45).

The annual report of Her Majesty's Chief Inspector of Schools for 1997/1998 (OFSTED 1999a) includes a section summarising a series of OFSTED inspections of services designed to counter disaffection and social exclusion by means of educational approaches. These include pupil referral units (PRUs), secure accommodation, young offender institutions and a range of New Start partnerships aimed specifically at young people aged 14–17 who are among the 35,000 young people who leave school each year without any statutory qualifications. The OFSTED evaluations are variable, with some good results in PRUs in terms of teaching, learning and behaviour, but a picture of poor provision and resourcing in many of the other services.

Exclusions

The government's commitment to inclusion is hard to reconcile with the epidemic of permanent exclusions that characterised the 1990s. Many people now argue that we cannot think about inclusion and conveniently ignore exclusion (Booth *et al.* 1998; Booth 1999a). Both are locked into the same dynamic.

The dramatic rise in the number of excluded children does not reflect a sudden increase of disruptive behaviour in young people: the evidence from one major study suggests that the incidence of emotional and behavioural disorders has changed very little in 20 years (Croll and Moses 2000). What has changed is the tolerance level of the schools to pupils with disruptive behaviour. This in turn reflects the pressures on schools to put a premium on academic success, to secure a favourable position in league tables and to ensure that the local media report on their successes and achievements. Since their funding depends on parents opting into the school, it is hard for even the most caring school to retain pupils who appear to flout its values and priorities and who may prevent other pupils from reaching targets set by the government. This is the price we are paying as a society for allowing our schools to be put into the market place and forced to tout for custom in order to survive.

The figures speak for themselves (NCH 2000):
- The number of permanent exclusions increased by 450 per cent between 1990 and 1995 and was around 13,000 by 1997–98. For the first time, there has been a 3 per cent reduction in the most recent statistics.
- Only 27 per cent of these pupils are reintegrated into mainstream education.
- Children with special educational needs and Afro-Caribbean boys are each six times more likely to be excluded. Those in the care of local authorities are ten times more likely to be excluded.
- 137,000 pupils are temporarily excluded; that is, for more than five school days in any one term. This is a loss of 2 million days. Primary schools tend to use temporary exclusion but more than four-fifths of secondary exclusions are permanent.
- Permanent exclusion rates reflect enormous variations within and between LEAs. For example, the rate for Hammersmith and Fulham was four times that of Newham. A quarter of schools never exclude. Another quarter account for two-thirds of all exclusions. If these cut their rates to the national average, exclusions overall would be halved (Parsons and Castle 1998; Social Exclusion Unit 1998).
- Three-quarters of excluded children have reading ages between 8½ and 10. Two-thirds of school-age offenders have either been excluded or truanted.

A recent NFER survey of 30 LEAs suggests that exclusion rates are now rising for Bangladeshi boys and Afro-Caribbean girls and that certain ethnic groups (e.g. Croatians) are not reflected in the figures (Kinder *et al.* 2000). In one LEA, pupils with statements accounted for 20 per cent of excluded pupils. Staff in pupil referral units complained about poor teaching resources for students and lack of training opportunities for staff.

A survey carried out in 1994 (summarised in NCH 2000) summarised the reasons given by schools for exclusions (percentages):
- bullying, fighting and assaults on peers (30)
- disruption, misconduct and unacceptable behaviour (17)
- verbal abuse to peers (15)   • drugs (smoking, alcohol, cannabis) (4)
- verbal abuse to staff (12)   • vandalism and arson (2)
- theft (6)   • physical abuse and assault on staff (1)
- defiance and disobedience (5)   • miscellaneous (8)

Behind each of these figures there are obviously real dilemmas and agonising decisions. A few children leave head teachers little alternative to exclusion (e.g. assault on staff), but it is clear that such emergencies form only a very small proportion of the total. The OFSTED report on secondary exclusion concludes that 'Some schools are so anxious to avoid exclusions that they incur some danger to themselves as institutions, to staff and pupils. Others are only too ready to exclude. A few are irresolutely profligate in the use made of exclusion, devaluing it as a sanction' (OFSTED 1996).

Perhaps the most depressing aspect of what we know about excluded children has been the lack of official interest in meeting their needs. Once excluded, there are no clear lines of responsibility for ensuring that they receive educational help and that their families are involved in attempts to reintegrate them into schooling. Many receive only a few hours of home teaching and some seem to slip through the net altogether. The excluding school does not want them back and other schools are not queuing to meet their needs either. The NFER survey reported that around 80 per cent of secondary aged pupils and half of those at Key Stage 1 were out of school for more than a term and more than 20 per cent for two terms (Kinder *et al.* 2000). At LEA level, reintegration rates ranged from 23 per cent to 100 per cent for primary level and from 9 per cent to 100 per cent at secondary level.

The priority given to this problem by the Cabinet Social Exclusion Unit has certainly helped to put exclusions on the agenda. Information about individual school exclusions is much more in the public domain than in the past.

From September 1999, all pupils excluded for more than 15 days have to receive full-time appropriate education, instead of receiving a few hours of teaching at home or in pupil referral units. Circular 10/99 (Social Inclusion: Pupil Support) also provides guidance on prevention and on the development of pastoral support programmes; ironically enough, these draw on the 1989 Elton Report *Discipline in Schools* (DES 1989a), which was warmly welcomed as constructive and sensible and then quietly forgotten. The government also wants to see all LEAs develop behaviour support plans and teams and to agree new mechanisms for collaborating across agencies (e.g. for looked after children). Circular 10/99 provides encouraging examples of good practice. What is not clear at this stage is whether schools will receive additional support in working with pupils at risk of exclusion.

Truancy

The number of children who exclude themselves by truanting is a matter of dispute, partly because it is not easy to define unauthorised absence and also because this information has become sensitive since it has had to be published in league tables.

Official figures suggest that one million children truant each year (15 per cent) but the Social Exclusion Unit suggested that the true figure is probably twice as high. Official records fail to reflect the fact that children tend to disappear after registration. A great many children truant for an odd day or so but others are persistent. In one study, nearly one in ten 15-year-olds truanted at least once a week, and up to 2 per cent truant for weeks at a time (Social Exclusion Unit 1998; NCH 2000).

Truancy has major long-term consequences. Over and above the fact that truants tend to come from families with multiple poverty related problems, 38 per cent of truants in one study left school without any GCSE examination passes, compared with 3 per cent of non-truants. Only 8 per cent obtained the desired five good passes, compared with 54 per cent of non-truants. Truants are more than three times likely to criminally offend: 40 per cent of robberies, 25 per cent of burglaries, 20 per cent of thefts and 20 per cent of criminal damage were carried out by 10–16-year-olds during school hours (NCH 2000) .

The government has set a target to reduce truancy and exclusion by one-third by 2002. To this end, £22 million was made available through the Standards Fund in 1989/1999 for locally developed projects to tackle attendance and behaviour problems.

Projects funded from this and other DfEE sources include:
- Fresh Start, which works with local schools and pupil referral units to support young people aged 13–19 who have been or are at risk of being excluded from school by providing a mentoring scheme and personal support;
- a free service to all teachers in Merton providing advice on dealing with pupil disaffection;
- a mentoring scheme to help black pupils promote better links between home and school (in Bristol and through Barnardos);
- electronic pagers to let parents know where their children are (in Durham);
- 'Return to work' tutors who work individually with children reluctant to return to school (in Devon).

The Social Exclusion Unit summarises 'what works' in tackling truancy, For example, acting quickly, involving parents immediately and making home–school agreements raises attendance rates by 10–15 per cent. In addition, all schools should have unambiguous discipline policies, deal with academic problems early and broaden the range of extra-curricular activities (all recommended by the Elton report in 1989).

The government's own signature is reflected in the insistence on LEA and school targets, a proposal to fine parents and require them to take their children to school, giving the police powers to return truants to school, and OFSTED inspections for high excluding schools. Young people will also be able to appeal against exclusion. Most important of all, full-time and appropriate education will have to be provided for all excluded pupils.

Improvements for some

In reviewing the government's responses to these challenges, we distinguish between initiatives aimed at children and young people in areas of disadvantage and those that target the country as a whole. Some of the former are pilot programmes that may be extended nationally at a later stage.

Education action zones

Within days of taking office, the government announced plans for 25 new EAZs: 'a £75 million programme to drive up educational standards' (DfEE 1998b). A second round of EAZs was launched in the autumn of 1999, making a total of around 100 EAZs up and running at the beginning of 2000. A typical EAZ consists of a cluster of around 20 primary, secondary and special schools working with the LEA and business and community groups. The lead can be taken by any of these groups.

In launching the first 25 successful EAZs, David Blunkett was clear that 'traditional solutions are not working in these areas':

> We cannot afford to continue to have areas of inner city, or suburban, or rural blight where young people are given a wholly inadequate education, and tend to pass that on from one generation to another . . . These zones are testbeds for innovation, and each one of the proposals is full of fresh and energetic ideas . . . The objective is simple – that schools in our most difficult areas should provide as good an education as schools elsewhere . . . At the heart of each zone is a partnership approach. We want schools and LEAs to join together with their community and with business to ensure that these zones work. The Standards and Effectiveness Unit will be monitoring progress and providing help and guidance. (DfEE 1998b)

Each zone receives £1 million a year for three years, government providing 75 per cent and private sponsors finding the rest.

There has been a good response to this initiative, with many areas setting clear targets and committing themselves to new developments that might otherwise not have been funded.

Examples of targets include:
- a 25 per cent reduction in the number of pupils leaving school without employment or training and a 20 per cent improvement in pupil attainment at all stages (in Birmingham);
- an increase in the percentage of five GCSE grade C or higher examination passes from 11 to 31 (in New Addington and Croydon);
- 60 per cent of the age group to enter colleges of further education (in Herefordshire);
- elimination of all permanent exclusions (in Grimsby).

Among the innovations listed are:
- 24 hour classrooms and all-year round schooling;
- a tailor-made TV channel bringing the classroom into the living room (in Grimsby);
- increasing opening hours of schools by 50 per cent (in Birmingham);
- nursery provision for 52 weeks each year from 8 a.m. to 6 p.m. (in Brighton)

Other initiatives are not expressed as clearly but sound encouraging: a one-stop shop for health and social services in schools for parents and pupils (in Newcastle); learning with football (in Middlesbrough); family literacy centres open to all (in Birmingham), specialist family and counselling services (in Sheffield). Others are in jargonese: 'wrap around services', 'reaching across local authority boundaries'.

No government initiative is complete without the need to draft in a taskforce of super teachers who will work with more modestly endowed colleagues and show them the way. Some areas propose to make use of the new breed of 'advanced skills teachers', who will 'work alongside classroom teachers in Lambeth; work in teams to tackle poor behaviour in Hereford and drive up standards of literacy in Grimsby and Newham' (DfEE 1998b).

More detailed guidelines were provided for applicants to the second round (DfEE 1999f). As expected, the priority is on raising standards through improving teaching and learning but applicants are encouraged to propose a wide variety of strategies. The targets listed above include a few that are directly relevant to pupils with exceptional needs.

In response to my enquiry, the DfEE has provided further examples, including:
- the inclusion of 28 special schools in the first round of 25 EAZs;
- additional funding for LSAs, releasing SENCOs to spend more time on their own professional development (in Herefordshire);

- links between mainstream and emotional and behavioural difficulties (EBD) special schools (including joint INSET and mentoring) focusing on behaviour management (in Plymouth and Southwark);
- social inclusion mentoring in high schools (in Salford and Trafford); and
- additional teacher training to meet individual pupils' needs in the classroom (in Leicester).

The EAZ initiative has undoubtedly generated some excellent responses, although on rather narrow school-focused foundations. 'Special needs' issues have been addressed in many of the first round proposals but it is a pity that very few initiatives have been concerned with the development of better links between home and school, despite the clear guidance from the DfEE that support to families is one of five major headings under which proposals might fall. Examples of ongoing government support to families given in the DfEE guidelines are limited to language and literacy support rather than the development of partnerships based on shared expertise. In future, it may be necessary to earmark funds for improving home–school links and other priority areas listed in the DfEE guidelines but that is not being taken up (see Chapter 10).

The notion of EAZs is not unlike the old educational (social) priority areas (EPAs) of the late 1960s and early 1970s. Have the lessons of that project been learned? One lesson was that not all schools in the designated areas had problems, whereas many schools outside the areas were in greater need (Halsey 1972; Silver and Silver 1991). A second lesson was that practitioners in EPA areas resented the assumption that they had been wasting their time and that new methods were needed, just as parents resented the assumption that living in EPA areas must mean that they were not thought fit to be parents and needed special help.

Finally, the government itself could also have done more to raise both teacher morale and standards by committing itself to funding a reduction in class sizes in all EAZs to the end of Key Stage 2, since it would not be practical or economical for EAZs to spend most of their allocation in this way. The election promise to reduce class sizes is now being implemented for all children at Key Stage 1. Surely the next step is to extend that commitment to Key Stage 2, starting with schools in EAZs and Excellence in Cities programmes? Similarly, SENCOs working in such areas should be given additional time (see Chapter 8).

Excellence in cities

In March 1999 the government published an ambitious action plan for the inner cities (*Excellence in Cities*, DfEE 1999h). The first target areas are parts of inner London, Manchester/Salford, Liverpool/Knowsley, Birmingham, Leeds/Bradford and Sheffield/Rotherham. Others will be added and there are plans to extend the scheme to the whole country.

The proposals contain a mixture of new ideas and well rehearsed but rather vague print bites, starting with 'Excellence must become the norm' and 'We must transform this culture of fatalism'. In considering these proposals, we have again to ask ourselves whether they are consistent with the government's stated commitment to inclusion, whether the reforms will reach and be relevant for the whole range of pupils in our schools and whether they build on existing initiatives such as the Code of Practice. This depends not only on government or funding but on the readiness of the schools themselves and the parents and communities that they serve to take advantage of such new opportunities.

- By 2003 there will be 800 specialist and 1,000 beacon schools, with priority for inner cities 'so that every community has a beacon of excellence'.
- There will be extended opportunities for gifted and talented children, with special programmes for the highest performing 5 to 10 per cent of pupils in each secondary school, including university summer schools and the introduction of new 'world-class tests' in mathematics and problem-solving.
- There will be a new network of learning centres, developing existing schools as centres of excellence to link with neighbouring schools, involving advanced information and communications technology (ICT) and providing after school and holiday opportunities for learning.
- Setting is encouraged, to meet individual aptitudes and abilities.
- A learning mentor will be provided for every young person who needs one 'as a single point of contact to tackle barriers to pupils' learning'. These mentors will liaise with primary schools at the point of transfer to identify children who will need extra help; oversee a progress review of every child at the end of the first year and again as they enter Key Stage 4; draw up and implement an action plan for each child who needs support; and have regular contact with each pupil and their families.
- Disruption in schools will be tackled more effectively by ensuring that every school has access to a learning support unit where children can be referred when necessary and by giving support to head teachers and teachers in establishing high expectation and standards.
- There will be new emphasis on literacy and numeracy; better transition from primary to secondary school, especially for pupils 'not up to standard'; expansion of the number of summer schools and after school programmes; and publication of schemes of work for Key Stage 3.
- New, smaller EAZs will focus on low performance in small clusters of schools.
- There will be a new scheme of low-cost home computer leases for pupils and adults who face particular disadvantage, together with subsidised loans to enable teachers to buy computers.

In addition, there are the usual references to 'strengthening school leadership', 'turning round' the 200 weakest schools', 'modernising LEAs' and 'bringing in contractors where necessary'.

The extent to which this list of targets can be considered inclusive is a matter of debate. Clearly, there are those who believe that specialist and beacon schools can promote inclusion but the process has not been very clearly spelled out so far. Similarly, reliance on setting is not necessarily consistent with inclusive class-rooms, since the emphasis is on grouping pupils by achievement in a subject area, rather than by differentiation of the curriculum in ways that would enable pupils to support as well as learn from one another.

The document as it stands does not seem to have been written with full knowl-edge of the policies clearly set out in the DfEE SEN *Programme of Action* (DfEE 1998a). For example, the mention of 'learning mentors' is puzzling. Where are these mentors to come from, how will they be trained and supported and how will they relate to SENCOs and support services?

Improvements for all

Whatever the strengths and achievements of many of the government's new initia-tives such as EAZs, Excellence in Cities and Sure Start, they only reach a small section of the population. Even when the number of participating areas is increased, many schools and communities will still not have been touched by these innovations. This creates divisions between some areas and others and is therefore not inclusive in its approach unless systematic plans are developed to disseminate good practice across all schools and all areas. In contrast to these schemes, we have several examples of policy initiatives and developments that are intended for all schools and all pupils and are therefore potentially inclusive.

National literacy and numeracy strategies

The introduction of the National Literacy Strategy (NLS) and National Numeracy Strategy (NNS) is an example of a more universalist approach, which is intended for all schools and all pupils, regardless of social background or educational level. All children, it is argued, will benefit from increased attention to literacy and numeracy, whatever level they have reached. Although critics disliked the prescriptions and time allocations, early indications are that the NLS has made a positive impact across the board and has benefited children with special educational needs.

The most recent figures quoted by the Secretary of State for Education in his speech to the North of England conference (Blunkett 2000) certainly reflect substantial improvements. The extent to which credit for these gains can be attrib-uted to the NLS may be a matter of debate among researchers but the facts speak for themselves: 'At the time of the election when the targets were set, 57 per cent of 11 year olds reached the target expected for their age in English and 54 per cent in Mathematics. This year the corresponding figures are 70 and 69 per cent' (Blunkett 2000: 15).

Particularly encouraging is the fact that nine out of ten LEAs reporting the greatest gains in mathematics and eight out ten in English are in deprived areas, with Tower Hamlets and Blackburn, respectively, in the lead. By September 2000, an additional 20,000 LSAs will be appointed across the country, mainly to support the literacy and numeracy strategies.

Despite the fact that the initial guidance on the NLS failed to mention children with exceptional needs, teachers seemed to accept this as a challenge (Berger and Gross 1999; Berger et al. 1999), including those working with pupils with severe learning difficulties (Atkins 1999). Although guidance was provided at a later stage, we are still left with the question of which children have gained most from the literacy hour. Is it those who were below or above average or is there no difference?

OFSTED evaluations provide encouraging evidence on the effectiveness of the NLS. An interim report (OFSTED 1999b) includes the conclusions that:
- teachers' attitudes are positive in the overwhelming majority of schools;
- the training provided by LEAs, especially for the coordinators, has generally been well received;
- the quality of teaching in the literacy hour was satisfactory or better in 80 per cent of lessons;
- the main weaknesses noted concerned the word and sentence level strands and the teaching of phonics, especially in Years 3 and 4, and in the relative neglect of writing.

The NNS, which became operational in September 1999 included guidance on pupils with exceptional needs from the outset and early reports of its implementation are positive. OFSTED (1998b) reports findings from a pilot project in which 'pupils in Years 2, 3 and 5 at the start of the project made significantly greater progress than predicted over the first five terms in both written and mental tests across all LEAs involved' (1998b: 7). Year 4 pupils were, on average, about 12–16 months ahead of the results achieved by Year 4 pupils in the same schools two years previously.

Particularly encouraging is the finding that 'pupils at Stage 1 of the SEN Code of Practice made very significant gains, as did pupils with statements, exceeding the progress made by pupils in the control groups who were not part of the Project for Years 2, 3 and 5' (OFSTED 1998b: 7). The project also 'succeeded in closing the attainment gap between all ethnic minority groups and white pupils by enabling the former groups to make greater progress' (1998b: 7). Good progress was also recorded for pupils whose first language was not English.

A problem identified for both literacy and numeracy is the lack of integration between work targets set as part of the child's IEP and those set within the literacy and numeracy initiatives.

Improvements at Key Stage 3

The Secretary of State for Education's speech to the North of England conference in January 2000 announced some new measures directed at pupils between the ages of 11 and 14, based on findings from the most recent OFSTED annual report (OFSTED 2000b).

> At the end of the first year of secondary education, around a third of pupils perform worse in tests than they did a year earlier. Test results change little from year to year; science results have not improved since 1996. Boys show less progress than girls and are more likely to become disaffected in years 7 and 8. OFSTED reports say that 11 to 14 year olds are at the receiving end of more poor lessons than any other pupils. (Blunkett 2000: 18)

In response to this challenge, the Secretary of State for Education announced some new policy initiatives:
- Teachers working with this age group will receive additional support and opportunities for professional development.
- The literacy and numeracy strategies will be extended into the first year of secondary school.
- Pupils leaving primary school who have not reached Level 4 will be encouraged to attend summer schools.
- Children who entered secondary schools with achievements below Level 4 in English and mathematics will be tested at the end of their first year and helped accordingly. These tests will be available free of charge, to encourage all schools to assess all pupils at this stage. Additional targets for 14-year-olds will be introduced for English, mathematics and science.

The number of summer schools has risen from 50 in 1997 to 2,300 in the summer of 2000, of which 500 will be targeted at gifted and talented children. The plan is to make summer schools available to all 11-year-olds in the community.

A particularly interesting development for pupils in secondary schools is the official adoption of research on the teaching of higher order thinking skills, based on the Cognitive Acceleration through Science Education (CASE) and Cognitive Acceleration through Maths Education (CAME) projects developed at King's College, University of London. We can only hope that this approach will be used with underachieving children, since it was for this group that the materials were originally developed by Reuven Feuerstein in Israel (Feuerstein 1980).

Can effective schools be inclusive?

In our attempt to address the question 'Can schools prevent learning difficulties?' we have been considering ways in which the government is responding to the challenge of underachievement in general but with particular reference to children living in areas characterised by poverty, deprivation and social exclusion. In parallel with these developments, we also need to consider the relevance of a much earlier concern with school effectiveness which goes back some 20 years. What does the school effectiveness movement have to say about the impact of poverty on underachievement? If learning difficulties can be created by schools, can they also prevent them?

Characteristics of effective schools

Attempts to define school effectiveness have a long history, starting with a series of major UK research studies such as *Fifteen Thousand Hours* (Rutter *et al.* 1979) and its primary counterpart *Schools Matter* (Mortimore *et al.* 1988). These studies examined how schools differed in their impact on the learning and development of their pupils and the extent to which the organisation and management of the school might affect educational achievement.

> The NCE's (1993) summary of ten features of school effectiveness provides a good starting point. The features are:
> * strong, positive leadership
> * a good atmosphere, shared aims and values, and good physical environment
> * high and consistent expectations of all pupils
> * clear and continuing focus on teaching and learning
> * well developed procedures for assessing how pupils are progressing
> * shared responsibility for learning
> * pupil participation in the life of the school
> * rewards and incentives
> * parental involvement
> * extra-curricular activities that broaden pupils' interests and experiences, expand their opportunities to succeed and help to build good relationships with the school (NCE 1993).

A similar but slightly fuller summary can be found in a review of school effectiveness commissioned by OFSTED from the London Institute of Education (Sammons *et al.* 1995).

The features identified are:
- professional leadership
  - firm and purposeful
  - participative
  - leading professional
- shared vision and goals
  - unity of goals
  - consistency of practice
  - collegiality and participation
- a suitable learning environment
  - orderly atmosphere
  - attractive working environment
- purposeful teaching
  - efficient organisation
  - clarity of purpose
  - structured lessons
  - adaptive practice
- high expectations
  - communicating expectations
  - providing intellectual challenge
- positive reinforcement
  - clear and fair discipline
  - feedback
- monitoring progress
  - pupil performance
  - school performance
- pupils' rights and responsibilities
  - raising self-esteem
  - positions of responsibility
  - control of work
- home–school partnership
  - parental involvement in children's learning
- learning organisation
  - school based staff development.

Although most of these criteria could be described as 'inclusion-friendly', they are in fact blandly neutral when it comes to the core of inclusion, namely the reorganisation of structures and curricula to ensure that they meet the needs of all pupils. They have nothing to say about selection or grouping of pupils, whether on the basis of admission interviews, proficiency in a specialism offered by the school, setting and banding by subject or other forms of internal segregation within the school, far less about the school's legally required special needs policy, the role of the SENCO or how the school meets the needs of pupils with statements or works with neighbouring special schools.

It seems as though the school effectiveness and inclusion movements have been developing independently of one another. Despite having many points in common, there are also areas where they conflict. Now that inclusion is central to government policy, we need to ask whether effectiveness and inclusion can be brought together within a wider framework of diversity of achievement and culture. From an inclusion perspective, we can argue that an effective school should also, by definition, be inclusive and that criteria for school effectiveness, and therefore school improvement, should reflect inclusive principles and practice.

But are effectiveness and inclusion compatible? The school effectiveness movement has been criticised for narrowing its focus to academic excellence and for its concern with schools as organisations without reference to their social and political context. Slee and Weiner (1998) are highly critical of its perceived irrelevance to disadvantaged children, its 'silence on the impact of the National Curriculum, the marketisation of schooling, the press for selected entry and grant-maintained distortions of the relative performance of schools' (1998: 5). The chapter by Slee (1998) includes a salutary account of the collapse of a well meaning inclusion policy in the Australian state of Victoria that is highly relevant to our own government's new-found commitment to inclusion.

Despite this, the headings in both the NCE and OFSTED lists are mostly relevant to a school run on inclusive lines. High expectations are particularly important since they reflect values and attitudes that go to the heart of inclusion. Low expectations can be found at the level of the institution, as well as in the attitudes of individual teachers. No matter how competent a teacher may be in the classroom, low expectations and underestimation of pupils' abilities and strengths reflect pernicious and pervasive forms of exclusion. Teachers have to make many decisions on grouping and setting, in advising on subject choices at around age 14 and in entering pupils for particular bands in public examinations. These decisions profoundly affect the extent to which pupils feel included in or excluded from the life of their school and, by definition, their participation in the life of their community.

In his speech to the North of England conference, the Secretary of State for Education referred to some essential features of secondary schools that more clearly reflect inclusive principles. His speech singles out:

- diversity within the campus;
- meeting the needs and aspirations of all children, whatever their diverse talents, abilities or learning needs
- schools which remove barriers to learning
- schools which develop their strengths and contribute to a network of diverse provision across an area.   (Blunkett 2000: 9)

This reads like an inclusion-friendly list but is it consistent with his unequivocal call in the same speech to 'abandon any residual dogmatic attachment to mixed ability teaching' (Blunkett 2000: 10)? We have here another example of a major policy tension that is too often conveniently ignored. In promoting academic excellence and higher standards, are we in danger of segregating children within mainstream schools? Is the government's emphasis on grouping and setting consistent with an inclusive school?

Do specialist and beacon schools sit comfortably with inclusion? By 2003, one in four secondary schools will have specialist status. How will this affect the self-esteem and morale of the other three, given the information in his speech that specialist schools have improved their performance at 'twice the rate of the average comprehensive'. Diversity and excellence are good aims but not if they relegate three out of four schools to what parents may perceive to be a lower status. Are we in danger of reinventing secondary moderns, defined as schools that are not in special schemes?

Although school effectiveness and school inclusion are both central policy objectives at the moment, there is an unresolved tension between them, particularly if school effectiveness is defined in terms of academic achievement and examination results. A school can be consciously becoming more inclusive by changing its curriculum and assessment arrangements to meet a wider range of needs but still fail to produce the 'good' examination results demanded by parents and politicians (Mortimore and Whitty 2000).

A second dilemma is presented by exclusions. At one level, a school can fully meet all the criteria for an effective school and still exclude a substantial number of its pupils. Such a school cannot claim to be inclusive because inclusion is not just about children with learning or behaviour problems but about all pupils. This is one of many examples of the 'dilemmas' facing special needs education at this transitional period (Dyson 1999).

It is sometimes suggested that identification of the needs of a particular group of pupils, whether defined by gender, ethnicity, disability or exceptional needs, undermines the whole principle of inclusion and is therefore counter-productive. The example of 'colour-blind' school policies shows such a position to be invalid. We can no longer assume that children from ethnic minorities will automatically benefit from school reform. A conscious, focused attention on their needs is necessary to avoid marginalisation and unwitting discrimination. We have known for over 30 years that Afro-Caribbean children are much more likely than other minority groups to be sent to special schools (Coard 1971; Tomlinson 1981) and we now know that they are six times more likely to be excluded from school. The reasons are far from simple but institutional racism cannot be ruled out, although this would not be the only explanation. The ethos of the school and the extent to which it understands and celebrates the varieties of culture in its local community are clearly important. There are also major issues about the impact of a nationally prescribed ethnocentric curriculum and how far a school can go in making it relevant to the needs of an ethnically diverse student population (Diniz 1999; Tomlinson 2000).

David Reynolds, one of the leading school effectiveness researchers and now a key government adviser, has tried to disentangle some of the strands relevant to inclusion and exceptional needs within the school effectiveness and improvement movements and identified some points of similarity as well as difference (Reynolds 1995). Points in common include an emphasis on 'whole-school' approaches, which work to ensure that the learning and social experiences offered by a school are examined and if necessary changed to make them accessible to all pupils. This in turn reflects an assumption that children's difficulties in learning can be created or complicated by the curriculum and by the way in which schools are organised and managed and are not simply the results of deficiencies in the child or the family.

Using information from a wide range of school effectiveness studies, particularly those from the UK, Reynolds invites us to consider the issues under four headings:

- *How much do individual schools affect their pupils' academic and social achievement?*

  The research indicates that at least 10 per cent of the differences between pupils' examination results at age 16 can be attributed to school effects. Much of the earlier research was done on the former General Certificate of Education (GCE) Ordinary (O) level examinations, with results suggesting that the difference between the most and least effective schools is as much as two O level examination passes per pupil.

- *Are effective schools consistently effective upon all areas of pupils' academic and social development?*

  Despite earlier optimism, later research suggests that schools that achieve good academic results do not necessarily produce good social outcomes, expressed in terms of attendance rates and behaviour problems. In particular, the large-scale British study of effective primary schools by Mortimore reflected substantial independence in academic and social outcomes (Mortimore *et al.* 1988). However, we should note that 16 of the 50 schools did achieve both academic and social effectiveness, even though the remainder were not able to be equally successful on both fronts.

- *Are schools effective for all pupils?*

  The evidence here suggests that pupils from disadvantaged backgrounds derive the greatest benefit from effective schools. As suggested by Smith and Tomlinson (1989) some schools are particularly effective in narrowing the achievement gap between children from different social backgrounds. Some evidence for this is claimed for the NLS (OFSTED 1999b). Unfortunately, we have very little new information on how such schools achieve these results 'against the odds'.

- *What factors exist in schools that are effective?*

  The discussion here largely revisits the major headings identified in the NCE (1993) and OFSTED reviews (Sammons *et al.* 1995) but ends on a note that can be characterised as pessimistic or cautionary, depending on one's point of view:

Whole-school policies may not be productive of changed classroom experience for children with special educational needs. Schools may be involved in complex 'trade-offs' in which certain goals have to be maximised (academic ones) which may lead to deficiencies in goals in other areas. Different subgroups of pupils may be advantaged differentially by different ways of running schools. Schools cannot even be told from research what the ways are of maximising the social outcomes so appropriate to children with special educational needs. Schools that have higher proportions of children with special educational needs may well be the least able to progress their children and may, if this is true, be the least able to change their organisational functioning.   (Reynolds 1995: 120)

This conclusion is based on a review of what we know about school effectiveness but becomes more alarming if it is set in some wider policy contexts, particularly the standards drive and the continuation of open enrolment, league tables and OFSTED inspections in their present form and the none too encouraging research about teachers' attitudes to inclusion. Reynolds also looks further afield to Hong Kong, Taiwan and Korea, where, he claims, education policies have 'in effect knocked the bottom of their distributions into the middle' rather than having the elongated `tail' of low achieving children that we know here. He attributes this to the insistence in these countries on children understanding and finishing tasks, if necessary during breaks and in after school catch-up periods or by spending more time on homework. We have also had a first call from Her Majesty's Chief Inspector of Schools to follow the practice of other countries by making children repeat a year if they do not reach the necessary standard.

Conclusions

In this chapter we have been considering the impact of innovation and change on schools and asking how far schools can go in using new opportunities to work for more successful educational and personal outcomes for all children but particularly those who experience difficulties in benefiting from what schools have to offer. Such children have been repeatedly overlooked in earlier reforms but the present government seems determined to ensure that their needs are met right from the start.

Most of these children are living in the poorest and most disadvantaged sections of society. Although many of them are successful both in school and later in employment, a disproportionate number encounter significant difficulties during and after school. Many children in our society still experience exclusion and marginalisation, including those who are regular attenders but who fail to learn or to be motivated for learning and who leave school without any qualifications.

Schools cannot be expected to meet this challenge in isolation. Some will go further than others but all will need to find new partners among parents and in their local community. They will also need leadership and resources from government. In Chapter 6 we will look more closely at government policies on inclusion and consider their likely impact on pupils, parents and professionals.

Chapter 6

Towards Inclusive Policies

Introduction

In this chapter we will look more closely at some emerging policies on inclusion in education and consider what impact they might have on practice in schools and on the lives of children and families. We can start in the present by looking at the most recent developments, such as the Green Paper *Excellence for All Children* (DfEE 1997a), followed by the firm proposals set out in the *Programme of Action* (DfEE 1998a), the recommendations of the Disability Rights Task Force (DfEE 1999e), the impact of the *Code of Practice on the Identification and Assessment of Special Educational Needs* (DfE 1994) and proposals for its revision. We also need to consider the impact of the very explicit commitment to inclusion in the revised National Curriculum (DfEE and QCA 1999), which will be discussed in Chapter 7.

There can be no doubt of the government's commitment to the principle of inclusion and to its determination to achieve positive changes for children with exceptional needs. Neither can there be any doubt about the relevance of most of the targets that the government has set or about the significant amounts of new money that are being invested to reach them. What is still in question is the extent to which the avalanche of change will achieve high quality inclusion on the ground and make a significant impact on the quality of education and inclusion of children and their families. This in turn depends to a large extent on the ways in which schools, governors, teachers and communities respond to the challenges and opportunities that are now available. Some of these are explicitly related to children with exceptional needs but many others are designed for all children and therefore include children with exceptional needs. The stage is set as never before.

Excellence for All Children (DfEE 1997a)

Within days of the new government taking office, a National Advisory Group on Special Educational Needs started work under the chairmanship of the Minister of State, Estelle Morris. The resulting Green Paper *Excellence for All Children* was published in October 1997 and given a generally warm welcome.

The Green Paper built on the earlier White Paper *Excellence in Schools* (DfEE 1997b). Although this made reference to children with special educational needs, further work was clearly needed to ensure that these objectives were developed within an inclusive rather than a separate framework.

The proposals are built on what are by now familiar themes. These include:
- high expectations
- inclusion within mainstream provision 'wherever possible'
- redefining the role of special schools to develop a network of specialist support
- new regional arrangements
- enhanced support for parents
- greater emphasis on prevention and early intervention
- improvement in statements
- better opportunities for staff development

The consultation following the publication of the Green Paper resulted in over 3,600 responses, most of them favourable. The main reservations came from parents, who expressed concerns that an emphasis on reducing the number of statements might lead to loss of entitlement to additional resources. There was also concern that special schools would be closed or phased out, despite the clear commitment both in the Green Paper and in the subsequent Programme of Action to 'protect and enhance specialist provision for those who need it' and to 'redefine the role of special schools to bring out their contribution in working with mainstream schools to support greater inclusion' (DfEE 1997a).

Programme of Action (DfEE 1998a)

Taking the Green Paper as an agreed starting point, the Programme of Action sets out an ambitious and wide-ranging agenda, with generally clear definitions and time-lined targets. In the event, the government began to implement many of the targets without waiting for the consultation to end or the Programme of Action to be published. Since then, progress in implementing the targets has been regularly summarised in regular DfEE *SEN Updates* and also on the DfEE website.

The document itself provides a summary chart in box form with cross-references to further information. Because such lists date quickly, more recent developments have been added here. The proposals are summarised under convenient headings mostly drawn from the Green Paper and the Programme of Action itself. Some developments have been discussed in earlier chapters; a number of others will be discussed briefly in this and later chapters.

Summary of the Programme of Action

Funding
The DfEE has provided significant additional funds to implement the Programme of Action. For 1999/2000, the Standards Fund was almost doubled to £35 million and increased again to £55 million for 2000/2001. Other funds have also been earmarked to meet specific objectives.

High expectations
- Helpful guidance has been given (somewhat belatedly) on implementing the NLS and National Year of Reading for children with special educational needs. £22 million has been allocated to provide training and support through the Additional Literacy Support Programme to help pupils in the middle years of primary education who have fallen behind. An extra £48 million has been made available to expand the Booster programme, which provides additional literacy and numeracy support to pupils in Year 6. LEAs have also been invited to bid for funds for early intervention projects to help children experiencing literacy difficulties in Year 1.
- Advice on SEN was incorporated into the initial guidance on the NNS.
- Early years initiatives, such as Sure Start (see Chapter 3), have been introduced.
- LEA development plans must include proposals for raising achievement of pupils with special educational needs.
- £200 million Lottery funding to support out-of-school activities in all schools, including special schools, has been made available.
- Secondary special schools have been included in the specialist schools programme in areas such as technology, languages, sports and arts. They are also included in the Beacon Schools initiative, which will involve 1,000 schools by 2002.
- Guidance on target setting, including the new P scales for children below Level 3 has been published by DfEE and QCA: their impact is being evaluated by the University of Durham. Work is also in progress to develop richer criteria for assessing the achievements of pupils with emotional and behavioural difficulties.

Effective support for parents
- Parent partnership schemes are to be extended to all parts of the country. All parents of children identified as having special educational needs are to have access to an independent parental supporter, including parents of children below school age and those not on statements (legislation is going through parliament at time of writing).
- LEAs are required to establish independent conciliation arrangements to reduce the number of appeals to the SEN Tribunal.
- There are improvements to SEN Tribunal procedures: e.g. legislation to require LEAs to comply with SEN Tribunal rulings, strengthening parents' rights of appeal to the SEN Tribunal where the school rather than the parent asks for an assessment that is refused by the LEA. The SEN Tribunal is to have regard to the views of the child (see Chapter 10).

Promoting inclusion wherever possible
- There was a review of the statutory basis for inclusion in the light of the recommendations of the Disability Rights Task Force (DfEE 1999e), and the Disability Rights Commission was launched in April 2000.
- £20 million was allocated under the Schools Access Initiative to improve physical access in mainstream schools (increased from £11 million).
- £8 million was provided from the Standards Fund to promote inclusion and develop better links between mainstream and special schools, particularly for children with emotional and behavioural difficulties.
- LEAs are required to publish their plans to promote inclusion; these will be monitored by the DfEE and challenged if necessary. National and local inclusion targets are not planned at this stage but the possibility is to be kept under review. LEAs will also be required within the new Admissions Code of Practice to monitor the admission to mainstream schools of children with special educational needs.
- Examples of good practice in developing practical links with mainstream schools are to be promoted and disseminated (CD ROM to be published).
- DfEE commissioned research is to be disseminated. Subjects covered include: providing for pupils with emotional and behavioural difficulties in mainstream schools (University of Birmingham); cooperation between special and mainstream schools (University of Manchester); and on the relative costs of educating children with moderate learning difficulties in special and mainstream schools (University of Newcastle upon Tyne).

Shifting focus from procedures to practical support

- The implementation of the revised Code of Practice is to be postponed to September 2001, to allow time for other legislation and initiatives to be included: e.g. early years and post-school provision and a review of the work of educational psychologists and the SEN Tribunal.
- There will be increased pressure on LEAs (e.g. through OFSTED inspections) to speed up statementing procedures and to publish information about timescales.
- LEAs are required to publish information on what schools are expected to provide from their own budgets under each stage of the Code of Practice, as well as LEAs' own plans for providing SEN support to schools.
- There is to be more transparency for the SEN element in each school's budget allocation.
- Independent schools catering mainly for children with special educational needs may have to be approved by the Secretary of State.

Boosting opportunities for staff development (Chapter 9)

- There is to be an extra £21 million for training of all staff in SEN.
- The TTA has published standards for newly qualified teachers, SENCOs and specialist teachers.
- New training and guidance will be available for LSAs, and there will be funding to enable LEAs to work with other providers to plan and deliver such training.
- Clarification on the future role and training of educational psychologists is to be provided.
- There will be peer support for staff of special schools and units catering for pupils with emotional and behavioural difficulties.
- There will be guidance on training of governors in SEN.

Promoting partnerships

- New regional coordination arrangements will be developed in all areas. Experience of five pilot areas is now to be extended to all LEAs. Pump priming funding will be provided for two years. Collaboration is planned in training and in provision for pupils with emotional and behavioural difficulties, autism and sensory impairment.
- There are plans for legislation to facilitate joint funding and working partnerships between the NHS and LEAs. The Social Exclusion Unit will make suggestions for a more integrated local planning framework for all children's services, including those for children with special educational needs.

- There will be a new 'scoping study' to review speech and language therapy (SLT) services for children with special educational needs in mainstream and special schools, followed by pilot projects to develop innovative approaches to the provision of SLT and to provide guidance for parents on access to SLT provision.

Transition post-16

- There will be entirely new structures for post-16 learning opportunities, including the merging of the functions of the Further Education Funding Council (FEFC) and local Training and Enterprise Councils (TECs) into 57 new Learning Skills Councils under a national Council. These are likely to abolish the present funding restrictions on courses that are not likely to lead to employment.
- There will be improved access and provision in colleges of further education and implementation of the recommendations of the Tomlinson report (FEFC 1996).
- There will be improvements in standards of careers service guidance.
- There will be research into the experiences of young people with special educational needs once they have left school.
- The means testing of Disabled Students' Allowances in higher education will be ended, and the scheme will be extended to part-time students; there will be improvements in learning support for disabled students.

The Disability Rights Commission

The Disability Discrimination Act 1995 was the result of innumerable parliamentary battles, some of which hit the national headlines and caused the resignation of Nicholas Scott, the minister who had in fact conscientiously supported the legislation. It split the disability movement into those who rejected the Act because it lacked teeth and those who were prepared to use the Act as a stepping stone to stronger anti-discrimination mechanisms. The new government set up a Disability Rights Task Force, which reported in December 1999, and which will be placed by the Disability Rights Commission (DRC), which started work in April 2000.

The setting up of the DRC is therefore a major milestone in the history of the struggle of disabled people to achieve basic human rights and to outlaw institutional discrimination. For the first time, disabled people will have an enforcement agency comparable to those provided by the Equal Opportunities Commission and the Commission for Racial Enquiry. The work of the Disability Rights Task Force was in fact greatly helped by the McPherson report on the Stephen Lawrence inquiry, which emphasised the pervasiveness of institutional discrimination in British society, and which helped to create a climate in which discrimination against disabled people could be identified and confronted.

Education was originally excluded from the Disability Discrimination Act 1995 but the report of the Disability Rights Task Force now proposes to bring education within the framework of the Act. The report welcomes the proposals set out in the Programme of Action (DfEE 1998a) and the government's commitment to inclusion but is careful not to create new requirements at a time when so much is happening already. Their report, *From Exclusion to Inclusion,* contains new proposals on education that have been accepted by government and that will be enforced by the Commission (DfEE 1999e). They propose that:

> Disabled pupils will have a new right not to be discriminated against unfairly by schools and LEAs and to have 'reasonable' adjustments made to policies, practices and procedures which place them at a substantial disadvantage to others'. [A Code of Practice may be needed to clarify the concept of reasonableness and the allocation of responsibility for various levels of provision.]
>
> A new duty on schools and LEAs to plan strategically and make progress in increasing accessibility for disabled pupils to school premises and the curriculum.   (DfEE 1999e: 33–4)

A number of recommendations concerned further and higher education, in line with the recommendations of the Tomlinson report, *Inclusive Learning* (FEFC 1996).

Their proposals fall short of requiring every school to make reasonable physical adjustments and favour a requirement on LEAs to increase accessibility in the area as a whole. This could increase the number of 'resourced' schools where physical changes will be made to increase access. All schools should, however, be under a duty to provide access to the curriculum.

Revising the Code of Practice

The impact of the *Code of Practice for the Identification and Assessment of Special Educational Needs* (DfE 1994) on schools and teachers has been greater than any other single initiative taken by government since the Warnock report.

When the Code of Practice was being developed as a consequence of the statutory commitment made in the Education Act 1993, the then Department for Education won rare praise for taking immense trouble to consult and to listen to parents and practitioners representing a wide range of interests and needs. The final document was warmly welcomed as a major step forward but concern was expressed from the outset that the requirements of the Code would place a very heavy burden on teachers at a time when many other demands were being made on them. It was a time when morale and motivation were at a low ebb, due partly to innovation fatigue and partly to the constant denigration of their work by politicians and media pundits. It is a tribute to teachers that so much progress has been made under such difficult circumstances.

Strengths of the Code of Practice

The Code of Practice is a landmark document because it promotes inclusion by setting out as clearly as possible the principle that all schools and all teachers, without exception, are responsible for the teaching of all children and that new mechanisms will need to be put in place to provide them with appropriate support in this task. This support includes the requirement in the Education Act 1993 for every school to produce a special needs policy under a series of prescribed headings and to appoint a SENCO with clearly defined roles and responsibilities.

The Code sets out the steps that every school is expected to take to identify children who may need additional support as early as possible; to make arrangements to adapt what the school has to offer to meet their individual needs; to set targets both for the child and for staff and to review those targets in the light of the child's response. This policy is inclusive in so far as the onus is on the school to modify its provision to meet the needs of individual children who are experiencing difficulty. The initial aim is to provide whatever support the child needs in order to make progress. If the child does not respond, the school has to review its targets and the intensity of support and to go on doing so until it is clear that additional external support is needed.

Proposals for a revised Code of Practice

In the light of OFSTED and other research findings, the DfEE is consulting on some proposals to change the Code of Practice. Many of these are relatively small-scale changes.

The more important proposals include:
- reduction of the present three school based stages to two stages: 'School Action' and 'School Action Plus'. Guidance will be given on prevention and work at the pre-Code stage and criteria for movement in and out of stages;
- more guidance on IEPs, including examples of formats and short-term targets;
- guidance on the time required for SENCOs to do their work;
- cross-referencing to TTA Standards documents, including those for SENCOs;

- more guidance for teachers in secondary schools: e.g. on target setting and monitoring;
- strengthening guidance on provision for under-fives in relation to other early years initiatives and the National Childcare Strategy;
- more guidance on children whose first language is not English; children looked after by the local authority; and the rights of disabled children to personal support;
- detailed guidance on role and function of parent partnership schemes, which all LEAs are expected to provide, including the role of the independent parental supporter;
- removal of categorical, specific needs examples;
- strengthening of guidance to ensure that children's own views are taken into in the assessment process and by the SEN Tribunal. Tribunals will be able to accept appeals against LEA refusals to assess when requests are made by schools or other agencies.

Limitations of the Code of Practice and the proposed revision

The government's proposals for a revision to the Code of Practice focus largely on improvements to its day-to-day operation and on responding to teachers' complaints about 'bureaucracy' and workload. The proposed changes have on the whole been welcomed and there can be little doubt that an improved Code will emerge from the consultation process. Nevertheless, some fundamental questions remain and the proposals do not take us very far: at best they are fine tuning, at worst tinkering.

The fundamental defect of the Code of Practice lies in the lack of engagement with issues that lie at the heart of inclusion. True to its title, it focuses on identification and assessment but has little to say on classroom teaching or curriculum. The Code fails to reflect the growing consensus that inclusion is about whole-school restructuring and reform both of the curriculum and of assessment practices available to all pupils, not just those with special educational needs. It underestimates the key role of the head teacher and governors in promoting inclusion and limits itself to their contribution to the development of an effective special needs policy rather than seeing this as an integral element of the school development as a whole.

The separation of assessment from curriculum recapitulates the decision by the authors of the Education Reform Act 1988 to create two statutory councils, one concerned with assessment and examinations, the other with curriculum, despite strong advice that separation of assessment from curriculum was not sensible. A late marriage had then to be arranged between two warring empires, giving birth to the SCAA, later replaced by the QCA. Fortunately the QCA has done an excellent job in laying the foundations for an inclusive curriculum (see Chapter 7). This only serves to highlight the relatively limited brief of the Code of Practice, which reflects the historical preoccupation of special education with assessment and identification at the expense of teaching and learning.

This historical legacy was also reflected in the amount of space allocated in the Code of Practice to advice under categorical headings such as specific learning difficulties, emotional and behavioural difficulties, physical disabilities, sensory impairments, speech and language difficulties and medical conditions, all the more so since the advice given does not differ very much from group to group and categories were supposed to have been abandoned 20 years ago. Although the DfEE now proposes to drop these headings, officials at the time justified their use by saying that this was the form in which such advice was most useful to teachers. We can also detect the influence of lobbies representing particular parent interest groups (e.g. dyslexia), who worked hard to ensure that the children whom they represented were clearly identified.

The work of SENCOs

With hindsight, we can also see that more guidance should have been given on the role of SENCOs, who are the key to helping schools to develop more inclusive policies but who have not generally been given anything like the amount of time, status or management support to enable them to fulfil the immense responsibilities entrusted to them in the Code of Practice. Many SENCOs are allowed only one or two hours a week for this work and the government has so far failed to provide any clear guidance on time allocation. Some clarification is promised in the revised Code but the matter is too urgent to be left that long. Many SENCOs are over-whelmed with work and are physically and professionally exhausted. There is also no clear career structure and their levels of pay rarely reflect the scale of their re-sponsibilities.

The amount of time needed by a SENCO will vary from school to school, depending not only on its size and location but on the progress already made in moving towards more inclusive practice. A case can be made for allocating the equivalent of at least two days a week, rising to three days in areas of disadvantage, starting with schools taking part in the Excellence in Cities initiative and schools in EAZs, and all areas where children are well below the levels of educational attain-ment expected for their age and stage. Time is particularly needed for SENCOs to undertake collaborative planning with class or subject teachers; to liaise with parents and with agencies and services outside the school, to maintain the register and to prepare IEPs.

The TTA national standards for SENCOs, developed after extensive consultation, are both awesomely impressive and burdensome (see Chapter 9). The standards particularly emphasise their leadership and management roles: 'The SENCO's fundamental task is to support the head teacher in ensuring that all staff recognise the importance of planning their lessons in ways that will encourage the participation and learning of all pupils' (TTA 1998a: 5). This quotation seems to take it for granted that the head teacher is already committed to an inclusive policy. Later in the same document there is a strong hint that one of the tasks of the SENCO may be to persuade head teachers to review their policy where such commitment may be lacking or merely tokenistic:

> Effective coordination of SEN results in headteachers and other senior managers who recognise that the curriculum must be relevant to all pupils by taking SEN into account in the formulation and implementation of policies throughout the school; understand how best to support those with responsibility for SEN coordination.   (TTA 1998a: 6)

The TTA standards distinguish between outcomes for pupils, teachers, LSAs, parents, head teachers and senior management teams, governors and LEAs.

Headings include:
- professional knowledge (e.g. identification and assessment, IEPs, resources including ICT, legislation, effective teaching and learning styles, research and inspection);
- skills and attributes (e.g. leadership; fostering commitment and confidence, setting standards, providing direction, using specialist resources, record systems, confidentiality; communication, self-management).

Even these few extracts conjure up a paragon of professional perfection rather than a harassed coordinator with an hour or two a week in which to deploy these attributes.

The SENCO initiative illustrates the dilemmas inherent in attempts to promote inclusion. The role of the SENCO within the school is rightly seen as that of a facilitator and manager, someone whose task it is to support their mainstream colleagues in meeting the needs of all the pupils in their class. Paradoxically, their arrival in some schools has resulted in a collective sigh of relief from their colleagues that at last an expert in special needs education has arrived, who will either suggest instant solutions or help to remove certain children from their classroom or even from the school as a whole. This situation can only be avoided or confronted by full support and understanding for their role by the head teacher, the governors and the senior staff of the school.

Individual education plans

Although special schools have been using IEPs for some 20 years, their sudden incorporation into mainstream practice for all children from Stage 2 of the Code of Practice has been something of a professional culture shock. Very few opportunities have been available for teachers to undergo training or supervision in the writing and implementing of IEPs. It is a tribute to SENCOs and others that so much progress has been made in introducing them into schools. Indeed, the UK has so far avoided some of the problems experienced in the USA, where parents' dissatisfaction with 'worthless pieces of paper' has resulted in litigation and breakdown of trust.

IEPs have very quickly acquired an aura of orthodoxy and have come to be regarded as a hallmark of good practice and therefore a target for OFSTED inspections. The DfEE may have overestimated what they could achieve and underestimated the problems that would arise by their sudden arrival from outer space. It now looks as though the revision of the Code of Practice in the light of the OFSTED report (1999a) and other reports will lead to a strong drive to improve the quality of IEPs. Although this is probably the right policy, it is important not to pin too much faith in the IEP as a route to higher standards.

The OFSTED report on the third year of the SEN Code of Practice (OFSTED 1999c) is largely concerned with IEPs, since the writing and reviewing of IEPs was identified as 'the biggest single problem' in an earlier report on the Code (OFSTED 1997). The later report provides useful examples of good practice across all phases of mainstream education and makes a number of recommendations for more detailed guidance to be provided in a revised Code.

A review by Janet Tod (1999) provides a balanced account of the strengths and weakness of current IEP practice.

Positive features
IEPs:
- are a vehicle for collaboration with parents and a mechanism for enabling pupils to become more involved in their own learning plans;
- direct teacher attention towards the setting and resetting of clear, educationally relevant targets;
- involve staff in meeting targets and thereby improving and sharing classroom practice;
- are a mechanism for evaluating the effectiveness of additional SEN provision;
- harness available resources;
- can establish mechanisms for raising the achievement of all pupils; and
- emphasise monitoring of pupils' response to teaching.

Areas of concern
- Written IEPs are not always translated into practice;
- too much time spent on administration diminishes SENCO expertise in SEN teaching and coordination;
- IEP procedures can be perverted by the prospect of increased resources;
- adherence to behavioural objectives and SMART targets (measurable, achievable, relevant and time-related) may narrow learning opportunities;
- IEPs can become resource-led rather than needs-led;
- checklists and commercial IEP schemes tend to be defect-oriented; and
- IEPs can become static documents or so simplified that their educational benefit is questionable.

A number of reports from the UK as well as from overseas suggest that the time has come to rethink the whole basis of IEPs and in particular to question their contribution to inclusion.

The more inclusive the school, the less need there is for IEPs because such schools would already have a curriculum that was appropriately differentiated to meet the needs of all children. In so far as IEPs seem to have helped some pupils to acquire basic literacy and numeracy skills, they will have facilitated access to the curriculum as a whole. Achieving IEP targets is only one small step to inclusion.

IEPs may be needed during the long period of transition towards more inclusive practice but their very existence can create segregation within the mainstream school, unless the process is very skilfully managed (Ainscow 1999). IEPs need not be limited to children with learning difficulties. Many other children might benefit from them; for example, to enable them to overcome a learning obstacle at a particular point in a programme of study. The advent of appropriate ICT software can also provide the means of helping any child to overcome such a learning block. Recently, there have been ministerial statements that all children need individual learning plans. Although this is not a reference to IEPs as such, the principle of individualised and alternative pathways through the curriculum for all pupils would set IEPs for a minority of children in a broader and less exclusionary context.

Conclusions

We have reached a stage where 'special needs education' as it developed during the 1980s and early 1990s has in effect been overtaken by the inclusion agenda. This challenges all forms of exclusion and discrimination, whether arising from society's response to disability, gender, race, sexual orientation or poverty and social disadvantage. It mirrors the global UN EFA movement, which aims to provide or improve schooling for 200 million children world-wide, of whom a significant minority are disabled or have exceptional needs (Chapter 2).

In Britain, it is in fact the second 'takeover', the first occurring in 1978 when the Warnock report announced a ten-fold expansion of special education, from the 2 per cent of children who were mostly in special schools to the 20 per cent experiencing difficulties in mainstream schools. The traditional field of special education quickly reconstructed itself to embrace its new constituency and has now laid claim to the whole territory of education by demanding radical structural and organisational changes that would enable all children to enjoy access and entitlement to the wider range of learning opportunities offered by schools. Some of the most powerful advocates for inclusive education have firsthand experience of segregated schools and services.

But history is not so easily abandoned. Despite much talk of 'the 18 per cent', both government and the professions continued in their old ways to equate special needs with disability or at least with segregated provision, since many of the children in special schools could not be described as disabled. Indeed, the Warnock report itself, although appearing to usher in a new era, was in fact much more concerned with the needs of the 2 per cent than the 18 per cent, particularly in its three priority areas of under-fives, over-16s and (to a lesser extent) teacher training. Mary Warnock herself has publicly regretted the naiveté of her report, which was based on the assumption that government would give greater priority to children with special educational needs in ordinary schools, most of whom were living in areas of poverty and disadvantage.

The government is now pursuing policies that are directed both to reducing the impact of poverty and disadvantage and to achieving a more inclusive agenda in schools. The changes now proposed and still to come could change the face of education in this country from one that catered well for the needs of its ablest students but failed to meet the needs of the majority to one that is designed from the outset to prevent failure and marginalisation and to offer richer opportunities for growth and development to all. The goals of inclusion and social justice involve fundamental change in society and in our assumptions about human potential. Its foundations lie in the quality of the educational experiences that we provide for all our children.

Chapter 7

Curriculum and Assessment

Equality of opportunity is one of a broad set of common values and purposes which underpin the school's curriculum and the work of schools. These also include a commitment to valuing ourselves, our families and other relationships, the wider groups to which we belong, the diversity in our society and the environment in which we live.

(Secretary of State's Foreword, DfEE and QCA 1999).

The inclusion–exclusion continuum

The new National Curriculum, which will be introduced into all schools in September 2000, contains the strongest commitment to inclusion so far given by any UK government. It also provides the fullest account of what inclusion means in the context of ordinary classrooms. This chapter will set the new curriculum policy in a wider social and historical context.

Inclusion and exclusion begin in the classroom. No matter how committed a government may be to inclusion, it is the day-to-day experiences of children in classrooms that define the quality of their participation in the whole range of learning experiences provided by a school. Just as important are the interactions and social relationships that children have with one another and with the staff of the school. The ways in which schools promote inclusion and prevent exclusion go to the heart of the quality of living and learning experienced by all children.

The process of educational exclusion begins when children do not understand what a teacher is saying or what they are supposed to do. Teachers know this and are constantly on the alert to ensure that this does not happen and are ready to take action to restore communication if it seems to have broken down, for any reason. But even when children are attentive and eager to learn, there will always be some for whom the lesson or the task seems too difficult, even when teachers explain it in a different way or make it easier. It is not surprising that children who experience such difficulties day after day sooner or later decide that the fault lies with them, rather than with the school or the curriculum or with an individual teacher who is failing to make the lesson accessible to every child in the class.

Children who feel educationally excluded are more likely to feel socially isolated. They can also experience loss of confidence in themselves not only as learners but as individuals. This may be disguised by bravado or disruptive behaviour, which in turn can trigger punitive measures from the school or from peers and isolate the pupil even further, possibly to the point of exclusion. One way to break into this vicious circle is to try to prevent learning difficulties from arising in the first place by planning an accessible curriculum and ensuring that teaching is planned in ways that ensure successful learning.

The influence of the Education Reform Act 1988

The starting point for inclusion must be a curriculum and individual lessons that are accessible to all pupils. But the freedom of the teacher to determine the content of the curriculum and the timing of its delivery has been constrained by the introduction of the National Curriculum, with its programmes of study, SATs and national tests. Although these do not prescribe how teachers should teach, they have had a powerful effect on teachers' priorities and job satisfaction.

The balance of received wisdom today seems to be that the introduction of a national curriculum was necessary and has on the whole been beneficial, although the same cannot be said of national testing. It can also be argued that the National Curriculum has benefited children with exceptional needs by setting standards and benchmarks and by introducing a single common language, which could facilitate the transfer of pupils from special to mainstream schools, although in fact very few pupils have made the journey. There is also good evidence that it has particularly benefited children in special schools where curriculum planning and delivery were often weak (OFSTED 1999d).

What is debatable is whether the speed with which the National Curriculum was launched in 1988 and the political momentum behind it have in effect created new obstacles to learning by setting standards that too many children were unable to reach. A counter-argument might be that this has always been the case but that at least since the Code of Practice children experiencing difficulties are now identified and better supported at an early stage.

In some ways, the context within which the new National Curriculum is being launched in 2000 is more favourable to children with special educational needs than it was in 1988. Although the Code of Practice has little to say about curriculum or teaching, it has certainly brought about a major reorientation of policy and practice in mainstream schools, with the result that children experiencing difficulties are less likely to be overlooked or forgotten. Teachers are now much more aware of their pupils' needs and of strategies for meeting them.

Learning from history

Although today's climate is more positive and inclusion is at the heart of government policy and central to the new National Curriculum, it was not always thus. A brief look back at the past may provide some lessons for the future.

The only mention of special needs in the original consultation document that led to the Education Reform Act 1988 was a brief paragraph that indicated that such children could be exempted from the National Curriculum. This created a storm of protest among teachers and parents and the growth of a powerful lobby, which has influenced parliament and decision making at all levels.

Margaret Peter has provided an illuminating account of the working of this lobby, which is still active and reconstitutes itself to respond to each opportunity to effect change (Peter 1996). At present it is immersed in the detail of the Special Educational Needs Bill, which is going through parliament. There are also accounts of advocacy in the field of learning disability (Mittler and Sinason 1996).

It would be hard to deny that children with exceptional needs were overlooked by the authors of the Education Reform Act 1988. Many readers will remember that a six-week consultation period (four of them in August) was available for the public to comment on what was the most ambitious and revolutionary piece of educational legislation since 1944 or even 1870. In fact, no serious consultation could take place on any of the provisions of the proposed legislation.

Some early concessions were made. Professor Ron Davie and I were rather hurriedly appointed to serve on the NCC and the Schools Examination and Assessment Council (SEAC) respectively. Special needs HMIs began to appear at meetings and to provide input to the decision making process between meetings. Furthermore, official publications and pronouncements by ministers began to make more explicit references to children with special educational needs, providing assurance that the National Curriculum was for all children, 'including those with special educational needs'. While these ritualistic references were at first welcomed as reassuring, as time went on they became redundant and tokenistic because it was felt that their inclusion should by then have been self-evident.

At the same time, government publications provided helpful guidance by setting out clearer principles and examples of practice. For example, the DES issued a widely disseminated guidance document, which stated: 'The principle that each pupil should have a broad and balanced curriculum which is also relevant to his or her particular needs is now established in law' (1989b: 2). Ironically enough, the same document included this classic of ambivalent thinking: 'Information about the attainments of some pupils with SENs might be excluded from the aggregate figures which must be published . . . that way, schools need have no fears that the overall picture of attainments for their pupils will suffer because children with SEN have been included' (DES 1989b: 8.5). Although this policy was later changed, it does reflect deep ignorance in the drafters. Who was to be exempted: only children with statements or the whole spectrum comprising 20 per cent or more of the total school population?

A more positive and particularly influential document was NCC Circular 5, which was limited to two sides of A4 and is still relevant today (NCC 1989a). The circular moved beyond words like 'access' and 'entitlement' and talked about 'participation', which is now regarded as the key to inclusion. It encouraged flexibility at a time when there was much uncertainty in schools about what degree of flexibility was `allowed in law': 'Access to the curriculum should be facilitated by whatever means necessary to ensure that success is achieved . . . Participation in the National Curriculum by pupils with SEN is most likely to be achieved by encouraging good practice for all pupils' (NCC 1989a: 2).

Circular 5 was rapidly followed by a 45-page report of an NCC Task Force chaired by Professor Ron Davie (NCC 1989b). This very clearly spelled out not only principles of entitlement, access and participation for the whole range of pupils with special educational needs but provided many examples of how these could be applied in the classroom for the core subjects of English, mathematics and science. This and other reports also stressed that learning difficulties are often related to factors within schools, which can create or exacerbate problems, and which could therefore be prevented by changing aspects of the school's structure or organisation. This is an early statement of inclusive principles that have now moved nearer centre stage (Ainscow 1999).

At the same time, the early versions of the subject orders in English, mathematics and science made explicit reference to ways in which the curriculum could be made accessible to pupils with exceptional needs. The examples given (enlarged print, use of audio and video tapes and alternative means of communication) made it clear that it was disabled children rather than the broad group of children with learning difficulties whose needs were being discussed.

Teachers in special schools responded to the challenge of the National Curriculum by forming their own working parties and producing guidance materials that showed with inventiveness and creativity how children with exceptional needs could gain access to what seemed a highly inaccessible and inflexible curriculum, from which children who had patently not reached Level 1 were in effect excluded (e.g. Fagg et al. 1990; Sebba 1994, 1995). In addition, the NCC (1992) funded a study illustrating good practice in adapting the curriculum to meet the needs of pupils with severe and complex learning difficulties. This tradition was continued by its successors, the SCAA and the QCA, which have produced useful guidance materials with the help of teachers with first-hand knowledge and experience.

However, most of these initiatives were directed at teachers working with pupils with severe and complex learning difficulties. Much less support has been available for teachers working with children with emotional and behavioural difficulties or moderate learning difficulties – two of the largest groups who also lack professional or parental advocates. Children with emotional and behavioural difficulties are only now being given serious consideration, the DfEE *Programme of Action* devoting a whole chapter to their needs (DfEE 1998a).

The Dearing review (1993) of the National Curriculum prompted a reconsideration of priorities and, in theory at least, released the equivalent of a day a week for other activities. Unlike the 1988 curriculum, each subject and Key Stage committee included members with experience of children with exceptional needs who monitored the modified curriculum to ensure that it was accessible. The Dearing review gave scope for more flexibility to relate the programmes of study and the assessment arrangements to the needs of individual pupils and provided time and freedom to design school experiences accordingly.

Seven years after the Dearing review, there is growing evidence that teachers have adapted well to the National Curriculum both in mainstream and in special schools. It is less prescriptive and far less overcrowded and the intervening years have seen some relaxation of the strict requirements imposed by the 1988 legislation and regulations.

Curriculum 2000

The new National Curriculum builds as far as possible on the lessons learned from the past 12 years and at first sight does not differ from the old National Curriculum in any radical way. Once again, care was taken to ensure that each subject committee included at least one member with appropriate experience of children with exceptional needs and that detailed advice was consistently incorporated at subject level (DfEE and QCA 1999).

From an inclusion perspective, the documents mark a major watershed. Firstly, the new National Curriculum is based on a set of explicit values, which are the product of an independent consultation process. Secondly, these values are reflected in a clear and detailed statement on inclusion. Thirdly, the new proposals on citizenship and on personal, social and health education reflect a wider vision of the purpose of education.

Statement of values

The quotation at the start of this chapter is taken from the opening sentence of the Secretary of State's introduction to the whole National Curriculum. The more detailed statement of values reflects a vision of a caring, inclusive society.

The values are organised under the following headings, each of which is followed by a range of examples of ways in which these values could find expression:
- *The self* – We value ourselves as unique human beings capable of spiritual, moral, intellectual and physical growth and development.

- *Relationships* – We value others for themselves, not only for what they have or what they can do for us. We value relationships as fundamental to the development and fulfilment of ourselves and others, and to the good of the community.
- *Society* – We value truth, freedom, justice, human rights, the rule of law and collective effort for the common good. In particular, we value families as sources of love and support for all their members, and as the basis of a society in which people care for others.
- *The environment* – We value the environment, both natural and shaped by humanity, as the basis of life and a source of wonder and inspiration.

The inclusion statement

Each of the new National Curriculum packs, which were sent to all schools in September 1999, contains a seven-page statement: 'Inclusion: providing effective learning opportunities for all pupils'.

Subject specific documents provide further non-statutory guidance and information on access issues relevant for that subject area. The new statement sets out three key principles for developing a more inclusive curriculum.

In planning and teaching the National Curriculum, teachers are required to have due regard to the key principles:
- setting suitable learning challenges
- responding to pupils' diverse learning needs and
- overcoming potential barriers to learning and assessment for individuals and groups of pupils.

Setting suitable learning challenges

Teachers should teach the knowledge, skills and understanding in ways that suit their pupils' abilities. This may mean choosing knowledge, skills or understanding from earlier or later key stages . . . where it is appropriate for pupils to make extensive use of content from an earlier key stage, there may not be time to teach all aspects of the age related programmes of study.

(DfEE and QCA 1999)

For pupils whose attainments fall significantly below the expected levels at a particular key stage, a much greater degree of differentiation will be necessary.

(DfEE and QCA 1999)

Responding to pupils' diverse learning needs

Although diversity is not officially defined, the following quotation is indicative of the range of pupils whose needs have to be considered.

> When planning, teachers should set high expectations and provide opportunities for all pupils to achieve, including boys and girls, pupils with special educational needs, pupils with disabilities, pupils from all social and cultural backgrounds, pupils of different ethnic groups including travellers, refugees and asylum seekers and those from diverse linguistic backgrounds.

Gifted and talented children are not mentioned in this list but it is clear from the rest of the document that they are included.

Teachers should take specific action to respond to pupils' diverse needs by:
- creating effective learning environments;
- securing their motivation and concentration;
- providing equality of opportunity through teaching approaches;
- using appropriate assessment approaches; and
- setting targets for learning.

Overcoming potential barriers to learning and assessment for individuals and groups of pupils

Pupils with special educational needs

> In many cases, the action necessary to respond to an individual's requirements for curriculum access will be met through greater differentiation of tasks and materials . . . a smaller number of pupils may need access to specialist equipment and approaches or to alternative and adapted activities.
>
> (DfEE and QCA 1999)

Pupils with disabilities

> Not all pupils with disabilities will necessarily have special educational needs. Teachers should take specific action to enable the effective participation of pupils with disabilities by:
> - planning appropriate amounts of time to allow for satisfactory completion of tasks
> - planning opportunities where necessary for the development of skills in practical aspects of the curriculum
> - identifying aspects of programmes of study and attainment targets that may present specific difficulties for individuals.
>
> (DfEE and QCA 1999)

Pupils who are learning English as an additional language

> The ability of pupils for whom English is an additional language to take part in the National Curriculum may be ahead of their communication skills in English. Teachers should plan learning opportunities to help pupils develop their English and should aim to provide the support pupils need to take part in all subject areas.   (DfEE and QCA 1999)

Detailed examples are offered under the headings.

Personal, social and health education and citizenship

Personal, social and health education

The new National Curriculum provides a framework for personal, social and health education (PSHE) and citizenship throughout all Key Stages. This is available in the form of non-statutory guidelines. Citizenship will become a statutory subject for Key Stages 3 and 4 in 2002.

> Personal, social and health education and citizenship help to give pupils the knowledge, skills and understanding they need to lead confident, healthy and independent lives and to become informed and active, responsible citizens . . . They learn to understand and respect our common humanity, diversity and differences so that they can go on to form the effective, fulfilling relationships that are an essential part of life and learning.   (Key Stages 1 and 2)

> PSHE gives pupils opportunities to reflect on their experiences and how they are developing . . . It also develops pupils' well-being and self-esteem, encouraging belief in their ability to succeed and enabling them to take responsibility for their learning and future choice of courses and career.
>   (Key Stages 3 and 4)

> Pupils should be taught:
> * about the diversity of different ethnic groups and the power of prejudice
> * to be aware of exploitation in relationships
> * to challenge offending behaviour, prejudice, bullying, racism and discrimination assertively and take the initiative in giving and receiving support
> * to work cooperatively with a range of people who are different from themselves.   (Key Stage 4)
>   (DfEE and QCA 1999)

A strong argument for personal and social development permeating all aspects of the work of both mainstream and special schools had already been made by

Sebba *et al.* (1995) and Rose *et al.* (1996) and further developed by Byers (1998). These authors see personal and social development as concerned with the development of personal autonomy and self-determination, rather than with the acquisition of skills *per se*. They argued that planning such a curriculum involves a reconsideration of the nature of the power relationship between teacher and pupil and the extent to which the aims of schooling should be concerned with 'empowerment and liberation rather than remediation and normalisation' (DfEE and QCA 1999). The aim is to foster environments that reduce dependency and to remove practices that disempower pupils (Mittler 1996b and in press).

Citizenship

The programmes of study for citizenship are set out under three headings (DfEE and QCA 1999):
- *Becoming informed citizens*. For example:
  - legal and human rights and responsibilities
  - diversity of national, regional, religious and ethnic identities (Key Stage 3)
  - opportunities to bring about social change
  - the UK's relations in Europe, with the Commonwealth and the UN; global interdependence and responsibility, including sustainable development (Key Stage 4).
- *Developing skills of enquiry and communication*. For example:
  - thinking about and justifying topical issues, and analysing information and its sources, including ICT.
- *Developing skills of participation and responsible action*. For example:
  - using imagination to consider other people's experiences and being able to think about, express and explain views that are not held personally
  - reflecting on the process of participating.

These aims could hardly be more relevant to pupils with exceptional needs and to preparing the next generation of young people to work for and live in a more inclusive society. At one level, the pupils with exceptional needs will benefit if the next generation of citizens has a clearer understanding of issues concerned with social justice and human rights. On a day-to-day level, these values address the experience of bullying, exclusion and discrimination faced by marginalised groups, since all too often they are the victims of denial of human rights and of unfairness and injustice.

Testing, testing, testing

Political imperatives

Although the principle of a National Curriculum was widely accepted when it was first announced in 1987, the same cannot be said of the proposals for national testing. These introduced compulsory national testing at the ages of 7, 11 and 14, and were bitterly opposed by teachers and teachers' organisations, although public opinion polls reflected a greater degree of support, especially from parents of school-age children. Nevertheless, teachers cooperated well with the early SATs, especially for Key Stage 1, but opposition to national testing later led to industrial action and caused the resignation of John Patten, the Secretary of State for Education.

Unfortunately, it took no time at all for SAT results to be used by politicians and in public debate as though they were written on scientifically validated tablets of stone. More recently, they have been used for target-setting by schools, LEAs and at national level and the Secretary of State for Education has promised to resign if certain targets are not met by the nation's children by a given date.

People in high places who should know better have gone on record as disgusted with the finding that one-third of the nation's children are below average at one or other Key Stage. Such statements reflect a lack of understanding of the concept of average.*

The publication of national test results in league tables is obviously part of the political objective of enforcing accountability. Although the league tables now contain additional information, the information reported fails to do justice to the work of schools in teaching 'the whole curriculum', nor can such tables reflect the 'ethos and values' of a school. The government is encouraging attempts to define and quantify the 'value-added' element but this is proving to be a technically challenging task (Saunders 1996).

Now that a new National Curriculum is about to be launched, it is apparent that no parallel matching proposals have been made for a major review of national testing. What we have inherited is the 1988 framework of end of Key Stage national tests, in parallel with teacher assessment, which has been greatly slimmed down and made more flexible.

On the other hand, we now have baseline assessment at the beginning of the Reception year (i.e. close to the child's fourth birthday) and informal assessments in the light of the *Early Learning Goals* (QCA and DfEE 1999) (see Chapter 3). Very recently, the Secretary of State for Education has proposed further tests at the

---

* See Level 4 mathematics at Key Stage 2: 'pupils should know that mode is a measure of average and that range is a measure of spread, and to use both ideas to describe data sets; draw conclusions from statistics and graphs and recognise when information is presented in a misleading way'.

end of the first year of secondary education as part of a policy of identifying and helping pupils who have not reached Level 4 when they leave primary school and of raising standards within Key Stage 3 as a whole. 'World-class' tests are also being piloted to identify potential high flyers in mathematics who will be encouraged to take GCSE examinations before they even leave primary schools. It seems that testing is definitely here to stay.

Is there another way?

The hostile reception given to national testing was in part a response to the confusing pot pourri of reasons given by the government to justify national tests. Some of these are mutually contradictory; others cannot be achieved with the assessment tools at our disposal. Since the present government has not made any serious proposals to change the system of assessment, it may be useful to look at some of the arguments and issues (see Cline (1992) and Gipps and Murphy (1994) for more detailed data and discussion).

While it is true that there is little point in launching a new National Curriculum without at the same time assessing the progress that children make within that curriculum, the same purpose could be achieved in a variety of ways. For example, we could assess large representative samples of children in core subjects at regular intervals, rather than testing every single child. We could also scrap national tests at Key Stages 1–3 but greatly strengthen teacher assessment. The experience in Scotland, where a more flexible system avoiding end of Key Stage national tests was adopted, could now be considered as an alternative approach to the assessment of children in England.

Before the Education Reform Act 1988 we had a government funded Assessment and Performance Unit (APU) under the aegis of HMI, which regularly carried out careful and systematic testing of the performance of large but representative samples of pupils in particular subject areas (Gipps and Murphy 1994). These sweep tests were meticulously constructed in the light of the best available knowledge of test design and interpretation and the APU reports were models of scientific respectability. Perhaps that is why they had so little impact.

Through the work of the APU we have inherited the experience and the technical know-how to devise tests that are administered to a carefully constructed sample of children. If governments want information on how the new curriculum is working, they could well commission the QCA or an independent body to propose alternative models to the present system and discuss whether the APU model could be adapted to today's conditions. The existence of a National Curriculum would now make the task much easier.

The refusal of the 1988 government even to consider any alternative to the testing of every child at the end of each Key Stage reflects a political imperative rather than an educational need. It sprang from a determination to develop a new system of national accountability in which the scores of all the children in a school at a given stage could be compared with other schools and with local, regional or national norms so that parents were provided with information to enable them to select a school of their choice. This policy is even stronger today than when it was first introduced. League tables, modified and contextualised and with a touch of context and value-added, have become a political imperative.

But governments have gone further by claiming that regular testing would at the same time identify children with learning difficulties at an early stage, so that they could be given appropriate help. This argument has resurfaced in the debates about baseline assessment, with the government still pinning its faith on the tests' diagnostic functions.

There are many difficulties with this argument. Firstly, neither the early SATs nor the later national tests were ever developed as diagnostic tests but as a means of providing a snapshot assessment of a child's performance on nationally laid down ATs in the core subjects. The results are not likely to reveal much about an individual child that a good teacher did not know already.

Neither the early SATs nor later national tests were ever standardised and contained no norms against which individual children could be compared. They therefore differ from standardised normative reading tests. The test items in the SATs had of necessity to be related to the statements of attainment of the National Curriculum.

National tests can never provide more than a broad-brush assessment or overcome some basic problems of interpretation. For example, how do we know that Level 1 in English is comparable to Level 1 in mathematics? The levels were developed on the assumption that it takes children two years, on average, to move from one level to another. Each level includes a wide range of achievement so that two children who are reliably assessed as being at a particular level may still differ greatly in their mastery of the subject.

This is not to dismiss national tests as having no value. Great care has been taken in their construction. Teachers have been involved in their preparation and they have been improved in the light of field tests and pilot studies. Furthermore, teachers themselves administer the tests in their own classrooms.

Some of these issues were well anticipated by the Task Group on Assessment and Testing (TGAT), which was set up by the DES (1987a) under the chairmanship of a distinguished academic, Professor Paul Black. The TGAT report marked a turning point in the government's fortunes because it met the concerns of many teachers about the government's plans for national tests. TGAT recommended that the SATs should be matched by teacher assessments and that both should have equal value. In other words, teachers would make an estimate of where each child stood in relation to the official attainment targets of the National Curriculum, based on their knowledge of the pupil's response to teaching over a period of time and not just on a given day. Teachers were encouraged to discuss schemes of assessment with their head teacher and with an assessment coordinator in each school or cluster of schools and their assessments could be moderated by locally appointed assessors.

This scheme was in fact put into place but soon downgraded by the government, who ruled that where the results of SATs differed from teacher assessments, the SAT results were to 'take precedence'. Fortunately, the balance was restored in the Dearing review, so that teacher assessment is now recorded alongside national tests and can replace national tests where this is agreed to be more appropriate. Teacher assessment is in fact much richer than the national tests, as the following quote from QCA makes clear:

> The tests provide a standard 'snapshot' of attainment at the end of the key stage, while teacher assessment, carried out as part of teaching and learning in the classroom, covers the full range and scope of the programmes of study and takes account of evidence of achievement in a range of contexts, including that gained through discussion and observation.   (QCA 1997: 9)

If these words mean what they seem to mean, is there not a case for phasing out national assessments and raising the status of teacher assessment? Such a proposal would have been rejected in the political climate of the late 1980s and early 1990s because ministers argued that the public would not have confidence in teacher assessment alone and that independently constructed national tests were needed to 'guarantee objectivity'. But can such an argument still be sustained? Teacher assessment is already much more comprehensive than national tests; for example, it covers all ATs and programmes of study. Furthermore, there are various external checks to ensure consistency, including clear criteria on aggregating weightings. If we can have confidence in teacher assessment, do we really need to retain national tests at Key Stages 1–3?

One counter-argument that might be advanced against such a proposal is the evidence from OFSTED national reports, which indicate that the quality of assessment and record keeping across all schools is not as good as it should be for all pupils (OFSTED 1999a). On the other hand, another OFSTED report also illustrates examples of good inclusive practice: 'the most effective assessment practice for pupils with SEN occurred where schools linked their . . . practice arising from the Code with their procedures for assessing and reporting on the progress of all pupils in the schools' (OFSTED 1997: 8).

One other finding about teacher assessment that should be mentioned is the occasional reference in the research literature to teacher assessments being on occasion lower than SAT results (Lewis 1996), particularly for children with low attainments or from disadvantaged backgrounds. This would be consistent with other evidence that the abilities of such children are liable to be underestimated. This interpretation assumes that the SAT assessment is more objective and nearer 'the truth'. Of course, the opposite explanation could also be offered, but since neither assessment has proven reliability or validity, there is no reason to expect anything like perfect agreement between them.

With the emphasis now given to assessment and reporting, a new professional development strategy is needed to ensure that all teachers are given support to develop their assessment skills, not just for Key Stage assessments but across the board. Because initial teacher education cannot provide enough time for this in universities and colleges, students depend on whatever assessment practices they see in schools. In the light of OFSTED findings about major weaknesses in this area, new initiatives are called for.

For example, if we have to have specialist and beacon schools, why not allow them to bid for such status through the excellence of their work in assessment and recording? Gaps in professional knowledge and skills in assessment and monitoring of pupils' achievements across the school as a whole could also be met through the TTA (or its successor). OFSTED inspection guidelines already include criteria for ensuring quality control in the school's assessment and recording systems.

There is also scope for local initiatives led by LEAs or clusters of schools that not only want to improve their assessment and monitoring systems but also become proficient in the use of diagnostic tests. This is an opportunity for educational psychologists to share their distinctive skills with teachers. This suggestion was made 30 years ago, repeated more recently (Mittler 1970, 1990) and is worth revisiting one more time now that the government is completing a major review of the role of educational psychologists.

National tests and children with exceptional needs

All children with exceptional needs in mainstream schools are assessed at the end of each Key Stage, unless specifically exempted by the appropriate section of the Education Reform Act 1988. This is permissible only if they have also been exempted from a programme of study or a whole subject. Since few schools exempt any their pupils from national assessment, the league tables will reflect the scores of all assessed pupils, whether or not they are on the special needs register or a have a statement.

This clearly has major implications for publication of results in league tables. For some time, the government refused to sanction the publication of any contextual information, such as the number of children on the special needs register or on free school meals, arguing that such information must not be used to provide 'excuses' for poor school performance. More recently, this information has been made available but it is still difficult for parents or governors to know how to interpret it.

Schools are thus faced with a dilemma. If they identify or accept 'too many' children with learning difficulties, this may well have an adverse effect on their published results. Many schools have enough confidence in their work and in their commitment to inclusion to live with the possible effects of the league tables. They rely on good communication and relationships with their parents, their local community and their LEA to offset their position in the league tables. Schools that have retained and developed a good reputation because of the quality of their work seem to take league tables in their stride.

Some helpful guidance has been provided by the statutory bodies to support teachers in making national tests accessible to the largest possible number of pupils with exceptional needs and in planning their own teacher assessments (e.g. SCAA 1996c). Nevertheless, a tension remains between continuing with national assessments in their present form and the government's stated commitment to inclusion. This tension could be partly resolved by shifting the emphasis of assessment more firmly in the direction of teacher assessment.

Children below Level 1

Some pupils may take many years to reach Level 1, and others might never reach it before leaving school aged 16 or 19. Such a system is manifestly unfair in what purported to be a curriculum for all children.

Faced with this dilemma, teachers were reluctant to use the provisions of the Education Reform Act 1988 that would allow them to exempt pupils from statutory assessment. Although they had to use the W (working towards Level 1) category, which was 'awarded' to virtually all pupils in schools for children with severe learning difficulties, it is clearly inappropriate for any pupils to remain on W for the rest of their schooling.

Teachers therefore devised their own solutions to this problem by designing and publishing their own 'steps to Level 1' and incorporating these into teacher assessment as a way of recording progress and reporting such progress to parents and pupils themselves, as well as to LEAs and ultimately to government. The NFER was commissioned to undertake a study reviewing the variety of practice being developed in schools. Their helpful report had a direct impact on official policy (Fletcher-Campbell and Lee (1995). Eventually, the principle of step-by-step progression to Level 1 and between Levels 1 and 3 became 'official' in the P (progress) levels adopted by the QCA (DfEE and QCA 1998; Wade 1999). This guidance encourages target setting beyond the statutory requirements and includes performance criteria in personal and social education.

Assessment at Key Stage 4

The overall aims of the government's proposals for the 14–19 age group were summarised by the Secretary of State for Education in his speech to the North of England conference. The aim is to ensure that 'virtually no pupil will leave school at 16 without any qualifications. All will be involved in education from 14 to 19 and in many cases beyond' (Blunkett 2000). In order to meet this aim, the range of qualifications is being extended beyond GCSE. A bewildering variety of new initiatives is under way or under discussion for the 14–19 age group.

Although the GCSE was originally devised as a course of study and assessment framework which rewards achievement at all levels and for all pupils, this aim has been subverted by the obsession of governments, parents and the media with performance at the higher grades of C or above, thus downgrading the achievements of students who gain passes with grades down to G. About ten years ago, further damage was done to the GCSE when the then Prime Minister, John Major, criticised coursework assessment as too easy. This immediately led to a massive reduction in the amount of coursework assessment, which had provided an access route to many young people with learning difficulties. This change was bitterly criticised by all teacher unions and professional bodies as a loss of entitlement but was justified by ministers by reference to the need to raise standards. Their decision involved a return to the 'sudden death' examination, which had disenfranchised a previous generation from school-leaving examinations and qualifications. Research commissioned by SEAC at the time also reflected enormous differences in the proportion of pupils who were entered for GCSE, some schools entering close to 100 per cent of the age group, and others far fewer. Very few special schools entered any pupils for GCSE.

Alternative qualifications

During the 1990s, GCSE was complemented by a range of alternative qualifications, mostly with a strong vocational element (e.g. GNVQ), which were meant to be of equal standing with the 'more academic' GCSEs. The QCA has now developed criteria and standards to enable work below these levels to be recognised within a wider qualifications framework. 'Entry level awards are available which are broadly equivalent to National Curriculum Levels 1, 2 and 3' (Wade 1999); these were specifically excluded from recognition by an earlier ministerial decision of the previous government, again in the name of standards.

Progress files: achievement planners

In addition to, and in place of formal qualifications, students in this age group have benefited from the national records of achievement. These provide a written record of interests and achievements outside as well inside the National Curriculum and include interests such as sport and community service. What goes into the record is largely decided by the student.

The Programme of Action announced that new guidance materials are being developed in place of the records of achievement; these will be known as 'progress files: achievement planners'. The needs and interests of students with exceptional needs are specifically included in these developments.

Conclusions

A school curriculum that is accessible and that provides all pupils without exception with opportunities to participate fully and to experience success is an essential foundation for inclusion. The new National Curriculum has been explicitly designed to be accessible to greater numbers of pupils. All schools and local communities should now have better support systems for those who do experience difficulty at any point.

But the new National Curriculum does not operate in a vacuum and has itself to grapple with many obstacles. Some of these spring from the traditional elitist nature of the education system, which has brought success to a few and exclusion to many. These legacies are deep rooted in our schools and in society at large. They cannot be discounted by politicians or reformers. Nearly 20 years ago David Hargreaves (1982) made a plea for comprehensive schools to loosen the stranglehold of the 'cognitive academic' and subject and examination dominated curriculum. The aim of a broader and richer curriculum was reflected in series of reports from the former Inner London Education Authority (ILEA) (1984) including the Fish report (ILEA 1985), which was the first to map out an inclusion terrain. These reports were interred with the ILEA but their message is even more relevant today.

The current reforms have to challenge traditions that have erected obstacles to learning. The content of the curriculum has not captured the interest of many children and has failed to reflect the diversity of the communities and cultures in our society. As a result many children have not been reached by what schools have to offer. Lessons may be pitched too high, children may fail to understand what is required of them, and the language of instruction may create further obstacles to understanding and participation.

Another major obstacle to inclusion lies in the practice of testing, assessing and classifying children, which we have inherited from previous generations and which have been traditionally used to separate children from one another. We cannot hope to achieve a more inclusive curriculum or more inclusive schools unless we also undertake a fundamental review of the assessment system and its impact on the lives of children and families. A small start has been made with widening the assessment framework at 16. The time has come to replace national assessment tests in the first three Key Stages with a strengthened system of teacher assessment and regular sweep tests of samples of pupils.

Designing an accessible curriculum and assessment framework is only the first step to inclusion. In Chapter 8 we will review what has been said about the characteristics of an inclusive system as it impacts on children in the classroom.

Chapter 8

Towards Inclusive Practice

> We will know that inclusive education has fully arrived when designations such as 'inclusion school', 'inclusion classroom', 'inclusion student' are no longer part of our educational vocabulary. Inclusion survives as an issue only so long as someone is excluded. (Giangreco 1997: 194)

Introduction

What does inclusion mean in day-to-day practice? What difference does it make to the work of teachers and above all how does it affect pupils? Can we define and describe some of the core features of inclusion from a classroom and pupil perspective? Although a great deal has been written on this subject, it is impossible to do justice to the rich variety of practice. All we can do is to attempt to provide signposts under a few convenient headings.

Elements of inclusion

Many writers have tried to distil the essence of inclusive practice. Some have described a vision but most now stress that inclusion is a journey without end. Some schools are well equipped for the journey; others will find that the baggage that they carry is unsuitable and may need to be adapted or even discarded. Each school will encounter different obstacles along the way but all schools will find that the most difficult barriers spring from deeply ingrained but not necessarily expressed doubts about whether the journey is worthwhile in the first place.

Chapter 1 summarised attempts that have been made to define the core essentials of inclusion. Briefly, these are:
- all children attend their neighbourhood school:
  - in the regular classroom
  - with appropriate support;

- all teachers accept responsibility for all pupils:
  - receiving appropriate support and
  - opportunities for professional development;
- schools rethink their values:
  - restructure their organisation, curriculum and assessment arrangements
  - to overcome barriers to learning and participation and
  - to cater for the full range of pupils in their school and in their community.

This list contains items that are still controversial. To take just one example from the first item, there are those who insist that 'all children' means exactly what it says and includes children now in special schools or special classes. Clearly, this is not the view of the government, which envisages a continuing role for special schools.

There is also some ambiguity about the meaning of 'neighbourhood school'. To some, it means the school that the child would normally have attended if there had been no obstacle to doing so. This implies that every school in the country would have to meet the criteria for inclusion. Since we have not yet arrived at this point, many LEAs are developing 'resourced schools'; strategically placed and accessible mainstream schools that are additionally resourced to cater for all children and that may meet all the criteria for inclusion except that of being the child's nearest local school. Furthermore, as Booth (1999b) points out, the government's policy of open enrolment encourages all parents to look beyond their neighbourhood school, so that the principle of attending the nearest school is already breached for all children. It may therefore be somewhat doctrinaire to insist on it for children with exceptional needs.

Index for Inclusion

Schools wishing to explore what is actually involved in developing inclusive practice can now make use of a travel companion known as the *Index for Inclusion: Developing Learning and Participation in Schools* (Centre for Studies in Inclusive Education (CSIE) 2000). The Index developed from a collaboration between the CSIE, the University of Manchester Centre for Educational Needs and the Centre for Educational Research at Christ Church University College, Canterbury.

A first superficial glance may suggest that it is yet another checklist of bullet-pointed targets or the latest OFSTED framework for the inspection of inclusion. A closer look at the introductory text will make it clear that the Index is a tool for the use of schools themselves rather than the latest example of government prescription. Although the DfEE is funding the distribution of the Index free to every school and LEA in England, and some pump-priming funding came from the TTA, all the development work on the Index was carried out by a partnership of practitioners and academics in the field: a team of teachers, parents, academics, LEAs and schools, who have tried it out and improved it in a range of different settings across the country.

The Index is a tool for a process of self-evaluation of policy and practice. It is not a checklist that can be given to the SENCO to complete in their 'spare time'. It is designed to be used as a contribution to a process of school review involving all staff, governors, students, parents and carers. Their collective task is to examine the work of the school as a whole. No one is coming to inspect whether schools have used the Index in this or any other way. The way in which they use it is a matter for them. The exercise is voluntary.

The Index is organised under three dimensions, each with two sub-sections. Each of these leads to a list of indicators, which in turn result in a series of specific questions that form the core of the self-evaluation process. We can look briefly at all three dimensions and their sub-sections and then at all the indicators relevant to the third dimension, since these lie at the heart of classroom practice, which is the concern of this chapter. Finally, we can look at an example of the specific questions arising from one of the indicators.

- *Dimension A: Creating inclusive cultures*
  Section 1: Building community
  Section 2: Establishing inclusive values

- *Dimension B: Producing inclusive policies*
  Section 1: Developing schools for all
  Section 2: Organising support for diversity

- *Dimension C: Evolving inclusive practice*
  Section 1: Orchestrating learning
  Section 2: Mobilising resources

All three dimensions are of equal importance but for purposes of illustration we will focus on Dimension C, which is explained as follows:

> This dimension is about making school practices reflect the inclusive cultures and policies of the school. It is concerned with ensuring that classroom and extra-curricular activities encourage the participation of all students and draw on their knowledge and experience outside the school. Teaching and support are integrated together in the orchestration of learning and the overcoming of barriers to learning and participation. Staff mobilise resources within the school and local communities to sustain active learning for all.
>
> (CSIE 2000)

Indicators for sub-section C1: Orchestrating learning

- Lessons are responsive to student diversity.
- Lessons are made accessible to all students.
- Lessons develop an understanding of difference.
- Students are actively involved in their own learning.
- Students learn collaboratively.
- Assessment encourages the achievements of all students.
- Classroom discipline is based on mutual respect.
- Teachers plan, review and teach in partnership.
- Teachers minimise barriers to learning and participation for every student.
- LSAs are concerned to support the learning and participation of all students.
- Homework contributes to the learning of all.
- All students take part in activities outside the classroom.

Indicators for sub-section C2: Mobilising resources

- School resources are distributed fairly to support inclusion.
- Community resources are known and drawn upon.
- Staff expertise is fully utilised.
- Student difference is used as a resource for teaching and learning.
- Staff develop shared resources to support learning and participation.

Questions for C.1.2: Lessons are made accessible to all students

- Is particular attention paid to the accessibility of spoken and written language?
- Do lessons build on the language experience of students outside the school?
- Is technical vocabulary explained and practised during lessons?
- Do curriculum materials reflect the backgrounds and experience of all learners?
- Are all lessons made equally accessible to all boys and girls by including a range of activities that reflect the range of interests of both genders?
- Are there opportunities for students who are learning English as an additional language to speak and write in their first language?
- Are students able to participate fully in the curriculum, in clothes appropriate to their religious beliefs, for example in science and physical education?

- Are adaptations made to the curriculum, for students who have reservations about participating because of religious beliefs, in, for example, art or music?
- Do staff recognise the physical effort required to complete tasks for some learners with impairments or chronic illnesses and the tiredness that can result?
- Do staff recognise the mental effort expended by some students, for example using lip reading and vision aids?
- Do staff recognise the additional time required by some students with impairments to use equipment in practical work?
- Do staff provide alternative ways of giving experience or understanding for students who cannot engage in particular activities, for example using equipment in science, some forms of exercise in physical education, or optical science for blind students?

Foundations for inclusive practice

The Index for Inclusion takes as its starting point a range of fairly typical primary and secondary schools and works on the assumption that many of the elements of inclusive practice are already in place as an expression of good practice for all pupils but can still be further developed. Other areas may be weaker and need rethinking. In the following section we will look more closely at some of the major headings under which schools are planning to develop their inclusive practice and provide a few pointers to publications and good practice.

Differentiation

'Differentiation of classwork within a common curriculum framework will help the school to meet the learning needs of all pupils' (DfE 1994). This confident assertion from the Code of Practice reflects the official endorsement of differentiation as the royal road to inclusion. This finds further expression in the SCAA guidelines (SCAA 1996b) and in the Programme of Action. Helpful definitions and `worked examples' of differentiation in action are now available (Bearne 1996; Sewell 1996; Westwood 1997). Nevertheless, it is important to avoid the danger of differentiation leading unwittingly to segregation within the mainstream classroom (Hart 1992).

Visser (1993) and Phillips *et al.* (1999) offer the following definitions:

> Differentiation is the process whereby teachers meet the need for progress through the curriculum by selecting appropriate teaching methods to match an individual child's learning strategies, within a group situation.
>
> (Visser 1993)

> Differentiation is a process whereby planning and delivering the curriculum takes account of individual differences and matches what is taught and how it is taught to individual learning styles and needs. It seeks to provide opportunities for ALL children to participate and make progress in the curriculum by:
> - building on past achievement
> - presenting challenges for further achievement
> - providing opportunities for success.   (Phillips *et al.* 1999: 33)

They also distinguish between seven ways in which the curriculum may be differentiated: input, task, outcome, output, response, resource and support.

McNamara and Moreton (1997) contrast 'progressive' with 'traditional' approaches to differentiation. They associate progressive approaches with differentiation by outcome, where different standards of work are expected from children of different abilities, as well as with differentiation by resource involving 'extension' activities such as more time for explanations for the least able pupils. Traditional methods include grouping by ability and differentiation by task, both of which are said to lead to underestimation (McNamara and Moreton 1997: 3–4).

The SCAA (1996b) guidance provides particularly helpful suggestions on supporting access to the curriculum at Key Stage 3 and includes many examples of the work of both teachers and pupils.

Assessment and record keeping

Because the process and the outcomes of assessment can easily become instruments of exclusion, it is important for schools to develop assessment policies and practices that avoid this danger and that help to promote fuller access and participation in the learning experiences provided by the school. Unfortunately, assessment has come to be identified with assessment of pupils' progress on the National Curriculum and with the results of national tests rather than teacher assessment. This is a different purpose from using assessment to work with the pupil to plan the next steps in learning and mastery, although government statements consistently confuse the two aims, which are basically incompatible.

Available research suggests that teachers have worked hard to ensure that both the early SATs and later national tests and teacher assessment were adapted to meet the needs of pupils with special educational needs. Lewis (1995a, 1996) provides an excellent summary of early developments in primary schools.

There are few opportunities for teachers to learn about or learn to use the wide range of assessment tools that are now becoming available. In theory, SENCOs should have access to this information so that they can support their colleagues in learning about what is available and adapting it to the needs of their classrooms and students (Cline 1992; Gipps and Murphy 1994; Chapter 7).

Teachers already use records of achievement, which reflect a much richer picture of pupils' achievements outside as well as within the National Curriculum, including out of school interests and hobbies. Development work is now under way to incorporate these into broader pupil portfolios of work, with more emphasis on celebrating relatively small steps in learning (Wade 1999).

Keeping adequate classroom records is essential but is often overlooked, according to OFSTED national studies.

A national OFSTED (1998c) report on teacher assessment at Key Stage 2 offers the following summary of best practice:
- Teachers decide how and when they will assess pupils' attainment at the same time as they plan the work.
- Teachers are proficient in using a range of assessment techniques, including asking questions, observing pupils and setting tasks or tests at the end of a series of lessons.
- Manageable written recording systems are used alongside the sensible retention of evidence (portfolios).
- Teachers make accurate judgements about the standard of pupils' work based on reliable sources of evidence.
- There are effective procedures for reporting on pupils' progress and attainment.
- The best school policies on assessment are specific about what will be assessed and when.

The SCAA (1996b) guidelines summarise the aims of assessment to inform curriculum and lesson planning as to:
- allow pupils' progress to be monitored, within and beyond the National Curriculum;
- acknowledge pupils' physical, personal and affective development;
- enable appropriate objectives to be set, either for groups of pupils or for individuals;
- support pupils in determining options (for Key Stage 4); and
- provide evidence for reports to parents.

The guidelines stress the importance of assessment and record keeping as a continuous classroom based process that, *inter alia*:
- allows progress, however limited to be demonstrated
- provides appropriate starting points and challenges for individual pupils
- acknowledges pupils' oral and practical as well as written responses
- allows individuals to respond with help from their peers, an adult or an older pupil.   (SCAA 1996b: 32)

The Index for Inclusion (CSIE 2000) also has *Indicator C.1.6. Assessment encourages the achievements of all students*, as follows:
- Are assessments (even national assessments) always used formatively so that they develop the learning of all students in the school?
- Are there opportunities for assessment of work done in collaboration with others?
- Are students given feedback that indicates recognitions of what they have learnt and what they might do next?
- Are students involved in assessing and commenting on their own learning?
- Can students set clear goals for their future learning?
- Is there monitoring of the achievement of different groups of students (boys/girls, ethnic minority students/students with impairments) so that particular difficulties can be detected and addressed?

Collaborative learning

Pupils learning together has been a feature of most schools but has been somewhat undermined by government and OFSTED pronouncements on the importance of whole-class teaching. Pupils experiencing difficulties can benefit greatly from small-group learning but teachers have to ensure that all pupils are benefiting and that the group is not forced to work at the pace of the slowest or fastest learners. This is a form of differentiation not so much of the curriculum as of the opportunities presented by work in small groups.

Examples of relevant questions from the Index for Inclusion come from *Indicator C.1.5. Children and young people learn collaboratively*:
- Do group activities allow students to divide up tasks and pool what they have learnt?
- Do students learn how to compile a joint report from the different contributions in a group?

- When others in the class are troubled, do students help to calm them down rather than wind them up?
- Do students recognise that every student should have their share of the limelight?
- Do students share responsibility for helping to overcome the difficulties experienced by some students in lessons?
- Are students involved in assessing each other's learning?
- Are students involved in helping each other to set educational goals?

Support in theory and practice

The provision of a support system is the key to progress. But what is 'appropriate support' and is it for teachers or pupils? Does support come from the school itself or from outside? Must we assume that all children with exceptional needs necessarily need support?

Our starting point on the road to inclusion must be classrooms and teachers that already provide support naturally and as part of day-to-day practice. This includes ensuring that all pupils take the fullest part in a lesson, that they have opportunities to interact with the teacher and with each other and that they achieve success. The concept of support should not, therefore, devalue or deskill existing good practice. It may be useful to think of a continuum of support, beginning in the natural environment of the ordinary classroom and using the experienced teacher's natural repertoire of skills in ensuring that all pupils participate and are included.

Support has become a major enterprise. No publication or document on inclusion is complete without frequent references to 'support'; a word that carries many meanings and overtones. We now have a SENCO in every school and some 40,000 LSAs, who play a crucial role in working with a wide range of children in mainstream and special schools. There are LEA support services (e.g. for specific learning difficulties, sensory impairment or behaviour support), a well regarded professional journal called *Support for Learning* and many books and articles on the subject.

Is it possible to disentangle the different ways in which the word 'support' is used? To some, it has a reassuring warmth, conjuring up images of understanding and benevolence. To others, it means extra money, equipment and above all additional staff. Support tends to be welcomed because it is nearly always thought of as something additional to what is there already: 'provision beyond that which is generally available'. But who decides what kind of support a child needs and how do we know that what we define as support is seen in the same way by the child?

- A student who has Down's Syndrome was working very satisfactorily in an ordinary secondary classroom and taking a full part in the lesson. His support assistant was sitting next to him with nothing to do because he was fully involved. At the end of the lesson, a visitor to the school asked the pupil how he had enjoyed the lesson. His reply was, 'Fine but can you get that woman off my back?'
- In another class, a support assistant is sent home without pay because the pupil she is supporting is away sick.
- Another child is sent home because his support assistant is away sick.

Teachers supporting each other

One form of support comes from structures that enable teachers to support one another. This is in addition to informal sources of support that teachers develop whenever they have an opportunity to discuss problems, however briefly.

There is no set or preferred pattern but the common feature of the published accounts is that a small group of teachers meet regularly to discuss either a particular child or, more commonly, a more general concern relating to barriers to learning and participation for groups of pupils. An early account of 'teacher assistance teams' was provided by Chalfant *et al.* (1979) and has recently been adapted to the very different setting of Hong Kong (McBrayer and McBrayer 1999). Typically, members of the group suggest possible solutions that may (or may not) be tried out, with results reported back to the next meeting. Such meetings may be encouraged and supported by school management but they are intended as a grass roots initiative under the control of members of the group, who take it in turns to chair the sessions and take any further action on behalf of the group as a whole.

A variant on this theme is the addition of a visiting consultant, whose job it is to facilitate the exchange of information and ideas, not to offer instant solutions in the manner expected of consultants in business and industry. An English example of such 'light touch' consultancy can be found in the work of Gerda Hanko (1995), who has many years' experience of collaborative consultation in mainstream schools in inner London. The role of the consultant is rather like that of a trained counsellor who helps people to clarify problems and solutions for themselves. Their success is measured by the extent to which groups continue to meet when the consultant's given number of sessions has been completed. The fact that the consultant is brought in by the school and is not an employee of the LEA makes it easier to share problems and solutions (Platt 1989).

Collaborative teaching

The presence of a second adult in the classroom is a new experience for most teachers in mainstream schools and one for which they are unlikely to have been prepared in their training. Not surprisingly, the arrival of a second adult, either temporarily or permanently, can be at the least disconcerting and unsettling and at worst a permanent threat to the teacher's autonomy.

A good deal of information on collaborative teaching is now available. A book by Jordan (1994) is particularly useful as it is based on UK as well as Canadian experience. A practitioner's guide has been published by Doyle (1997) and an interesting book of readings has been brought together by Graham and Harris (1999). In the UK, the work of Lacey and Lomas (1993) has provided helpful guidance on teamwork and collaboration across professional boundaries.

> The Index for Inclusion also raises some relevant question in *Indicator C.1.8. Staff plan, teach and review in partnership:*
> * Do staff engage in partnership teaching?
> * Do teachers modify their teaching in response to feedback from colleagues?
> * Do classroom and support teachers share in working with individuals, groups and the whole class?

Children supporting children

Successful inclusion and participation in lessons and in the life of the school depends to a large extent on other children. In general, help and support are given casually and without teacher planning or intervention, although in countries with large classes teachers ensure that children of varying abilities are sitting next to each other, so that more able children are helping neighbours who may be struggling to understand what they are supposed to do. In China such support is regarded as a duty of a more able child.

In Western countries, the practice of peer tutoring is increasingly used. The best guide in Britain is still Topping's (1988) *The Peer Tutoring Handbook,* which gives many examples of the wide range of approaches that have been used to enable students to support one another's learning, as well as suggestions on how to plan and organise successful projects. A recent issue of *Support for Learning* was devoted to the theme of peer support (Charlton 1998). The articles emphasise the mutual benefits to be derived from such support and show that gains for the tutee go well beyond skill acquisition or mastery.

Peer tutoring has been shown to be particularly effective in the teaching of reading, provided the tutor is properly prepared and supported and the pupil is willing to accept such help. More recently, there have been reports of the successful use of peer tutoring in the context of helping to raise the achievements of children taking part in an 'integration pilot project' in Hong Kong (P. A. Mittler 1998). To quote Winter: 'Children can teach other children and they can learn from doing so . . . put simply, all school systems are full of students and all classes are rich in students, no matter what other resources they may lack' (Winter 2000).

Westwood (1997) summarises four essentials of peer tutoring as:
- clear directions as to what they are to do and how they are to do it;
- a specific teaching task to undertake and appropriate instructional materials;
- a demonstration of effective tutoring behaviours; and
- an opportunity to role play or practise tutoring, with feedback and correction.

Children also support one another informally and without teacher planning. Research reviews on inclusion of children with severe learning difficulties report that other children in the schools are generally supportive and accepting (Farrell 1997, Sebba with Sachdev 1997), although warm friendships are not frequently reported. A study by Lewis (1995b) of groups of children working together in one school provides more insight into the process of inclusion from the perspective of the children involved than any number of scholarly reviews.

Support from the SENCO

So far, we have been looking briefly at some examples of resources already available to schools and how they might be developed to support inclusion. We now turn to some comparatively recent resources that have been added to schools. The first of these is clearly the SENCO. Every school has at least one; some have two (e.g. one each for Key Stage 1 and Key Stage 2); secondary schools will have at least a small team of learning support coordinators, possibly attached to subject departments and also working within the pastoral framework of the school.

The SENCO's first task is to support ordinary teachers in carrying out their responsibilities to teach all children. Stage 1 of the 1994 Code of Practice (DfE 1994) envisaged a 'light touch' by the SENCO, who encourages teachers to make whatever adaptations are possible to classroom management and curriculum. In this sense, Stage 1 was intended to support inclusion because responsibility remains fully with the class teacher.

More recently, the government has been consulting on their proposal to merge Stages 1 and 2 under the new heading 'School Action', distinguishing this from 'School Action Plus' when some additional resources would be made available to the school, not necessarily for individual children. This proposal could provide more flexibility as well as reducing paperwork. It would also enable the SENCO and class teacher to use their discretion about when to draw up an IEP at any time within the School Action phase rather than at the beginning of Stage 2. However, very little information has been published on how the new Code of Practice would operate in practice and how patterns of funding might change.

The establishment of an effective working partnership between SENCOs and class and subject teachers depends largely on the amount of time that can be allocated and to the effectiveness with which the limited time available is used. The degree to which head teachers and governors understand and are committed to working towards inclusion will be reflected in the quality of the support given to the work of SENCOs and above all in the amount of time allocated to their work.

A case can be made for SENCOs to be given the equivalent of two days a week, rising to three in EAZs and schools taking part in Excellence in Cities (Chapter 5).

Support from LSAs

Many US examples are of two qualified 'equal status' teachers working together, whereas much of the British experience is of teachers working with staff who may not have any form of qualification, who are working part-time and may be funded through the LEA rather than from the school's own budget. Good management as well as good will can ensure that such differences do not erect barriers to collaboration. This depends to a large extent on the head teacher supporting and modelling collaborative planning.

Special schools have been working with LSAs for many years, under a variety of none too appropriate titles such as non-teaching aides, special support assistants and classroom assistants. Special schools with a much longer history of two (or three) adults to a class have tried out a variety of approaches to the sharing of roles and responsibilities in the classroom. Thomas (1992) has shown how this experience can be adapted for use in mainstream primary schools. For example, an LSA can work with the class as a whole while the teacher spends five or ten minutes in one-to-one interaction with a single child, perhaps on an IEP target. Roles can then be reversed. This is an example of how clusters of schools that include both mainstream and special schools can work together to adapt strategies to different settings.

LSAs have now arrived in mainstream schools in large numbers. At the last count, there were 40,000 LSAs and another 20,000 are being recruited specifically to support the NLS. Until recently, governments and LEAs have shown no interest in their conditions of work or career structure. All of them are on appallingly low rates of pay, considering the importance and quality of their work. The government commissioned a major piece of research on LSAs (Farrell *et al.* 1999), is funding a vast expansion of recruitment and also beginning to plan training opportunities. These measures are long overdue and should lead to real improvements not only for LSAs but for schools in which they work.

As with SENCOs, the major obstacle to effective collaboration between teachers and LSAs is the lack of planning time. Although both may be working in the same classroom day after day, and may in fact have developed good working relationships, the lack of time to sit together and consider alternative ways of working makes the presence of the second adult less effective than it might otherwise be. Here again, leadership from the head teacher and SENCO can make an enormous difference (Balshaw 1999).

Planning collaborative teaching is made difficult not only by lack of time but by changing perceptions at every level about the role of the LSA. Initially, most LSAs worked in special schools. As time went on, they were recruited to support individual children on statements in mainstream schools. Nationally, more than 60 per cent of all children on statements are in mainstream schools and the numbers are likely to rise further. Because many statements specify a number of hours of LSA support per week, there is an implication that much or most of the LSA's time must be spent with the individual child. Moreover, parents are likely to resist anything that reduces the number of hours spent with their child on the grounds that this is their child's entitlement in law.

This is the price we pay for relying on the statement to provide additional support. In future, schools should be funded to enable them to recruit LSA support as part of the regular budget. Although a few children do need intensive one-to-one support, the time of LSAs may be much more productively spent in working as a second adult in the class as a whole. The LSA may keep a close eye on a particular child and offer one-to-one support when it is clearly needed, but for the rest of the time, the LSA is working with a larger group or with the class as a whole. Many patterns of collaboration are possible but time is needed to consider the best possible strategy for all pupils and to change this in the light of different needs and demands, including those of the child with the statement.

The recent University of Manchester research report on LSAs (Farrell et al. 1999) confirms the key role that many LSAs play in acting as the main source of support for children with exceptional needs in mainstream schools. Some work with children who are based in the special school but spend parts of each week in a mainstream setting. Others spend the whole of their time supporting one or more children in a mainstream setting. Although teachers were often responsible for planning schemes of work that were then implemented by LSAs, in many cases, especially when LSAs were working in non-resourced schools or employed by LEAs, 'they took the lead in adapting programmes of work and in planning new programmes' (Farrell et al. 1999: 17).

The report includes many examples of excellent working relationships and reflects a strong consensus among teachers and LSAs on how effective in-class support should be organised.

- LSAs must be fully informed about the aims and objectives of a lesson and about the learning needs of pupils who need assistance.
- LSAs need to be familiar with additional materials and equipment.
- Teachers and LSAs must get on well together, trust each others' judgement and have enough time to plan together.
- Pupils, teachers and LSAs were in agreement that they wanted support to be given from a distance – that is they preferred LSAs to 'float around a class' but to be immediately available when needed.

The report provides some useful insights into practitioners' definitions of effective practice. These are highly relevant to the questions posed in the introduction to this chapter. The report concludes with a review agenda (rather than a set of recommendations) that can be used by schools, LEAs and providers of training as a framework for evaluating practice. This consists of a series of questions and issues grouped under three major headings of role, management and training, each of which has three or four sub-headings. These in turn result in a large number of detailed questions (not reproduced here) (Farrell *et al*. 1999).

Role
- LSAs work cooperatively with teachers to support the learning and participation of pupils.
- LSAs work with teachers to prepare lesson plans and materials.
- LSAs contribute to the evaluation of the outcome of lessons.
- LSAs make relevant contributions to wider school activities.

Management
- Teachers' management strategies provide clear guidance as to how LSAs should work in their classrooms.
- Schools have policies outlining roles and responsibilities of LSAs.
- LEA policies ensure that LSAs' conditions of employment foster effective practice.

Training
- Teachers and LSAs learn together to improve the quality of their work.
- School staff development programmes foster the competence of LSAs and teachers to carry out their respective tasks.
- LEAs provide relevant additional training and support for LSAs.
- Use is made of (institution based) external courses, or courses run by voluntary organisations to extend the expertise of LSAs.

External supports

External support services vary in nature, quality and quantity between and within LEAs. One of the first tasks of a newly appointed SENCO must be to learn what is available to the school and to plan the most effective way of working with support services. These include educational psychology and a range of advisory services for language, literacy and numeracy, behaviour support and support for pupils with sensory impairments. Some of these services are directly funded by LEAs (e.g. psychology) but others depend on their services being purchased by schools or clusters of schools.

Educational psychologists

School psychological services are available in every LEA but there is an ongoing debate about how they can be used most effectively. In this context, the government has set up a working party to review the role of educational psychologists, the first since the Summerfield report in 1968 (DES 1968). The aim is to achieve a ratio of one educational psychologist for every 5,000 children of all ages, but very few areas of England have approached this target, although ratios are much higher in Scotland.

The profession faces at best a dilemma, at worst a crisis, that has been endemic for many years and that springs from the irresistible pressure for statutory assessment and report writing arising from the Code of Practice and the whole process of assessment and identification, placement and support; what Farrell (1995) calls 'a poisoned chalice'.

The source of professional frustration for educational psychologists arises from the lack of time to enable them to make a much broader contribution to schools, children and families. These possibilities are well summarised and clearly illustrated in a report from the British Psychological Society (1999; see also Farrell (1995) for a useful discussion of the range of work of educational psychologists). They include staff development on behaviour management, counselling, home–school liaison and, as suggested earlier, developments in assessment and individual planning.

From the perspective of an individual school or cluster of schools, it is essential to develop a working arrangement with the educational psychology service that aims to match the needs of the school with educational psychologists' resources of skills and time. Many educational psychology services enter into contractual agreements to work with schools on identified priorities and time allocations. Although at present, statutory assessment and support at Stage 3 of the Code of Practice takes up a great deal of time, the imminent publication of the DfEE working party report will provide opportunities for discussions between LEAs, educational psychologists and individual schools to consider alternatives and options for the future. For example, schools may find it useful to work in clusters, particularly for training and development work. As suggested in Chapter 7, educational psychologists are well placed to train and support school staff in selecting, using and interpreting a range of commercially available educational and attainment tests, leaving psychologists free to concentrate on specialist assessments that require more advanced training. Clearly, SENCOs are ideally placed to become more proficient in the use of a range of assessment measures and to act as mediators between the school and the school psychological service, but such a role would require a much greater allocation of time for SENCOs, as suggested earlier.

LEA support services

For some years there has been uncertainty about the funding and therefore the future of LEA support services. Unlike educational psychologists who are funded from monies retained by LEAs, support services are funded in a variety of ways. Although many schools are buying back support services, their survival is quite precarious. The government's Fair Funding policy implies that LEAs should only retain central funding for 'low incidence' sensory impairment services. This leaves language, literacy and behaviour support services to the vagaries of the market.

In this context, it is surprising to find so little reference to support services either in the DfEE Green Paper or in the subsequent Programme of Action, an omission noted in a useful NASEN policy options seminar (Norwich 1999). The scene-setting paper by Gray (1999) highlights some tensions and dilemmas; for example, schools may perceive behaviour support teams as pressuring them to retain pupils whom they would prefer to remove. By the same token, support teams may increase pressure for segregated provision if all the alternatives have been explored and rejected.

A further dilemma for support teams is to reconcile the two key priorities of supporting schools in working for whole-school development (especially in relation to behaviour policies) and focusing on individual pupils with the most severe and complex needs. A final irony is that support teams do not receive sufficient management support or training opportunities from their LEAs in meeting their delicate and complex responsibilities. For example, mainstream teachers have complained that they feel less confident and deskilled as a result of support worker involvement. Some support staff may need support themselves in learning to 'enskill' rather than deskill.

In the same symposium, Danks points out that support services will in future need to work in much closer partnerships with special schools as their work changes to providing support for mainstream schools, as part of local inclusive networks envisaged in the Programme of Action. Such a network will offer a 'basket of provision that is broad enough to meet a wide and ever changing range of individual local needs' (Danks 1999).

The example of the London Borough of Newham, where 90 per cent of pupils with statements are in mainstream schools and where only one special school remains open, may be a foretaste of the future. Burke (1999) summarised the work of Newham's support service, which employed 120 teachers and 130 LSAs in 1998. In addition to providing support to individual students on statements, which may involve an advocacy role for pupils in danger of being marginalised, support staff have a key role in school improvement initiatives, including work on adapting tasks and tests and deploying information on alternative accreditation pathways. In addition, they play a major role in training across the authority; this includes training for SENCOs and LSAs and on specific needs such as autism and promoting positive behaviour. A detailed account of one Newham primary school's response to inclusion can be found in Alderson (1999); this is one of many now available from the UK (see also Thomas *et al.* 1998).

Conclusions

The starting point for this chapter has been that much of what schools need on the journey towards inclusion is already in place. Above all, teachers already have the necessary knowledge and skills to equip them for the journey. What they often lack is confidence in their own ability to teach inclusively.

Many of the headings used in this chapter, such as differentiation, assessment and record keeping, informal support systems and good curriculum planning and delivery, are hallmarks of good practice for all children. Some of the new developments now being put in place, such as the Code of Practice and the work of SENCOs, are designed to build on and enhance existing practice.

Of course, it is more complicated than this. Teachers also need to work in schools that are committed to self-evaluation as part of the normal process of school development: schools that are prepared to review their practice and to experiment with different ways of working. They need head teachers, governors and LEAs that are open to change and will support them in moving forward. A list of requirements for what Ainscow (1999) calls a 'moving school' could be extended indefinitely until it becomes part of the classic litany of resistance of change: 'it's a good idea but . . .'; 'it wouldn't work here because . . .'; 'the money just isn't there . . .'; 'the parents would never agree . . .'; 'not another innovation, please!'

Teachers who are sceptical and who have genuine doubts about inclusion should not be dismissed as reactionary or labelled by politicians as representing 'the dark forces of conservatism'. Doubts and reservations are understandable because achieving inclusive practice is certainly not without its difficulties. In any case, our education system is anything but inclusive and the new policies are at odds with the competitive and divisive system that we have inherited and that seems set to remain on the scene for some time.

A pervasive obstacle to change lies in the mystique and the mythology that have been created around special needs education in general and about special schools and specialist provision in general. The very fact that specialist provision exists reinforces deeply held beliefs that special training and expertise are necessary to teach 'these children' and that this expertise is by definition absent in ordinary schools. Such an attitude is understandable in a system where a minority of children and their teachers have been separated from the majority.

The main obstacle to inclusion lies in beliefs and attitudes and not in the absence of readiness in schools and teachers. In Chapter 9, we will look more closely at teacher attitudes and beliefs and also consider the contribution that training and professional development can make to preparing all teachers to teach all children.

Chapter 9

Preparing all Teachers to Teach all Pupils

Unless the present favourable opportunity is taken to improve the professional qualifications of teachers in special education and hence the quality of special education itself, we fear that the next twenty years may yet again be a period of unfulfilled hope.   (Warnock report, DES 1978: para. 19.32)

We believe that all teachers should be entitled to relevant, high quality professional development.   (DfEE 2000: 1)

The challenge

The theme of this chapter is professional development from ITE right through to headship and beyond, taking in every single serving teacher along the way and not forgetting governors, politicians and decision makers at local and national level. No one can be excluded from training for inclusion. No one has nothing to learn about inclusion.

We have seen that inclusion is not a goal that can be reached but a journey with a purpose. During the course of that journey, teachers will build on their experience and increase their skills in reaching all children. But they also have a right to expect proper professional development and support along the way, just as parents have the right to expect that their children will be taught by teachers whose training prepares them to teach all children.

This task is nothing like as difficult as it may seem because most teachers already have much of the knowledge and skills they need to teach inclusively. What they lack is confidence in their own competence (Mittler and Mittler 2000). This is due partly to the lack of training opportunities and partly to a long-standing mystification of special needs expertise, which makes them believe that special training is a precondition for inclusion. Furthermore, few teachers have had the opportunity to teach all the children in their local community because some have been sent to special or independent schools.

This in no way justifies the lamentable lack of training opportunities that have been made available up to now, but it does represent a plea for basing further professional development opportunities on the foundations that are already there. Too many of us involved in special needs teacher education seem to have worked on the assumption that teachers in mainstream schools know little or nothing about children with exceptional needs or how to include them in ordinary schools. Although this is what teachers themselves often believe, tutors in this sector should be the last to have recourse to a defect model of teacher education and the first to practise what they preach about building on strengths.

Attitudes and feelings

Providing opportunities for training does not necessarily address or influence how teachers feel about inclusion. Such feelings are fundamental and need to be taken seriously. Any doubts and reservations should not be dismissed as reactionary or simply overridden. Teachers need opportunities to reflect on proposals for change that touch on their values and beliefs as well as affecting their day-to-day professional practice. They have already been subjected to an avalanche of change in which their views have not been seriously considered. It is important that inclusion is not seen as just another innovation.

Some teachers prefer to think through their attitudes to change on their own and resent being 'put into groups' to share their feelings on any subject. Each school has its own approach to the involvement of staff in bringing about change but there can be no doubt from the information we have available that providing opportunities for reflection and discussion is essential to the implementation of innovation of any kind.

This was one of the clearest findings of the first British national studies of what we then called integration carried out in the 1970s by the NFER (Hegarty et al. 1981). The success of the innovation depended on head teachers involving their staff in discussion and listening to their concerns. Enthusiasm and commitment on the part of head teachers alone was not enough.

So what does research have to say about teachers' attitudes to inclusion? A number of writers have tried to summarise a vast and complex literature in accessible form that will make sense to practitioners (Farrell 1997; Jenkinson 1997).

At the risk of oversimplification, there seems to be broad agreement on the following:
- most teachers in mainstream schools support the principle of inclusion but many have doubts about whether it would work in their school;

- teachers are much more positive about the inclusion of children with sensory or physical impairments than about those with emotional and behavioural difficulties or severe learning difficulties;
- class teachers have less positive attitudes than head teachers but much depends on the credibility of visiting specialist support personnel; and
- support for inclusion generally increases once teachers have directly experienced it and they feel the scheme has the full support of the head teacher and local authorities.

Of course, what teachers say and what they do are not necessarily consistent. In this context, a very recent and relevant account of both attitudes and practice can be found in a detailed study of 60 primary schools, most of which had also been involved in a similar study by the same team 18 years earlier (Croll and Moses 1985, 2000).

Interviews with 48 head teachers and some 300 class teachers revealed that virtually all agreed that there was a continuing role for special schools. Half the head teachers and a third of the teachers thought that more children should attend special schools, particularly those with emotional and behavioural difficulties. When teachers were asked about the 2,000 children on the special needs register of their own schools, nine out of ten thought the regular class was the right place for the child but that around 6 per cent of their pupils should be in a special class or unit and 4 per cent in a special school. These are aggregate figures for children at all five stages of the Code of Practice. For those at Stages 4 and 5, the percentages were 60, 19 and 21 for mainstream, special class and special school respectively. Because most of the children on statements would in earlier times have been in special schools, these figures still reflect a high degree of acceptance.

Teacher perceptions and attitudes are obviously fundamental to their response to new policies on inclusion and will also affect how they react to and implement training. Those who plan or provide training will need to take teacher attitudes into account, as will head teachers and SENCOs when it comes to implementation of change at the level of the school.

Low priority for training

Until recently, training has been a low priority for government. During the 1980s and early 1990s, the government did nothing to prevent the collapse of professionally relevant award-bearing courses, nor was there much evidence of sustained protest from the teacher unions about the virtual disappearance of opportunities for secondment to one-year courses or their part-time equivalents.

It now seems hard to believe that the transformation of our education system by the Education Reform Act 1988 and its aftermaths was achieved without a matching training initiative. It is true that a great deal of money was spent on one-off training days introducing teachers to the programmes of study, ATs and assessment arrangements of each new subject in the curriculum as it emerged from central government agencies. But an accumulation of training days does not make a training strategy.

Under the Grants for Educational Support and Training (GEST) scheme and its many predecessors, central government did make it possible for LEAs to bid for moneys to co-fund training in specific areas, such as sensory impairment and severe learning difficulties, as well as for support in mainstream schools. The operation of this scheme was very uneven. Some LEAs could not find the money to match the central government grant and the distribution of funds among the various areas of need reflected local pressures as well as national priorities. For example, autism and moderate learning difficulties secured equal shares of the funding (4 per cent of the total each) with a 13 per cent allocation to dyslexia, while mandatory areas such as hearing impairment were underfunded. Only half the teachers working with pupils with severe learning difficulties were additionally qualified (Mittler 1993, 1995a).

It was only when the Code of Practice was published that serious concerns were expressed about the absence of any matching DfEE plans to launch a staff development strategy for teachers in general and for SENCOs in particular. Here again, most LEAs provided training days for SENCOs but these were mainly used to discuss the requirements of the Code and how it could be related to local needs. This left little time for training on the specific requirements, such as planning and delivering IEPs, working with parents or liaising with other agencies (OFSTED 1997).

Since the 1980s, each school has been expected to identify and meet at least some of the costs of any training needed by its staff. Many LEAs did what they could to help schools to respond to their training needs but the pressure to delegate funding left little for training initiatives from the centre, although advisors and support services did their best to continue to provide professional training opportunities.

In addition to the five statutory training days, a great deal of training still takes the form of one day or twilight school based courses. While these fulfil a useful function and give the staff a sense of ownership, they are not a substitute for a sustained period of part-time or full-time study.

New initiatives

The early 1990s saw the beginning of a change of climate. In 1994 the government established the TTA with responsibilities for all ITE and, for a brief period, CPD.

Legislation creating the TTA was bitterly opposed by universities and colleges and also in the House of Lords on the grounds of political interference and infringements of academic freedom. More recently, its position has been weakened by the establishment of the General Teaching Council (GTC) and by the decision of the DfEE to take back responsibility for CPD.

Despite initial opposition and continuing suspicion from higher education, the TTA deserves credit for including exceptional needs in its planning and for maintaining this interest ever since.

The Special Educational Needs Training Consortium

The need for new training initiatives emerged very strongly from the consultation process following the publication of the Code of Practice. Even before this, the Special Educational Needs Training Consortium (SENTC) had been formed, consisting of an alliance of teacher unions, LEA representatives, voluntary organisations and training providers, as well as specialist interest groups who had been developing their own standards for teachers working with particular groups of pupils (e.g. those with hearing impairments, severe learning difficulties and specific learning difficulties). SENTC meetings were attended by official observers from the DfEE, OFSTED, the Local Government Association, the TTA and the SCAA.

Early in 1995 the DfEE agreed to fund SENTC to produce a report with the following terms of reference:
- to review the systems currently in place for the training of teachers of pupils with special educational needs; and
- to make recommendations on how these systems might be improved to make more efficient and/or effective use of resources in the light of the respective roles and responsibilities of those involved in the provision of SEN teacher training.

SENTC set up a working party to prepare a report, which was submitted to the Secretary of State for Education in February 1996 (SENTC 1996). The report was timely because it was published at a time when both the TTA and DfEE were ready to work on new initiatives. But because its recommendations have now been partly overtaken by later developments, I will refer to it only in passing or where its analysis or recommendations still appear to be relevant.

Initial teacher education

Ensuring that newly qualified teachers have a basic understanding of inclusive teaching and inclusive schools is the best long-term investment that can be made.

It would lay the foundations for good practice on which later generations could build and it would provide a 'critical mass' of young teachers who had some understanding and experience of inclusive practice.

Twenty-two years ago, the Warnock committee recommended that 'a special education element should be included in all courses of initial teacher training . . . those responsible for validating teacher training courses should make the inclusion of a special needs element a condition for their approval of training courses' (DES 1978: paras. 12.7, 12.11).

The responsibility for providing initial training is now shared between higher education and the partnership schools in which students spend up to two-thirds of their training. Students are almost entirely dependent on schools to ensure that they are exposed to the best practice under the guidance of the SENCO, who may arrange for them to spend time with visiting support staff such as educational psychologists and advisory teachers. In the absence of reliable data on whether this happens, we have to ask whether this is a high enough priority for mentors or whether SENCOs can find time to add the needs of students to their workload.

Although some training providers have done their best to implement the spirit of this recommendation, progress overall has been both patchy and slow, with the result that few young people entering the teaching profession have received more than a few hours of exposure to the teaching of children with exceptional needs and generally express themselves as dissatisfied with the quality of their preparation to teach such students. (Garner *et al.* 1995; Dew-Hughes and Brayton 1997).

TTA standards for the award of Qualified Teacher Status

The SENTC report addressed this problem in some detail and drew up a list of relevant areas of knowledge and skills that students should possess at the end of their training and that should then be further developed during their year first year of teaching (SENTC 1996). Since then, the TTA has included some relevant criteria into its National Standards for Qualified Teacher Status (TTA 1998b).

We can consider these standards from two different but complementary perspectives: standards that are specific to pupils with exceptional needs and those that, while relevant to all pupils, are particularly important for such pupils.

Specific standards

> Teachers must plan their teaching to achieve progression in pupils' learning through:
> - identifying pupils who have special educational needs, including specific learning difficulties; are very able; are not yet fluent in English and know where to get help in order to give positive and targeted support
> - being familiar with the *Code of Practice on the Identification and Assessment of Special Educational Needs*.

Examples of other relevant standards

- Setting high expectations for all pupils, notwithstanding individual differences, including gender and cultural and linguistic backgrounds;
- understanding how pupils' learning in the subject is affected by their physical, intellectual, emotional and social development;
- knowing pupils' most common misconceptions and mistakes in the subject; and
- setting appropriate and demanding expectations of pupils' learning, motivation and presentation of work.

There are also relevant references to knowing about the work of other agencies, child protection and effective ways of working with parents and carers.

The TTA standards illustrate a dilemma and a paradox common to all providers of ITE. On the one hand, an inclusive teacher training curriculum should include standards and criteria relevant to the whole range of pupils in schools without any need to make specific reference to those with exceptional needs. Such a strategy aims to ensure that inclusive practice permeates all areas of training, whether theoretical and knowledge based or practical and skills-oriented. But how do you assess something that is permeated and how do the TTA or OFSTED monitor that students are being adequately prepared for inclusive practice?

The specific standards quoted above could be regarded as minimum essentials, provided that the inclusion dimensions do indeed permeate the other standards. This in turns depends on mainstream teacher trainers, whether they are teaching curriculum specialisations or professional studies or whether they are teachers in schools who are themselves providers of ITE.

The ITE standards as a whole were initially well received because the standards themselves were mostly relevant. Since then, criticism has swelled on account of their sheer number and the impossibility of assessing each teacher training student on several hundred competencies. The inclusion standards are therefore at risk of being yet again overlooked because the exercise as a whole is proving unmanageable. In December 1999, the TTA issued a consultation document on how the ITE standards as a whole should be monitored but somehow omitted all reference to exceptional needs, while still referring to other equal opportunities issues such as gender and ethnic minorities. Although OFSTED inspects all ITE courses, the inspection of the inclusion element is very light touch, if it exists at all.

Induction

Although newly qualified teachers are not likely to attain all the standards expected by the TTA, the government's renewed emphasis on the process of induction in the first year of teaching provides an excellent opportunity to build on whatever foundations have been laid in ITE. As these will differ from course to course, each school receiving a newly qualified teacher will have to assess what knowledge and skills have been laid down during initial training in order to support new teachers in consolidating what they have already done and using this as a stepping stone for further development. Needless to add, this is yet another task for the SENCO.

The SENTC (1996) report offered some suggestions for competencies that could be developed during the induction period.

Students should:
- develop a thorough knowledge about the school's SEN policy and its implementation in relation to the Code of Practice;
- learn to collaborate with parents, support teachers, LSAs and other professionals;
- become proficient in different modes of assessment to demonstrate pupil achievements; and
- learn about different ways of eliciting pupils' views and perspectives.

Training for mainstream decision makers

Providing training and awareness for new teachers lays firm foundations for good practice in the next generation but it is just as important to reach head teachers and senior staff in mainstream schools, since their active leadership and support are essential to the achievement of change and reform along inclusive lines.

Several sets of TTA initiatives are relevant here, particularly standards for head teachers (e.g. National Professional Qualification for Head Teachers (NPQHT)), advanced skills teachers and subject leaders. Advanced management or curriculum courses clearly need to 'have regard' not just to an inclusion dimension but to inclusive planning and practice as a whole, in the light of government policies. Whether the courses do so or not is unclear. The TTA gives overall approval to NPQHT and other courses but it does not directly determine content.

Inexplicably, the national standards for head teachers (TTA 1998c) make no direct reference to inclusion issues as an essential management task. There is a brief mention of equal opportunities and race relations but the Code of Practice does not feature in the list of statutory documents, despite the fact that it is included in standards for qualified teacher status and also in the national standards for subject leaders (TTA 1998d).

The national standards for head teachers include one fleeting reference: 'Understand the expectations of others, including subject leaders and SENCOs and ensure that trainee and newly qualified teachers are appropriately trained, monitored, supported and assessed in relation to the standards for Qualified Teacher Status, the Career Entry Profile and standards for induction' (TTA 1998c: 11).

National standards for SENCOs (TTA 1998a)

A rather happier chapter in the history of the TTA sprang from the decision some years ago to make the training of SENCOs one of eight priorities for action. A former HMI was appointed to undertake a wide-scale consultation on the competencies required by SENCOs. The resulting job description calls for a combination of Machiavelli and Mother Teresa: the latter not only for her saintliness but for her vow of poverty!

Although the SENCO standards are somewhat idealistic, the same could be said of those expected of a newly qualified teacher. No ordinary mortal could emerge from a Postgraduate Certificate in Education (PGCE) or Bachelor of Education (BEd) course endowed with the competencies listed in the ITE standards. Nevertheless, like inclusion, they represent a road to be travelled and a goal to be approached over a lifetime rather than a prescription for instant excellence.

In discussing the work of SENCOs in Chapter 8, we emphasised their key role in the management structure of the school. The national standards for SENCO build on this assumption and list a large number of standards under a series of headings concerned both with knowledge and understanding and with skills and attributes.

We can briefly list a few examples of the headings, without itemising the standards themselves:
- leadership skills, attributes and professional competence;
- decision making skills – the ability to solve problems and make decisions;
- communication skills – the ability to make points clearly and to listen and understand the views of others;
- self-management – the ability to plan time effectively and to organise oneself well; and
- attributes – e.g. personal impact and presence, adaptability, energy, vigour and perseverance, self-confidence, enthusiasm, intellectual ability, reliability, integrity, commitment.

The key areas of SEN coordination are considered under the following headings, each of which has a number of examples:
- strategic direction and development of SEN provision in the school;
- teaching and learning;
- leading and managing staff; and
- efficient and effective deployment of staff and resources.

National Special Educational Needs Specialist Standards (TTA 1999)

The TTA's most recent work in this field has been the publication of standards for specialist teachers. This has been the most difficult task so far, mainly because of the diversity of views on the role of specialist teachers in an inclusive system and the intensive lobbying by different pressure groups.

The TTA has made a helpful distinction between core standards and extension standards. They also usefully distinguish between three roles and responsibilities that specialists are likely to be asked to fulfil (advisory, curricular and managerial). A final section lists essential skills and attributes concerned largely with attitudes and values.

Core standards

> Core standards set out the professional knowledge, understanding and skills common across the full range of severe and/or complex forms of SEN. They constitute a starting point for the development of further specific expertise and are listed under five headings:
> * strategic direction and development of SEN provision nationally and regionally
> * identification, assessment and planning
> * effective teaching, ensuring maximum access to the curriculum
> * development of communication, literacy and numeracy skills and ICT capability
> * promotion of social and emotional development, positive behaviour and preparation for adulthood.   (TTA 1999: 4)

Each of these headings is followed by up to ten standards. The combined 43 standards are comprehensive and have been well received.

Extension standards

Agreement on extension standards was much harder to achieve because of pressure from disability specific interests who wanted to list standards under categorical headings. The final version is based on four headings, each of them stressing the teacher's role in promoting students' development and access to learning and curriculum.

> Extension standards provide a summary of the additional specialist knowledge, understanding and skills which teachers may need for the effective educational management of pupils with severe and/or complex forms of SEN. These standards will help teachers identify the further general and more need-

specific training and development opportunities they require to enable them to teach pupils with more severe and/or complex needs more effectively and/or to offer effective support and advice to other teachers working with such pupils in mainstream or specialist settings.   (TTA 1999: 4)

The extension standards are grouped under four headings:
- communication and interaction;
- cognition and learning;
- behavioural, emotional and social development; and
- sensory and physical development.

Each of these is further broken down into knowledge and understanding and skills, resulting in a total of 63 extension standards under the four headings. In addition, each area of knowledge and understanding and skills provides further standards under one or more disability specific headings from a choice of autistic spectrum disorders, deaf-blindness, deafness and visual impairment. Other areas of need are not listed.

Debates around specialisation

The core standards have been well received, but agreement on extension standards has been harder to achieve, although the end result reflects what will probably prove to be an acceptable compromise.

The debate has revolved around the issue of specialist training along categorical lines and in particular the status of the mandatory qualification for teachers of pupils with hearing and visual impairments who have for many years been required to obtain a mandatory qualification in their area of specialisation. Although the award is mandatory only for those who work in special schools, most teachers working in support services and mainstream settings have by now gained the award.

Understandably, teachers who hold the mandatory qualification resist any suggestion that this should be in any way diluted. When the government Advisory Committee on the Supply and Education of Teachers (ACSET) recommended its abolition in 1984, the proposal was quickly withdrawn as ministers and members of parliament (MPs) were bombarded with protests. Since then, the mandatory qualification has continued to be fiercely defended.

Unfortunately, this leaves other specialist teachers in a qualifications limbo. The SENTC report recommended that all specialist teachers should be expected to work for a recognised advanced qualification. This could be in modular form and taken over a period of years within agreed accreditation frameworks.

It is for the DfEE to decide whether the mandatory award should be retained and whether other specialist teachers should also be expected to work towards a recognised qualification. The task of the TTA is to develop specialist standards rather than to put them into a qualifications framework.

No one would argue with the proposition that teachers of children with hearing impairments need to have advanced knowledge and skills about, *inter alia*, sign language, amplification and the use of hearing aids, just as teachers working with children with visual impairments need to know about braille, low vision aids and mobility training. There is less agreement about whether the need for these highly specific skills justifies the continuation of forms of training that are separate in level and status from those available to colleagues working in other areas of specialist or mainstream provision. What is it about hearing and visual impairment that justifies a mandatory award that is not available to colleagues working with, say, children with emotional and behavioural difficulties, severe learning difficulties or autism?

Provision has changed out of all recognition even within the special school sector. Special schools and units no longer cater for clearly identified categories of disability. By far the largest and most heterogeneous group are in schools for children with 'moderate learning difficulties': a label that has long since failed to describe the complexity and variety of needs represented in schools, which are barely mentioned in TTA or DfEE publications, partly, one suspects, because of the absence of an active lobby. Similarly, schools for children with severe learning difficulties include pupils with a very wide range of additional impairments, including sensory and physical impairments, children with autism and those with challenging behaviour. Clearly, teachers working in these schools need knowledge and skills well beyond those once perceived to be specific to a single disability.

When specialist groups are asked to draw up their own lists of required competencies, many (but by no means all) of the items listed are either common to all teachers or are not specific to one area of identified need. This is reflected in the SENTC report and to a lesser extent in the TTA specialist standards. The challenge is to distinguish between areas of knowledge and skill that are required by all specialist teachers and those that are distinctive to specific groups. Could highly specific areas of knowledge and skill be concentrated into a specialist pathway, following a common core training taken together with broader groups of specialists?

Putting the standards to work

Taken as a whole, the TTA standards provide a comprehensive if rather overwhelming starting point for planning training and development experiences for individual teachers or larger groups. A head teacher or LEA officer could use the document as it stands in order to conduct an audit of training strengths and needs in a school or across a whole LEA and use them to identify priorities both for individuals and for training areas in need of development.

Although the standards have on the whole been welcomed, it is not at all clear how they can be used at local level. In the first place, some standards are more prescriptive than others; for example the ITE standards are in effect a national teacher training curriculum for which training providers are accountable and subject to inspection by OFSTED and monitoring by TTA. On completing their initial training, new teachers have a career entry profile, which potential employers can scrutinise and criticise. There are also a large number of subject-specific standards that relate to National Curriculum statutory orders. For different reasons, the NPQHT carries a good deal of weight and status.

This is not the case for other standards, including those for SENCOs and specialist teachers. They are there to be used but so far there has been no clear policy framework for doing so. For example, there is no requirement for SENCOs or specialist teachers to take part in a focused programme of continuing professional training leading to the possibility of an accredited award.

The TTA does not claim that the standards constitute an agenda for training, far less a curriculum for teachers working in particular sectors of education.: 'The national standards set out the professional knowledge, understanding, skills and attributes necessary to carry out effectively the key tasks of that role. It is the sum of these aspects which define the expertise demanded of the role, in order to achieve the outcomes set in the standards' (TTa 1998a: 1).

In summary, the main aims of the whole range of national standards are to:

- set out clear expectations for teachers at key points in the profession
- help teachers at different points in the professions to plan and monitor their development, training and performance effectively, and to set clear, relevant targets for improving their effectiveness
- ensure that the focus at every point is on improving the achievement of pupils and the quality of their education
- provide a basis for the professional recognition of teachers' expertise and achievements
- help providers of professional development to plan and provide high quality, relevant training which meets the need of individual teachers and head teachers, makes good use of their time and has the maximum benefit for pupils.   (TTA 1998a: 1)

These aims make it clear that the standards can be used to plan a programme of professional development. In that sense, they can be used by individual teachers to express their need or wish for training in one or more areas of understanding, knowledge and skills and to negotiate a programme of professional development to which they are entitled. They can also be used by head teachers and senior managers to plan to meet staff development needs of all members of staff or of staff with particular areas of responsibility or by LEA officers or other CPD providers to plan pathways for SENCOs or other groups of staff.

> The most recent TTA publication takes the form of six case studies showing how the national SENCO standards can be put to use in different contexts (TTA 2000). These include:
> - a performance review for a newly appointed SENCO in a primary school;
> - the effective deployment and review of staff resources across the school;
> - to inform job descriptions and set appropriate expectation and accountability;
> - to audit the school's performance in supporting effective coordination;
> - the identification of training and development needs by training providers; and
> - to inform regional planning of staff development for support services.

These are all useful examples but they seem to have been drafted without reference to the ongoing DfEE work on professional development, which provides an entirely new and funded framework for the professional development of all teachers.

DfEE consultation on professional development

The DfEE consultation paper, *Professional Development: Support for Teaching and Learning* (DfEE 2000), which was published in February 2000, marks a watershed in the history of the teaching profession. For the first time, a government has laid down the framework for a national strategy that is based on the entitlement of all teachers and other staff employed by education services to a programme of funded continuing professional development. The importance of this consultation document justifies quoting key extracts:

> We believe that all teachers should be entitled to relevant, high quality professional development . . .

> Good professional development requires time to reflect and set objectives; recognition and commitment; opportunity, particularly for work-based learning' a focus on schools and teachers; and high quality provision.

> We want to encourage in-depth career planning at regular points . . .

> We will pilot ways to make money available to individual teachers for their professional development, starting in September 2000. Teachers could use these bursaries towards the costs of workshops, courses, conferences or towards the cost of a Masters degree . . . teacher exchanges, international exchanges and study visits and business placements.

The new pay system will ensure that teachers receive fuller recognition for their achievements. We suggest that all teachers should have their own development portfolio which could be available through a disc or on the Internet.

Good teachers who apply for and pass an assessment against national quality standards will move to a new upper pay spine. They will receive an immediate pay rise of £2000 as well as access to further pay increases based on performance.

We are going to target funding for professional development through the School Improvement Grant which will increase to £290.5 million for 2000/2001, an increase of £40 million over the previous year. 90 per cent of the grant will be devolved to schools.

We want to support teacher research to enable teachers to conduct research in partnership with higher education institutions and other schools. We would initially suggest the inclusion of the following areas: special educational needs, achievement of boys; teaching gifted and talented children; managing the transition from primary to secondary school raising achievement at Key Stage 3; working effectively with teaching assistants; overcoming social barriers to achievement; closer working between home and school; information technology.

We also seek views from professionals on whether experienced teachers should be given a sabbatical period out of the classroom specifically for developmental activity and research.

We will . . . provide a Code of Practice for training providers to offer a checklist to schools and teachers of what to expect. We also want to encourage organisations such as professional associations to share information about professional development and to invite Ofsted to carry out specific exercises to identify and share information about provision.   (DfEE 2000)

Pathways to training

It is clear from these extracts that the government is committed to a programme of high quality, school based professional development. But where is the training to come from and how is it to be planned, organised and funded? Who will provide the study modules and experiences to enable coherent training pathways to be planned for individuals or groups?

A training sub-group of the National Advisory Group on SEN has been set up by ministers, with a remit to advise on a national training strategy, taking account of the TTA standards. Its members and masters have some major decisions to make concerning the next stage in the use of the SENCO standards and of standards for specialist teachers. The time is clearly right to design a framework that will enable teachers and others to plan coherent pathways to professional development that lead to recognised and valued qualifications in which parents, pupils and the public can have confidence.

The question of whether specialist teachers such as SENCOs should be expected to or required to work towards a recognised qualification is therefore still in a policy limbo. The examples given by the TTA of six ways in which the SENCO standards might be used seem to be based on the assumption that the standards could be used to design a series of staff development modules or training opportunities. This is not said explicitly but some of the examples (e.g. the identification of training and development needs by training providers) do suggest this. While the knowledge, skills and understanding underlying some of the standards could be acquired through school based or cluster based experiences, others would be more appropriately developed through an accredited modular course provided through an LEA, a region or a university. In the meantime, the most recent government proposals on staff development and the funding available from 2000, provide ample scope for local initiative.

Planning

Local planning is obviously the starting point for any new training initiative. Schools already have a responsibility to include both exceptional needs and staff development in their ongoing school development plans, although evidence from OFSTED suggests that staff development is not given much priority and sometimes does not feature at all in school plans. Even so, head teachers are responsible for monitoring and meeting staff development needs.

Planning for staff development can also usefully be undertaken by clusters of schools working together and sharing costs. The national research on school clusters by Evans *et al.* (1999) includes in-service education and training (INSET) as one of the activities undertaken by clusters and gives a variety of examples of effective collaboration for training. These include regular sessions for SENCOs to share ideas and experiences and plan collaboratively.

The LEA is obviously well placed to develop a strategic approach to staff development and to ensure that teachers working with pupils with exceptional needs are able to take advantage of the whole range of training opportunities that are available or at the planning stage. They may also be best placed to find and negotiate with a training provider, such as a local university or independent agency.

Regional initiatives

The government has given strong encouragement and some pump-priming funding to develop regional collaboration. Regional initiatives are already up and running covering the whole of England.

Regional collaboration is particularly useful in relation to 'low incidence' provision such as autism or physical and sensory impairments but can also be used for SENCOs, governors and head teachers. Because regional networks can include health, social services and the voluntary sector, it should be possible to plan new training initiatives across traditional local government boundaries: examples of 'joined-up training' involving, for example, speech and language therapists, early years practitioners or social workers. Such initiatives are very rare but could well result from the regional developments now being launched. The evaluation of regional collaboration that is being commissioned by the DfEE will provide evidence about the extent to which such potential is being realised on the ground and whether pupils and parents benefit.

New funding opportunities

Among the existing mechanisms, the Standards Fund, which has replaced and enhanced the former GEST can be used for both training and development. Although this is still largely organised along traditional disability lines, some broader headings have been added that add to the flexibility of the scheme (Chapter 11). Significantly increased sums of money will be released through school improvement grants, which will be almost entirely devolved to schools for staff development purposes. In addition, teachers will be able to receive direct grants to enable them to spend on agreed staff development purposes.

Conclusions

The launch of the government's strategy for professional development provides an opportunity for all teachers to have an entitlement to a funded programme of training opportunities that meets their individual needs, the needs of the schools and services in which they work and above all the needs of the children they teach. This strategy is more than welcome, following decades when training has been a very low priority and has not been well planned.

A number of new structures are in place that could lay the foundations for new staff development strategies and policies for all teachers. Being a single-focus agency, the TTA has been able to concentrate on training and has, on the whole, built exceptional needs and inclusion dimensions into its work from the beginning. Inevitably, its publications and prescriptions have not pleased everyone but it is hard to believe that more progress would have been made had it never been established in the first place. The belated launching of a GTC in England after decades of official hostility puts the teaching professions on a par with others in having their own regulatory body. The GTC will be well placed to advise on the refinement of the strategy now announced by the government.

These are all positive developments but vigilance and advocacy will be needed to ensure that inclusive principles are built into their foundations and permeate the new routes to professional development that are now becoming available. By the time today's newly qualified teachers retire in the 2040s, all teachers should be fully prepared to teach all pupils.

Chapter 10

Parents and Teachers

The closer the parent is to the education of the child, the greater the impact on child development and educational achievement.　　(Fullan 1991: 227)

It is the parents' unreasonable commitment to their child that makes them good parents.　　(Anon, quoted by Gascoigne 1995: vi)

Reaching all parents

Home–school links: a fresh start?

In this chapter I want to suggest that we need to rethink the whole basis of home–school relationships for all children. Devising new ways of bringing teachers and parents into a better working relationship is worthwhile for its own sake and would benefit all children, parents and teachers. It could also make an impact on children's learning and promote social as well as school inclusion, especially for those parents who are experiencing social exclusion themselves. Children with exceptional needs and their families would automatically benefit without the need for special principles and procedures.

Despite all the fine words about working with parents, there is still a velvet curtain between home and school. Teachers and parents may be friendly, helpful and polite to one another but there is an unavoidable underlying tension that arises from the imbalance of power between them. Many parents are apprehensive and anxious about going to schools because they are still carrying the history of their own experiences of teachers and schooling. Schools have changed out of all recognition in a single generation but many parents have had little direct experience of such changes and obtain much of their information from the media and from casual encounters with neighbours. Parents of children with exceptional needs have a particularly great need for working relationships with teachers based on understanding and trust.

The whirlwind of change that has been sweeping through schools in the 1990s has been focused on raising standards. This has left little time to develop new ways of bringing local parents into partnership with schools. 'Links with the community' are often equated with business and industry rather than with partnership with parents. Rooms earmarked for parents' use in the past have had to be brought into service as classrooms in response to the open enrolment legislation.

Every school has a 'reputation' in its neighbourhood that is based less on league tables and SAT results than on local perceptions about the quality of the relationships between staff and children and how approachable and welcoming the school is to them as parents and to the local community. These intangibles cannot be measured by inspectors but they lie at the heart of any attempt to develop better collaborative relationships.

Some schools have travelled further along this road than others but many parents are still unreached and at risk of being labelled as 'unreachable'. Some parents do not necessarily want to attend school meetings or may be alienated by some of the language and documentation that they encounter. They should not be written off as 'uninterested in their children's education'.

It seems ironic that at the very time when social inclusion and poverty are at the top of the government's agenda, many parents feel excluded from decisions being made or proposed in the schools that their children are attending, as well as those being taken at local or central government level. Information about good practice or new ideas is not widely known or disseminated and home–school links are not high on the priority list at any level.

Governments of both persuasions have sent out conflicting messages to parents. On the one hand, they have promoted the rights and interests of parents through for example, the Parents' Charter (DfEE 1995), which gives parents the right to information about their child's progress and achievements and about the work of the school as a whole. All parents (except, as we shall see, parents of children with exceptional needs) have the right to express a choice of school, to change the status of a school, to appeal against the decisions of schools and LEAs, to become school governors and to ensure that governors report to parents regularly. By these means, schools and LEAs are made accountable to parents. But governments have also encouraged parents to act as teacher watchdogs and to vote with their feet if schools do not match up to their expectations. This is not a good foundation for a climate of trust and partnership.

At the same time, parents are frequently blamed both by politicians and teachers' organisations for failing to ensure that children do their homework and do not roam the streets. Home–school agreements are being introduced to formalise relationships and ministers threaten children's curfews and fining parents whose children truant. Most recently, the DfEE guidelines on EAZs (DfEE 1999f) have highlighted the importance of support for families but the examples of desirable activities that they list seem to be concerned with compensating for parents' weaknesses in language and literacy, rather than helping parents and schools to work together as partners, each with distinctive contributions to make.

Lack of professional preparation

How many teachers can remember any attention being given to working with parents in their initial training? How many have had opportunities to attend training days or courses on the needs of parents and families and how they might work together? How many have had the opportunity to listen to parents speaking about their needs and perceptions?

Most teachers insist that there was no reference to parents and families in their initial training and that there have been few opportunities to attend courses or training days since then. It is depressing, therefore, to find that the most recent TTA national standards for qualified teacher status also have almost nothing to say on parents (TTA 1998b). Only in the additional standards for teachers working in nursery and reception classes do we find a reference to 'having a knowledge of effective ways of working with parents and other carers' and a further standard on 'managing the work of parents and other adults in the classroom'. Parents are not mentioned in the main standards for primary or secondary teachers and receive only a passing reference in standards for head teachers. They fare a little better in the SENCO and national SEN specialist standards.

It is not just a matter of training in the conventional sense, but of teachers having opportunities to heighten their self-awareness and to think about their attitudes to families, how they perceive them and relate to them and to consider whether there may be alternative approaches for them as individuals and for the schools and services in which they work. The use of role play and simulation, with or without videorecording, has been used in race awareness sessions and can provide insight into one's own styles of interaction with parents, but some may find such approaches too intrusive or too disturbing.

Home–school policies

Every school needs its own home–school policy to go beyond fine words and include concrete proposals for achieving better working relationships with its parents and with the local community. Despite much rhetoric about the importance of working with parents, there is no legal requirement for schools or LEAs to have a detailed written policy on working with parents and therefore no guidelines about the headings under which such a policy might be developed. However, the OFSTED frameworks for inspection say that inspectors must evaluate and report on:

> the effectiveness of the school's partnership with parents, highlighting strengths and weaknesses, in terms of:
> - the information provided about the school and about pupils' work and progress though annual and other reports and parents' meetings

- parents' involvement with the school and with their children's work at home
- the contribution which the school's link with the community makes to pupils' attainment and personal development.   (OFSTED 1995: 96)

There is a statutory requirement to obtain the views of parents on a school being inspected by means of a meeting between the registered inspector and parents and also through a questionnaire sent to all parents. Parents' views are sought under eight headings: pupils' attainment and progress; attitudes and values that the school promotes; information that the school provides to parents, including reports; help and guidance available to pupils; homework; behaviour and attendance; the part played by parents in the life of the school; and the school's response to their suggestions and complaints.

The evaluation schedules for the new inspection framework (OFSTED 2000c) include a section on 'How well does the school work in partnership with parents?' in which inspectors must report on:
- parents' views of the school;
- the effectiveness of the school's links with parents; and
- the impact of the parents' involvement with the work of the school.

A study of OFSTED reports by Blamires *et al.* (1997) indicates that schools that receive praise from OFSTED for their partnership with parents are characterised by:
- parents receiving a rapid response to requests;
- regular newsletters with a diary of forthcoming events;
- a member of staff or a working party being given responsibility for home–school liaison;
- information on children's progress being clearly presented to parents with opportunities for follow-up discussion;
- good use of home–school contact methods such as diaries and logs; and
- development of parental involvement in teaching their child through lending libraries for books/games or toys.

Schools also have a number of statutory requirement to report pupils' achievements to parents. The school SEN policy statements required by the Code of Practice must also include information about 'arrangements for partnership with parents' (DfE 1994: 8–9).

Over and above the legal requirements, it is difficult to find factual information on how mission statements and policies that look good on paper translate into practice. For example, what specific examples follow the 'blue sky' statements: 'all parents are welcome in this school at any time; we value parents as partners in their children's learning and development'? How do schools reach 'hard to reach' families who do not attend meetings or answer notes? How often do teachers and parents meet to share information and experiences? Is it possible for teachers to offer to visit parents in their own homes? How do parents and children react to such visits and do they have useful outcomes?

About ten years ago. the NFER carried out a national study of parental involvement in schools (Jowett and Baginsky 1991). Information was collected from 70–80 per cent of all LEAs in England and Wales, and from interviews with many parents and teachers. Although some excellent initiatives were found in some schools and LEAs, they were still few and far between across the whole country. It was clear that parents from all backgrounds were keen to be more involved by schools but that teachers tended to underestimate parental interest, particularly from parents in economically deprived areas.

Schools that want to review their home–school policies will find a great deal of valuable information and support in a series of publications arising from a major national project on home–school links, directed by John Bastiani. This project, which began at Nottingham University and was later brought under the auspices of the Royal Society of Arts, has resulted in a large number of practical publications and newsletters and has been an invaluable resource to schools that have wanted to use it. For example, the project has produced an audit questionnaire to enable parents and schools to identify strengths and needs and to improve the quality of communication between parents and teachers (Bastiani and Beresford 1995). A recent publication reviews the contribution of parents in the context of school effectiveness (Wolfendale and Bastiani 2000); others include a guide to home–school agreement (Bastiani and Wyse 1999) and reports of links with parents in multicultural settings (Bastiani 1997). An interesting comparative study of home–school links in nine countries, including England and Wales, has been published by the OECD (1997).

The publication *Early Learning Goals* (QCA and DfEE 1999) includes some useful indicators for 'parents as partners' most of which seem relevant to the whole age range.

> Parents are children's first and most enduring educators. When parents and practitioners work together in early years settings, the results have a positive impact on the child's development and learning. Therefore, each setting should seek to develop an effective partnership with parents.
>
> A successful partnership needs a two way flow of information, knowledge and expertise. There are many ways of achieving partnership with parents but the following are common features of effective practice:
> - practitioners show respect and understanding for the role of the parent in their child's education
> - the past and future part played by parents in the education of their children is recognised and explicitly encouraged

- arrangements for settling in are flexible enough to give time for children to become secure and for practitioners and parents to discuss each child's circumstances, interests, competencies and needs
- all parents are made to feel welcome, valued and necessary, through a range of different opportunities for collaboration between children, parents and practitioners
- the knowledge and expertise of parents and other family adults are used to support the learning opportunities provided by the setting
- practitioners use a variety of ways to keep parents fully informed about the curriculum, such as brochures, displays and videos which are available in the home languages of the parents and through informal discussion
- parents and practitioners talk about and record information about the child's progress and achievements, for example through meetings or making a book about the child
- relevant learning activities and play activities, such as sharing and reading books, are continued at home. Similarly, experiences at home are used to develop learning in the setting, for example, visits and celebrations.   (QCA and DfEE 1999)

Reaching the unreached

It is sometimes said that attempts to bring parents and teachers together using principles and practices such as those quoted above will not work for the poorest families, those who have literacy difficulties themselves or those whose first language is not English. Interviews with teachers taking part in the NFER study reflected pessimism and despair about the impossibility of reaching parents who never respond to notes or letters inviting them to attend parents' meetings. 'Good idea but it wouldn't work here' was a frequent response.

This pessimism is not borne out by the available research. The NFER survey (Jowett and Baginsky 1991) and Topping's review (1986) showed that parents living in areas of poverty and disadvantage were just as interested in helping their children to learn as other families. A number of community education projects have enlisted the support of parents living in areas of poverty and disadvantage, including many from ethnic minorities (Widlake 1985). Parents cooperate readily and reliably once they are convinced that a school or a particular project is genuinely committed to help their children to learn and, through education, to escape from poverty into a better life.

Similar findings were reported from other countries, including the US Head Start programmes (Sylva 1999). In many of these projects, parents who were living in very poor conditions went daily to nursery centres to work as volunteers with groups of children. They also worked in one-to-one play sessions with their own child, in partnership with a practitioner, making up games and activities that seemed likely to help the child learn a skill or enjoy an activity. The same parents were glad to receive teachers into their own homes once a week (see Chapter 3).

Parents reading with children

We have known for many years that children learn to read better and with greater enjoyment if their parents listen to them read even for only a few minutes a day and are greatly helped by parents reading to them. An early book edited by Topping and Wolfendale (1985) brought together many successful examples of collaboration. Later publications have added further evidence (Hannon 1995; Wolfendale and Topping 1996). It is difficult to know what impact these studies have had nationally. Although many schools have successfully involved parents in shared reading, the positive lessons that have come from the research have not been widely adopted across the country.

Knowing what we know about the importance of parents listening to and reading with their children does not justify putting pressure on parents to sign a home–school agreement in which they commit themselves to spending set periods on such activities. Where there is already confidence and trust between home and school and between individual teachers and families, such schemes will already be in place, although lack of time on both sides may mean that opportunities for sharing of ideas are just not available. Where such trust is lacking or where parents and teachers do not value one another, contractual agreements are worthless.

Gregory (2000) argues that many of our assumptions about parental involvement in reading do not reflect or respect the cultural diversity of our society. Parents are asked to read with their children using strategies suggested by the school on the assumption that the same reading practices are suitable in all linguistic and cultural contexts when this may not be the case. For example, there is no tradition of one-to-one bedtime stories in some cultures and reading is a formal group activity that may take up a great deal of time and is taken very seriously.

Teachers visiting families

Teachers do not generally visit families at home for what appear at first to be very sound reasons. They are not professionally trained or psychologically prepared to do so and many would feel uncomfortable in straying from their own territory. Similarly, parents might well be surprised and suspicious if teachers tried to arrange such visits and the child may not be too happy either. Such a practice clearly has huge resource implications and would require earmarked funding. And yet teachers working in community schools have been visiting families for decades and so have their colleagues working in special schools.

Following the publication of the the Plowden report, a number of LEAs funded schools to appoint home–school liaison teachers. These teachers were generally already on the staff of the school but were allocated up to 50 per cent of their time to make contact with parents in whatever ways were agreed to be convenient. Although these initiatives did not last long, the NFER survey did provide evidence of a small number of LEAs who continued to fund home–school liaison teachers up to the end of the 1980s. Examples were given of two large urban authorities who funded 60 and 127 teachers each.

Similar appointments could be revived today within some of the new programmes launched by the government, particularly EAZs and Excellence in Cities. Evidence available so far does not suggest that visits to families are a high priority among those bidding for funds under these initiatives.

Partnership or collaboration?

Many writers now agree that we need to make a distinction between partnership and collaboration. True partnership is a process rather than a destination. Like inclusion, it is a journey undertaken as an expression of certain values and principles. True partnership, as in any close relationship, implies mutual respect based on a willingness to learn from one another, a sense of common purpose, a sharing of information and decision making and, some would add, a sharing of feelings (Mittler 1995b).

These principles and values are relevant to work with all parents but they represent only the fundamental building blocks of a working relationship with families who are all different and who have unique needs. Getting to know the individuality of families is one of the most difficult tasks for any teacher because there are so few opportunities for them to get to know parents as people. This is why it is so important to meet parents on neutral territory.

Fundamental changes have taken place in the structure of families and in family life. Many children are experiencing the separation and divorce of their parents, are living in lone parent households or with one or more step-parents. They may suddenly find themselves with several new half brothers and sisters and rather more than four grandparents. The concept of the extended family has become much more complex, especially when we include members of a household who are not related. This means that many people will be involved in the life of a child with special needs, as with all children, and not just the parents.

Teachers in some schools have let it be known that, in addition to the 'normal' parent evenings, they were willing to meet parents living nearby in certain local pubs, with never more than one or two teachers in the same pub. Some parents who had never attended parents' meetings or any school functions were happy to talk informally on this basis, with not a register in sight. Similarly, school playgrounds and football pitches have been used for car boot and 'bring and buy' or 'good as new' sales just to enable parents to meet teachers socially without necessarily settling down for an earnest conversation about their child.

Not all parents will welcome such creative and original ways of reaching them and will take evasive action accordingly. Even when there is an atmosphere of mutual trust and confidence, the relationship is not between equals because power and authority are vested not just in the teachers as individuals but in the school as a publicly funded institution. However hard teachers try to break down barriers, some parents will feel that the power relationship is loaded against them.

Teachers in their turn can feel threatened by parents who imply that the child's difficulties are at least in part related to the learning opportunities and the quality of teaching provided by the school, such as access to the curriculum, the school's discipline policy or the way it is enforced. These issues may remain below the surface partly because they are so sensitive but mainly because there is not enough time and psychological space for them to be discussed.

Parents of children with exceptional needs

'Working with parents' has a long history in special needs education and countless books and articles have been written on the subject, describing difficulties and obstacles, as well as good practice. Many of these publications arose from work with families of children with significant disabilities, most of whom are or were in special schools. Rather less has been written about working with families of the much larger group of children with exceptional needs in mainstream schools but a number of recent publications written primarily for mainstream teachers usefully draw on experience gained in specialist provision and suggest ways in which such experience can be adapted to mainstream settings (Hornby 1995; Blamires *et al.* 1997; Wolfendale 1997). A number of parents have written about their own perspectives and experiences on partnership; such accounts are an essential starting point for the development of any new policies whether based on schools or other services (Rieser and Mason 1990; Gascoigne 1995; Mallett 1997). This is a field in which there is no shortage of experience and advice.

Such experience is relevant or can be adapted not only to the wider group of families of children with exceptional needs but to all families. This is for the obvious reason that the starting point of a working relationship with any family is valuing the uniqueness of that family, whether they have a child with exceptional needs or not. This means ridding oneself of any preconceptions about families, whether they are families who live in a particular area, have a child whose behaviour is particularly challenging or families who have already been labelled by others as 'difficult', 'rejecting', 'over-protective' or 'not yet come to terms with their child's difficulties', to give just a few examples of the most popular labels.

Changing patterns of parent–professional relationships

Relationships between parents and professionals have gone through various stages. At one time, parents were virtually ignored by professionals and left to get on with looking after their child. Professionals encouraged parents to 'put their child away' in an institution. Those who did not follow this advice received little encouragement or support.

The growth of the parents' movement

The end of the 1950s marked the beginning of parent organisations, which started as mutual support groups at local level but rapidly became powerful national bodies, such as the Royal Society for Mentally Handicapped Children and Adults (MENCAP) and SCOPE (formerly the Spastics Society). These societies were led by charismatic and influential people, often with a direct line to ministers and MPs. They campaigned to improve the appalling conditions in long-stay hospitals and succeeded, along with others, in halting the admission of children for long-term care. They also joined forces with professionals who were campaigning to transfer responsibility for the education of children with severe learning difficulties from health to education authorities (see Mittler and Sinason (1996) for a review of the impact of advocacy on services for people with learning disabilities).

With the growth of privatisation, organisations such as MENCAP have themselves moved into service provision, such as group homes and day-care facilities. SCOPE and the National Autistic Society have run their own schools, with fees usually paid by LEAs. In addition to the disability specific organisations, a number of national parent organisations have emerged since the 1980s, including the Alliance for Inclusive Education, Parents in Partnership, Network 81 and Campaign for Choice. These provide support, advocacy, information and telephone help lines to any parents who approach them (Paige-Smith 1997).

Parents as teachers

In the late 1960s and early 1970s, a number of psychologists and teachers began to run workshops for parents of children with special needs, with the aim of helping them to develop skills of observation and assessment with a view to designing and implementing a teaching programme for their own child. The best surviving example of such an approach is the Portage programme (White 1997; see also Chapter 3 and Mittler and McConachie (1983) for accounts of a range of approaches developed over a decade or so).

Many parents and family members not only collaborated willingly in such approaches but experienced considerable success in teaching their children, with varying degrees of support from professionals. Their success led professionals to expect even higher levels of commitment of time, resources and unlimited motivation.

We know that some parents are prepared to commit all their time and energy to their children. It is also clear that there are programmes that demand a degree of parental involvement that can be damaging and depriving to some members of the family. These examples may be at one end of a continuum, but they should alert professionals to the dangers of making demands for excessive or unreasonable degree of commitment from parents and other family members.

The early 1980s saw a reaction against parents being trained in professional skills. Objections came not only from parents but from professionals themselves, partly related to a swing of the pendulum away from overly behaviourist methods of teaching applied to children. This phase was dubbed 'the transplant model' and was gradually replaced by a 'consumer model' in which the family themselves were supposed to decide what kind of support they needed and what level of teaching and time commitment suited them best. Writing about early intervention, McConkey described the change of climate as follows: 'It's farewell to authoritarian experts prescribing similar treatments to "patients", and a welcome to professionals who meet people as people, striving to share their community and valuing the worth and dignity of each as they seek to overcome the adversities of life' (1994) .

As time went on, parents themselves became more assertive and began to insist on their right to be consulted at every stage of decision making concerning their child. Furthermore, many parents have made it clear that they do not necessarily see themselves in the role of teachers of their child but that they expect good quality teaching from those who are paid to do so.

Implications for services

Professionals therefore need to learn to look beyond the child to the family setting in which the child is living. If families agree, they should visit the child at home and learn to see the child in the normal family environment. They may also need to adapt their own working practices by getting to know fathers, sisters and brothers and other members of the household such as grandparents. It is only on this basis that they can begin to explore the various possible options for the nature and extent of collaboration and learn to negotiate with families what kinds of demands and routines are and are not realistic in the context of the individual family.

Parents' rights, the Education Act 1981and its successors

The Warnock report had made a strong case for the involvement of parents in decision making: 'The successful education of children with special educational needs is dependent on the full involvement of their parents; indeed, unless the parents are seen as equal partners in the educational process, the purpose of our report will be frustrated' (DES 1978: para 9.1). This quote is typical of much of the rhetoric about the importance of partnership with parents. But despite major improvements in many schools and services, the reality for parents is often very different from the official rhetoric.

Although many would argue that we are still in the consumer phase, some parents still feel that they are not given all the information to which they are entitled. A series of studies during the 1980s showed that half the LEAs omitted to include important information about parents' rights and entitlements under the Education Act 1981 (CSIE 1986; Armstrong 1995). Parents do not always feel welcome in schools and complain that they are sometimes ignored or patronised by teachers and other professionals. The notices saying 'No parents beyond this point' may have gone, but the attitudes remain.

The 1981 Act was a major landmark and has laid the foundations for all later legislation, particularly the Education Acts 1993 and 1996 and the Code of Practice. However, consultation is under way on a new Special Needs Bill, which will further strengthen parents' rights and bring education into the Disability Discrimination Act 1995.

The Education Act 1981 and the explanatory circulars and regulations that followed represented a radical departure from previous practice by putting a duty on LEAs to consult and work with parents.

Briefly, the Act gave parents the right to:
- request the LEA to conduct a formal assessment of their child;
- be involved in the process of assessment and in annual reviews;
- appeal against an LEA decision; and
- have their views taken into account in decisions concerning placement in special or ordinary schools.

The Act also gave parents the right to appeal to a local appeals committee and, under certain circumstances, to the Secretary of State for Education. The Education Act 1993 replaced this with an SEN Tribunal to deal with all appeals.

The Education Act 1981 stipulated that children with special educational needs should be educated in mainstream schools, where parents request this, provided that:
- the child can receive appropriate provision;
- it is compatible with the efficient education of other children;
- and with the efficient use of resources.

These clauses (which are now Section 316 of the Education Act 1996) have bedevilled the operation of the Act ever since; indeed, it is difficult to understand how the problems were not more clearly foreseen by legislators at that time. Now that new legislation has been promised, there will certainly be a battle about whether they should remain on the statute book.

Parents have complained that LEAs who did not want to place a child with exceptional needs in mainstream provision could easily marshall evidence on all three counts in order to refuse a mainstream placement. More fundamentally, they also argue that the three conditions place unreasonable restrictions on parental preference and put parents of children with exceptional needs on a different footing from all other parents. They are discriminatory in so far as children who do not have exceptional needs cannot be denied access to a school on the grounds that this would interfere with the education of other pupils or be an ineffective use of resources. For example, children from ethnic minorities would never be refused on such grounds.

Since the Education Act 1993, parents of children with exceptional needs have been able to express a choice for a mainstream placement but, unlike all other parents, cannot expect the LEA to agree to their choice of a particular school. Selection of the school remains the responsibility of the LEA, which should 'take parental views into account' but is not bound to act on them. The Education Act 1980 had given all parents the right to ask for a named school for their child, although their wishes could not always be met in practice. The Education Act 1981 did not extend this right to parents of children with exceptional needs.

Under the present system, LEAs in the course of preparing a statement should be considering which mainstream school would best meet the needs of the child, using their detailed knowledge of the schools in its area; for example, they might know that there were tensions and disagreements between the head teacher and staff, that there were problems of access to the curriculum or that resources allocated under a statement might not be effectively deployed. Since such information is highly sensitive, it can obviously not be shared with parents who express a strong preference for a particular school.

If the three conditions were removed, there would be an assumption that the LEA would have a duty to provide a mainstream school, unless the parents explicitly said that they wanted a special school placement or failed to express a view one way or the other.

Another issue concerns how the views of the children themselves can be heard. Despite the fact that this was recommended in DES Circular 1/83, which provided guidance on the implementation of the Education Act 1981 and became part of statutory provision in the Children Act 1989 and was strongly reiterated in the 1994 Code of Practice, all the evidence available suggests that this recommendation is being quietly forgotten in most areas.

The new Bill will provide a further opportunity to revisit this issue. For example, Section 316 could be amended to include the views of children as well as parents. If there was disagreement between parents and the child that could not be resolved through local mediation, the SEN Tribunal might need to be involved. Quite apart from the proposed Bill, the revised Code of Practice and other initiatives announced in the Programme of Action will contain new proposals to give greater weight to children's views in choice of school and also in SEN Tribunal hearings.

The Code of Practice and parents' rights

The Code of Practice provides by far the clearest and strongest affirmation of the rights of parents and the need for the closest possible working relationship between parents and teachers. This is reiterated throughout the document in relation to all stages of the Code. The consultation document on the revised Code reflects an even stronger commitment.

> Children's progress will be diminished if their parents are not seen as partners in the educational process with unique knowledge and information to impart.
>   Professional help can seldom be wholly effective unless it builds upon parents' capacity to be involved and unless professionals take account of what they say and treat their views and anxieties as intrinsically important.
>
> (DfE 1994: 2.28)

The Code of Practice requires that the school's SEN policy provides information to parents under the headings information, partnership and access for parents.

- Information on:
  - the school's SEN policy;
  - the support available for children with SEN within the school and LEA;
  - parents' involvement in assessment and decision making, emphasising the importance of their contribution;
  - services such as those provided by the local authority for children 'in need'; and
  - local and national voluntary organisations that might provide information, advice or counselling.
- Partnership:
  - arrangements for recording and acting on parental concerns;
  - procedures for involving parents when a concern is first expressed within the school;
  - arrangements for incorporating parents' views in assessment and subsequent reviews.
- Access for parents:
  - information in a range of community languages;
  - information on tape for parents who may have literacy or communication difficulties; and
  - a parents' room or other arrangement in the school to help parents feel confident and comfortable (DfE 1994: 2.33).

Named persons and named officers

The Warnock Committee had emphasised the importance of parents being given access to a 'named person' who would support them in stating their needs to decision makers and generally act as a single point of contact. However, they also suggested that the named person might be a health visitor for under-fives, a head teacher for children of school age and a careers officer for school leavers. While these individuals might be very helpful and supportive, they are all part of the decision-making process and therefore anything but independent. An obvious example would be the head teacher of a special school when a parent is fighting for a mainstream placement.

The notion of the named person was not accepted by the government in the sense proposed by Warnock and was changed in the progress of the 1981 legislation through parliament into the proposal for a named officer of the LEA who would be responsible for ensuring that parents whose child had a statement were given information from that point on, for example about annual reviews. It has, however, worked well in Scotland (Russell 1997).

The Code of Practice recommended a return to the proposal for a named person for children who already had or were about to receive a statement but stressed that it would be helpful for that person to be independent of the LEA and someone who would be trusted by the parent. The role of the named person was to give advice and information to parents about their child's special needs.

Parent partnership schemes

Since 1993, LEAs have been able to bid for 60 per cent of the cost of parent partnership schemes within the DfEE GEST, now replaced by an enlarged Standards Fund. Although most LEAs applied for and received funding, the new SEN Bill will place a statutory obligation on all LEAs in England to provide a parent partnership service. Guidelines for the new schemes are being drawn up in the light of the national evaluation, which has been carried out by the National Children's Bureau (Furze and Conrad 1997; Russell 1997; Wolfendale and Cook 1997). In the light of some major problems that have emerged from these evaluations, the DfEE has commissioned a new study with the aim of highlighting good practice (Vernon 1999).

One of the main functions of the new parent partnership service will be to recruit suitable local volunteers as 'independent parental supporters', the new name chosen in place of 'named person'. These can be members of a voluntary organisation or just friends who are prepared to support parents engaged in the process of securing appropriate provision for their children at any stage of the Code of Practice, not just those who have received a statement. So far, most named persons have been recruited from parents and carers, voluntary workers, preschool playgroup workers, school governors, retired teachers and LEA personnel. Nearly all are women.

According to Simmons (1997) very few of the pilot schemes were managed by the voluntary sector, many of whom were apprehensive about giving wrong advice to parents involved in legal disputes or preparing for a tribunal hearing without training and support. Although LEAs generally ran the schemes, a few 'kept their distance' and limited their role to 'pay and rations'. Even so, the parent partnership officer (now to be known as a coordinator) is an LEA appointment.

Reviewing the first years of the Code of Practice and the partnership with parents scheme, Russell (1997) summarises its lessons as follows:

- The Code of Practice is very time-consuming for everyone working with parents.
- Many parents find partnership onerous.
- The role of the named person requires training, support and a clear skill base that empowers but does not dominate.
- The named person is accessible and enabling and sees the eventual autonomy of the parent (i.e. facilitating help) as a key objective.
- Partnership often starts too late.
- The requirement for a school SEN policy has been a positive vehicle for change; the debate has moved from statutory assessment to the school based stages of assessment.
- Partnership with the voluntary sector has not been easy.

An early OFSTED report on the operation of the Code of Practice and the SEN Tribunal includes some disquieting findings about parental involvement (OFSTED 1997). For example, few schools were aware of the parent partnership scheme and were therefore not in a position to inform parents about how they worked. Many parents whose children had a statement did not appear to have a named person; this is problematic, since only a third of parents of disabled children belong to a voluntary organisation who could alert them to their rights.

The evaluation carried out by Wolfendale and Cook (1997) produced some disquieting findings that will need to be addressed now that the scheme is being extended nationally and made available to parents whose children are at any stage of the Code of Practice.

- The majority view of parent partnership officers (PPOs), LEAs, professionals and parents is that partnership goals in the spirit of the Code of Practice have not been achieved.
- PPOs view their role as primarily providers of information and advisory services but only at around Stage 4 of the Code of Practice, although

parents are approaching PPOs at Stage 3. PPOs seem to follow the LEA brief of reducing appeals to tribunal.
- Many schools do not make parents aware of the parent partnership service.
- SENCOs are beginning to take the initiative in making contact with PPOs and asking for in-service training.

SEN Tribunal

The SEN Tribunal was created by the Education Act 1993 to replace both the LEA appeal committees and the possibility of appeal to the Secretary of State for Education. In setting up the SEN Tribunal, the then government hoped that the Code of Practice would improve relationships between parents and LEAs and that the tribunal would be a last resort. This has not proved to be the case. The tribunal has not only been overwhelmed with appeals but its work has revealed major structural weaknesses in the system as a whole, with the result that it is now under review as part of the government's Programme of Action. The DfEE is consulting on new draft regulations and has also commissioned some examples of good practice in conciliation arrangements.

The main changes proposed are:
- changing the regulations to strengthen the rights of children;
- a change in requirements for lay panels;
- changing the time scales for LEAs to implement tribunal orders; and
- improved pre-tribunal conciliation procedures at LEA level.

The SEN Tribunal has published annual reports detailing the number, nature and outcomes of the appeals. The most recent records an increase of registrations from 1,161 in 1994–95 to 2,412 in 1988–99 and the rate is increasing by about 10 per cent year (SEN Tribunal 1999). The work of the tribunal has also been scrutinised by the House of Commons Select Committee on Education (1996) and reviewed by OFSTED (1997), and a critical review has been published by Simmons (1997) based on a survey carried out by the Independent Panel Supporting Special Education Advice (IPSEA).

These and other reports highlight the main problems that have arisen, as follows.
- A disproportionate number of parents who have used the SEN Tribunal have been well educated, articulate people, particularly parents of children with dyslexia, autism and speech and language difficulties. This

has created a two tier system at LEA level, as was made clear to the House of Commons Select Committee on Education (1996) by LEAs themselves. Relatively few parents from poor backgrounds or from ethnic minorities have used the tribunal. This is not the fault of the tribunal but reflects unequal opportunities for parents in the system as a whole.

- LEA employees, particularly teachers and educational psychologists, have been reluctant to appear as witnesses if their professional opinion differs from that of their employers. There have been reports of pressure on LEA staff not to appear, unless a formal summons was issued. Parents have hesitated to call professionals because they did not want to put them in a difficult position. This has weakened their case.
- Despite all efforts, hearings have become more formal and therefore more confusing and intimidating to parents. Although LEAs are able to call on legal advice, only parents with a very low income can receive legal aid in preparing their case but not in presenting it. The presence of a solicitor at a tribunal hearing costs at least £1,000. The original intention that tribunal hearings should be parent-friendly does not seem to have been fulfilled. Indeed, Simmons (1997) concludes that the present impasse makes for confrontation rather than partnership.
- There is a major problem for parents in receiving support in preparing their case and in being represented at the hearing because there are simply not enough volunteers who are willing and able to help. The major voluntary organisations are reluctant to become too involved and are understandably fearful about the vulnerability of their volunteers on legal grounds. Finding volunteers and independent parental supporters is the responsibility of the parent partnership coordinators, who, in the last analysis, are also employees of the LEA, whatever safeguards are put in place to secure their independence.
- Although LEAs are legally bound to implement tribunal decisions, there is evidence that some are taking too long to do so when the decision has gone against them.

Despite these problems, the work of the SEN Tribunal has provided an essential safeguard for those parents who cannot resolve their differences with the LEA and has enabled many parents to ensure that their child's education is in accordance with their wishes and priorities. Some LEAs are proud of their record in never having to defend their actions at a tribunal, while others appear several times in the same year. These range from none in Middlesbrough and one in Barnsley to 81 in Manchester and 89 in Kent.

What is particularly disquieting is the evidence that reflects a conflict of interest between the LEA and its employees before there is any question of an appeal to the tribunal. Some years ago an educational psychologist was dismissed by his LEA for giving advice to parents that was not acceptable to the LEA, although the decision was subsequently overruled by an employment tribunal. LEAs take the view that it is the job of their employees, such as educational psychologists and SENCOs, to give advice on the needs of the child and not on where those needs should be met; this, they argue, is a matter for the LEA, using its knowledge of available resources and provision in the area.

Conclusions

Evaluations of the operation of the parent partnership service and the SEN Tribunal have highlighted deep-seated and endemic tensions between parents and professionals. The tribunal is merely the tip of the iceberg for parents who have the tenacity and the support to use its services. Despite the rhetoric that surrounds parent–professional partnership, we have very little information on day-to-day practice on the ground or about how parents feel about decisions made on their children's education, far less their progress within the system or the quality of their working relationships with teachers. As far as children with exceptional needs are concerned, we have little information at national level about how satisfied parents are with their children being put on a register in the first place, whether they feel they are getting enough information from the school about the progress their child is making or what they make of IEPs.

The debates about parent–professional relationships within the field of exceptional needs education are merely one facet of the universal question about home–school relationships for all children and all parents. The gulf between home and school is not the fault of either and cannot easily be bridged. Over many decades, the education system as a whole has somehow distanced itself from the communities it serves. Although many individual schools have not only retained but developed and enriched their links with their local community, as well as with their own parents, many others have just been too overwhelmed with meeting government targets and responding to constant exhortation to change.

A government committed to inclusion has to tackle the exclusion of so many parents from participation in discussion and decision making about the education of their children. A useful start has been made: for example, the Sure Start projects seem to have been based on genuine community involvement within a very small area in which attempts were made to visit all families with children in the appropriate age range of the scheme. Are there ways in which parents and communities could be approached to give their views on how they would like to be involved in discussion and decision making about the work of schools? Schools in their turn could try to find new ways of asking parents for their views about how home–school links could be strengthened. Closer links between parents and teachers cannot be prescribed from on high; they have to be founded on the wishes and priorities of those who are at the grass roots.

The last word goes to a group of parents of children with special needs and disabilities (quoted by Russell 1997: 79):

- Please accept and value our children (and ourselves as families) as we are.
- Please celebrate difference.
- Please try and accept our children as children first. Don't attach labels to them unless you mean to *do* something.
- Please recognise your power over our lives. We live with the consequences of your opinions and decisions.
- Please understand the stress many families are under. The cancelled appointment, the waiting list no one gets to the top of, all the discussions about resources – it's *our* lives you're talking about.
- Don't put fashionable fads and treatments on to us unless you are going to be around to see them through. And don't forget families have many members, many responsibilities. Sometimes, we can't please everyone.
- Do recognise that sometimes we are right! Please believe us and listen to what we know that we and our child need.
- Sometimes we are sad, tired and depressed. Please value us as caring and committed families and try to go on working with us.

Chapter 11

Into the Future: Tensions and Dilemmas

As we start a new century, what are the prospects for a more inclusive society and a more inclusive school system? What changes will be witnessed by teachers starting their first job this year and what changes will they themselves initiate before they retire in the 2040s? Will they look back on the first decade of the 21st century as a new dawn or as a missed opportunity?

In this concluding chapter I will try to summarise some of the grounds for optimism about the future but also refer to tensions and contradictions underlying current policy and practice and identify some major decisions that still need to be made.

Education as a global imperative

Firstly, we can take heart that many governments around the world are giving greater priority to education. This springs from the conviction that education is the key to a better society, not just for today's children but for future generations.

All over the world, we find that heads of state and national leaders are beginning to reverse decades of under-investment in education and starting to see children as their most precious asset. It has taken a long time for politicians to accept what all parents have always known but all too often not been able to realise.

The Delors report (UNESCO 1996) gave voice to the vision but also expressed the obstacles to its realisation:

> Education is one of the principal means available to foster a deeper and more harmonious form of human development and thereby to reduce poverty, exclusion, ignorance, oppression and war.
>
> The coming century, dominated by globalisation, will bring with it enduring tensions to overcome: tensions between the global and the local, the universal and the individual, tradition and modernity, long-term and short-term considerations, competition and equality of opportunity, the unlimited expansion of knowledge and the limited capacity of human beings to assimilate it, and the spiritual and the material.

> Formal education systems tend to emphasise the acquisition of knowledge to the detriment of other types of learning; but it is vital now to conceive education in a more encompassing fashion . . . as built on four pillars of learning: learning to be, learning to know, learning to do and learning to live together.
>
> (UNESCO 1996)

Ten years ago at Jomtien, Thailand, the world's leaders committed themselves to the EFA programme, which set targets for universal primary education, adult literacy and the education of girls and women. A few countries can report real progress in approaching these targets but many others have failed to do so, mainly because of the burden of debt repayments but also because they had other priorities. For example, India and Pakistan still spend much more on armaments than on education, and children in many parts of Africa seem less rather than more likely to receive four years of primary education.

The Salamanca Conference in 1994 marked a turning point in reminding governments that children with difficulties and disabilities should be included in national plans to expand the number of children gaining access to schooling. The leadership provided by UNESCO over a 20-year period had encouraged many education ministries throughout the world to accept responsibility for the education of previously excluded children and to educate them in ordinary schools, with appropriate support. The Salamanca Framework for Education seems to have accelerated the process.

The example of Uganda shows that a commitment to universal primary education can at the same time be a commitment to inclusive education. Despite being devastated by civil strife and now by AIDS, Uganda has been able to bring schooling to an additional two million children in a period of two years. Four children in every family will be able to have access to free primary education and any child who has a disability has first priority. It is all a matter of political will and priorities.

Today, policy and practice around the world is moving towards inclusion (Daniels and Garner 1999) but this process seems to be happening with greater speed and greater commitment in some of the poorest countries of the world. In addition to Uganda, inclusive education is receiving strong government backing in countries varying in size from the two million people of the Kingdom of Lesotho to the 1.2 billion in the People's Republic of China. Vietnam, Laos, Guyana and parts of India are just some of the countries now leading the way, while some of the richer countries that were once leaders in the field seem more hesitant and half-hearted.

Within Europe, the Scandinavian countries set the example in the 1960s but the most radical step was taken by Italy, which passed legislation in the 1970s resulting in the closure of most special schools and the transfer of all children to their neighbourhood school, usually with one-to-one support. Spain adopted a more gradualist approach, inviting schools to volunteer, in return for a 25 per cent reduction in class size and the guaranteed services of a support team. Germany, the

Netherlands and France developed islands of inclusive practice while retaining special schools and systems at national level. The USA has gone through several waves of reform, starting with the Education of All Handicapped Children Act in 1975 through to the Individuals with Disabilities Education Act 1990, but still has many children in segregated classes in mainstream schools (Gartner and Lipsky 1997). Looking back, we now see these as mostly examples of integration rather than the much broader agenda involved in inclusion.

The national picture: tensions and dilemmas

It is heartening to find the UK government providing leadership in supporting the UN EFA initiative to provide education for all by being the first country to cancel the crippling burden of debt of many developing countries, on condition that the money released is invested in heath and education. It has rejoined UNESCO and is working within the UN and with national partners for basic literacy and universal primary education as a way to a better society (Chapter 2).

The government's priority for education is often expressed in terms of examination results but a broader vision of the purpose of education is reflected in David Blunkett's speech to the North of England conference in January 2000. He gave three, equally important reasons for prioritising education: economic, social and personal.

> The combined forces of globalisation and technological change will mean . . . that education will determine 'who has the keys to the treasures the world can furnish' . . . countries that respond astutely should experience extraordinary progress – with major social and economic benefits, including 'catch-up gains' for the poor and marginalised. Countries that fail to respond to the challenge risk stagnating . . . widening social and economic gaps and sowing the seeds of unrest.
>
> The second argument is a social one. Healthy, cohesive societies depend . . . on education because only through education can people gain the knowledge, learn the skills and develop the confidence to participate in shaping their communities.
>
> The third argument . . . is that education is the great liberator; it can unlock what William Blake called those 'mind-forged manacles'. Education gives people greater control over their lives, greater opportunity, more options in their working lives.
> (Blunkett 2000: 1)

We have seen that inclusion is central to government policy and that many new initiatives have been launched. But we must also be aware of deep-seated tensions, contradictions and dilemmas that arise from a divided education system and from the unequal nature of our society.

On the positive side, three long-standing but distinctive features of UK practice deserve mention. None of these is unique to the UK but all have been established for many years and have adapted well to changing circumstances.

> They are:
> - the redefinition by the Warnock committee of the field of special education to encompass what now appears to be one in four of the school population;
> - the development of a range of support services for children with exceptional needs in mainstream schools; and
> - the day-to-day working contacts between special and mainstream schools.

More recently, the Code of Practice counts as a major achievement, particularly the presence of a SENCO in every mainstream school in the context of a mandatory policy for children with exceptional needs. Despite early teething problems and lack of funding, the Code has marked a major shift of emphasis towards identifying and supporting children with difficulties in mainstream schools at an early stage. It has also provided a framework for the inclusion of children with more severe difficulties who would previously have been sent to special schools.

Diversity or divisiveness?

Among the many tensions listed in the quotation from the Delors report, that between competition and equality of opportunity has a particular relevance to the theme of this book. How can a commitment to inclusion and equality of opportunity be reconciled with an adherence to competition and market forces in education and other public services? How do market forces help children who fail to meet the standards set? When, as the government proclaims, excellence is the norm and there is zero tolerance for failure and for excuses, what happens to those who are not able to reach the targets? Are they supposed to opt out of the competition? Hegarty put it bluntly: 'As a rationale for educational reform, the belief that putting schools into open competition with one another will not merely jack up standards but do so in a benign way almost beggars belief' (Hegarty 1993b: 33).

The present government remains committed to competition and to separating schools from one another. Diversity has been increased by the arrival (and sometimes the departure) of grant maintained schools, City Technology Colleges, Beacon and specialist schools and most recently by the proposal for City Academies, removed from LEA control, funded by business and voluntary organisations and free to vary the National Curriculum and teachers' salaries. Schools are able to select a proportion of their students and to group them by levels of achievement at subject level. Mixed ability teaching has been discredited as outmoded and doctrinaire. Schools, LEAs and teacher training institutions that fail on the criteria selected by ministers or OFSTED are put in the modern equivalent of the stocks, publicly humiliated, put on probation or placed under new management by a new breed of super-head able to run five schools at a time for the right salary.

League tables are another example of an inheritance that has been taken over from the previous government without any evidence of a serious consideration of alternatives. Replacing league tables in their present form would probably do more for teacher morale than almost any other measure, since the criteria used for measuring the achievements of teachers as well as children are so limited. It should not be impossible for the government's legions of advisers to come up with a better alternative.

In a recent *Guardian* poll of 500 parents of primary and secondary pupils, 500 teachers and 100 university lecturers, as many as four out of five parents said they were not influenced by league tables in choosing a school and 38 per cent thought they should be scrapped, although 58 per cent still thought they were helpful or very helpful in understanding a school's performance. In the same poll, nine out of ten parents were very happy or fairly happy with the quality of their child's schooling. The majority of primary parents think their children's teachers are competent (54 per cent) or highly competent (39 per cent) (*Education Guardian* 29 February 2000).

There are arguments for and against each of these policies but their overall effect is divisive because they separate schools, teachers and children from one another in ways that are inconsistent with the government's stated commitment to inclusion.

Poverty and underachievement

The ten-fold increase in student numbers created by the Warnock committee should have resulted in a policy that responded to the challenge of poverty and its association with underachievement and educational disadvantage. But as we have seen (Chapter 4), it has taken more than 20 years for this link to begin to be addressed. The Warnock committee was explicitly forbidden to discuss the impact of poverty and social disadvantage on learning and the subject became taboo, despite the work of pioneers such as Midwinter and Halsey in the field of compensatory education and early intervention (Silver and Silver 1991).

Even now, politicians are speaking with different voices on different days. Major programmes are being launched to combat poverty, and at the same time the government rejects any association of poverty and educational underachievement as 'excuses'. It is ironic that a government committed to 'joined-up thinking' finds it so hard to integrate its policies for raising standards in schools with its wider social programme of combating poverty and disadvantage. Even OFSTED

(2000a) now criticises ministers for the continued repetition of the mantra 'poverty is no excuse' and argues for more money and for 'more realistic targets'. Their report indicates that only 10 per cent of secondary schools and 2 per cent of pupils in deprived areas even approach the national average of five good GCSE examination passes. In primary schools, only 4 per cent of pupils obtain average mathematics and English results. The report offers brief pen pictures of schools that 'beat prediction', despite having up to 70 per cent of pupils on free school meals.

Asked to account for their success, two head teachers mentioned the following:

[Working with surrounding schools] It may be unfashionable but schools round here support each other. It doesn't help in a disadvantaged area to think the school down the road is the enemy.

(Alasdair MacDonald, Head of Morpeth School, Tower Hamlets)

We don't just concentrate on exam results. A child cannot work if he is hungry or upset. I'd like to see more input from education welfare officers sooner. I'd like to introduce breakfast and homework clubs. I know if we can get into families coping with some of the difficult social problems when the children are very young, we turn those families around. We want the community and the parents to be proud of their children and their school.

(Patricia Deus, Head of St Hugh's RC School, Liverpool)
(*Times Educational Supplement* 10 March 2000)

We know very little about what if anything is distinctive about schools such as these and how they have such an impact on children's learning and motivation. Programmes such as Sure Start and other early years initiatives, EAZs and Excellence in Cities, which we have reviewed in earlier chapters, are all part of a wider social programme aiming to reduce poverty. What is not yet clear is just how these programmes will affect children and teachers and how they will make an impact on learning and achievement in general, not just on the holy grail of five good GCSE examination passes.

Inclusion and exclusion

Formal exclusion of pupils from schools is only one form of exclusion. Others are reflected in policies that separate children from one another on the basis of success and failure. Even more serious is the problem of children who virtually exclude themselves from learning and participation in the life of the school, even though they are physically present. Some of these are the children and young people are described as 'disaffected'. Hong Kong has even gone so far as to create a category of 'academically unmotivated' pupils who are removed from mainstream secondary schools and placed in schools that emphasise vocational training rather than academic achievement and examination results.

Quite apart from children who show outward evidence of disaffection, there are also many others whose abilities and imagination are not being stretched but who are not necessarily regarded as difficult or disaffected. Preventing underachievement in such children is another major challenge for schools.

There are no easy roads to preventing boredom and disaffection. Schools that can provide experience of success in learning have an accessible curriculum, good teaching and a pastoral support system that pupils can trust. The revised curriculum and the greater degree of flexibility at Key Stage 4 are more consistent with inclusive principles, although it may be difficult to avoid the stigma associated with non-academic study and qualifications. Similarly, the new emphasis on preventing underachievement at Key Stage 3 is welcome, as it should identify children who are beginning to fall behind their peers and prevent the damage to self-esteem associated with a growing sense of failure.

Managing change

Inclusion is about all pupils, not just a few. It involves changing the culture and organisation of the school to ensure access and participation for all pupils currently in the school and also for others who are now in segregated provision but who may be joining the school at some time in the future. Inclusion is not about the placement of individual children but about creating an environment where all pupils can enjoy access and success in the curriculum and become full and valued members of the school and the local community. Good management is about preventing underachievement, feelings of failure and loss of self-esteem. Dealing with the consequences of underachievement for pupils, parents, teachers and the community is a different, but equally challenging task.

There is no royal road to inclusion but there is agreement that it is a process and a journey rather than a destination. Nevertheless, studies of schools in action make it clear that some schools have travelled much further than others (Sewell 1996; Clarke et al. 1997; Ainscow 1999), not just because they have more pupils with exceptional needs or even because they make good provision for them but because the school as a whole is run along inclusive lines. The Index for Inclusion, which has now been sent to all schools and LEAs in England (Chapter 8), enables schools to address a wide range of questions that will enable them to make their own assessment of how far they have travelled and how far they have to go (CSIE 2000).

However well managed and led, inclusion is in the first and last analysis about what goes in classrooms. There are classrooms with up to 100 children in many parts of the world that are inclusive because each lesson and each activity seems naturally created to ensure that all the children can take part. By the same token, one can find classes with two adults and 20 children in which a few children are literally and metaphorically at the margins, not taking part in the lesson and isolated from other children.

Since all teachers have their individual styles of teaching, it is possible to find a great deal of variation in the extent to which teachers ensure participation by all pupils. Such variation may have little to do with the stated policy of the school as a whole but is a natural expression of a particular approach, or repertoire of approaches, that all teachers develop as a result of experience and reflection.

In Chapter 9 I suggested that many teachers already teach inclusively and display the 'knowledge, understanding, skills and attributes' to teach a much wider range of children. What they lack is not competence but confidence. Any head teacher – or indeed any government – engaged in the task of planning for more inclusive practice needs to build on these foundations and to avoid the assumption that 'training for inclusion' has to start from a clean slate.

After decades of neglect, the government is now introducing a new policy that is based on the entitlement of every teacher to funded and resourced opportunities for professional development. The TTA has laid the foundations for such a policy by defining the standards required by teachers at various stages of their career: newly qualified teachers, aspiring head teachers, advanced skill teachers, SENCOs and SEN specialists. Although many questions remain unanswered, the opportunities now available for professional development are a major landmark for all teachers and therefore all children.

Schools in partnership

No school is an island and no school can succeed without developing networks of partnerships with its local community, with its parents, past, present and future and with other schools and other agencies. In developing countries and in some rural communities, the school is at the heart of the community. Adults learn alongside and with their children; the buildings are in continuous use; and the staff of the school are valued for their knowledge and experience as well as for their key role in helping the community's children learn and develop.

Once again, government policy is fraught with tensions and contradictions. On the one hand, schools are encouraged to forge links with parents and the local community. But when schools fail to produce 'results', the government relies on bringing in new management to restructure the school without reference to the community around the school. Although some schools in inner city areas do raise achievement more than others and although school improvement and new management can yield results, it is simplistic to focus on schools alone without at the same time exploring ways in which schools can work with families and local communities. Common sense as well as experience and evidence tell us that this is likely to benefit all those involved, especially if parents can become more supportive of schools and schools can be more understanding of the difficulties that parents face.

We reviewed evidence of such attempts in Chapter 10, but also had to report that few LEAs and schools were investing time or resources in forging such links. This is a complex and sensitive area in which there are no easy solutions, but some schools have been able to find new ways of asking local parents about their ideas and suggestions. Difficult though it is, this should be a priority for development in the next decade.

Good foundations for a new kind of partnership are being laid in radical reforms to early provision, which we reviewed in Chapter 3. These are initially focused on children and families living in poverty but the principles underlying these developments are relevant across the board. For example, the Sure Start programme, which is for children in the first three years of life, is based on asking local parents individually what changes they would like to see and ensuring that they are involved in decision making and in the running of the scheme. Secondly, although the practitioners in early years provision have a variety of backgrounds and qualifications, they work together in a unified management structure created for the purpose by several statutory and voluntary agencies.

Education after school

The success of any system, whether inclusive or exclusive, can be best judged by the young people who are leaving it. On such a yardstick, our education system has succeeded for a few but failed the many. Too many young people living in areas of poverty have left school without qualifications and have faced long periods of unemployment and demoralisation. Opportunities for further education and training have been slow to develop, despite many new initiatives over the past 30 years. Very few young people have gone on to obtain advanced qualifications or entered higher education.

Looking to the future, there are grounds for optimism. Firstly, there have always been areas of excellence in the post-16 sector, implementing equal opportunities across the board and including students with severe disabilities of all kinds in post-16 provision. Secondly, the post-16 sector has never experienced the debate about the advantages and disadvantages of integrated versus segregated education. Nevertheless, although further education colleges are for everyone in the locality, some of the early provision was not inclusive because it was originally assumed that the needs of students with learning difficulties and disabilities could best be met through special classes, with as much integration as possible into the life of the college at other times. Even so, many colleges responded to the challenge of making inclusion work (see Johnstone (1995) for a critical evaluation of progress and problems).

The process was greatly helped by a whole series of curriculum and organisational guides from the then Further Education Unit, now the Further Education Development Authority. These guides were unique at the time in supporting the planning and implementation of a 'whole college approach' and in developing inclusive curricula. Some publications provided detailed information on the inclusion of students with specific disabilities that remain valid today. In addition, a DES report entitled *A Special Professionalism* (DES 1987b) provided a blueprint for staff development and awareness from the principal to the kitchen and portering staff, which was far superior in breadth and quality to any comparable publication for teachers and other staff working with school-age children at that time.

Unfortunately, the guidance was not always implemented or followed up in the colleges, so that many of these documents were neither known nor used. Nevertheless, they reflected a high level of interest on the part of official bodies; in addition a number of well placed individuals provided exceptional leadership within organisations such as SKILL (formerly the National Bureau of Students with Disabilities). There seemed to be a broad consensus that the way forward in further education and in the post-16 sector generally was based on inclusive principles and practice that were based on a zero reject philosophy.

Despite this, provision was patchy across the country as a whole and changes were held up by further education colleges becoming independent of LEAs in the Education Act 1992. The new funding structures imposed by the FEFC prioritised vocationally oriented courses likely to lead to employment, leaving some of the courses used by students with learning difficulties and difficulties vulnerable to closure.

Nevertheless, these developments can be said to have laid the foundations for the Tomlinson report, *Inclusive Learning* (FEFC 1996, Tomlinson 1996), which was set up by the FEFC and has been referred to as the Warnock report of further education. The report was warmly received and widely accepted and many colleges began to implement its recommendations as best they could, with limited resources.

In 1999, the government produced a White Paper, *Learning to Succeed*, which provides an entirely new framework for post-16 education and training, and which has the potential to bring about major improvements in access and provision for young people with learning difficulties and disabilities. Following extensive consultation, the main provisions of the White Paper are being incorporated in the new Special Needs Bill to be introduced in 2000.

The main generic proposals that will affect students with learning difficulties and disabilities are as follows:
- A new Learning and Skills Council will be established, replacing the FEFC and the former TECs, but with broader responsibilities, including adult and community education. There will be 50 local Learning and Skills Councils.

- This means that all learners, not just those in further education colleges, will be eligible for support under a common funding framework. The distinction between vocational and non-vocational courses will be weakened, enabling, for example, students with profound and multiple learning difficulties to have access to funded courses.
- OFSTED will inspect 16–19 provision and a new inspectorate will be established for all post-19 training outside higher education.
- A range of qualifications will be developed for all post-16 teaching and training staff.
- It seems likely that the new legislation will be strengthened by the adoption by the government of the recommendations of the Disability Rights Commission and report of the Disability Rights Task Force (DfEE 1999e).

Challenges ahead

In creating a more inclusive educational system, government needs to confront a number of interrelated major challenges.

The future of LEAs

Traditionally, LEAs have been at the heart of planning and provision for children with exceptional needs but it is no secret that their future role is uncertain. The previous government seriously weakened the roles, responsibilities and funding of LEAs and did its best through political and financial incentives to encourage schools to opt out of LEA control and become grant-maintained. Governments increased their range of duties but insisted that they in turn delegated greater proportions of funding to schools. At one time, it looked as though responsibility for exceptional needs would be all that was left of LEA duties: hardly a foundation for inclusion. The status of LEAs was partially restored with the change of government but ministers are quite prepared to replace an individual LEA if its performance falls short, by the criteria laid down by OFSTED for LEA inspection.

Whatever criticism may be levelled at LEAs, it is hard to imagine how planning and provision for children with exceptional needs across a large geographical area could take place without them. They have a statutory role in drawing up and implementing statements – now held by just under 250,000 children – around 1,500 for each LEA on average. They have to bid for and administer complex funding fairly and transparently and they have a key role in supporting schools involved in the management of change.

No doubt OFSTED will, in due course, publish a report of the performance of all inspected LEAs in the field of exceptional needs planning and provision. Existing reports reflect concerns about persisting delays in the completion of statements, complaints by schools of lack of professional support and advice in moving towards inclusive practice and in funding provision and growing evidence of parental dissatisfaction, as reflected in SEN Tribunal appeals. On the other hand, there is evidence that a number of LEAs that are not necessarily hitting the headlines are providing leadership and support in developing effective inclusive practice.

A recent DfEE funded study conducted by the Centre for Educational Needs at the University of Manchester provides a snapshot of LEAs at a critical transition point in moving towards more inclusive practice (Ainscow *et al.* 1998). With the help of LEA and school staff, an LEA review framework was developed to enable LEAs to evaluate their existing arrangements. The framework takes the form of a set of indicators that were considered relevant to the development of inclusive policies.

The indicators were:
- LEA policies encourage inclusive schooling;
- pupils attend a local mainstream school;
- schools are organised to respond to pupil diversity; and
- agencies work together to support the development of inclusive practice.

In general, although the 12 participating LEAs were strongly committed to inclusion and were able to report significant progress, the study reflected the need for greater clarity and more specific national guidance and leadership from the centre in relation to a number of key issues.

- How can LEA policies be designed to influence classroom practice?
- What are the areas of practice over which the LEA continues to have direct control?
- What other aspects of policy should be influenced (or permeated by) the inclusive agenda?
- In what ways can LEAs create a greater consensus among stakeholder groups about inclusive education?

In addition to policy, a number of other headings generated key questions and issues for discussion, including: funding strategies; processes and structures; the management of change; partnerships; and external influences. The study as a whole reflected not only the difficulties being experienced by LEAs but also the commitment to overcoming them within the limits of their powers and responsibilities. Funding issues proved to be particularly problematic. It was not simply a matter of LEAs demanding more resources to achieve change but of finding new mechanisms of allocating resources both to LEAs and to schools that would be seen as consistent both with the principles and practice of inclusion and with delegation of decision making to schools.

Alternatives to statements?

In looking to the future, we are bound to ask whether statements are here to stay or whether a better alternative can be devised. At first, it is hard to imagine how provision for vulnerable children would be protected without the 'guarantee' of a statement. There can be little doubt that without statements and their associated funding, we would not have arrived at a situation where 60 per cent of children with statements are in mainstream schools.

When statements were first introduced nearly 20 years ago, they were welcomed as a way of meeting the individual needs of children, giving rights to parents and at the same time providing a funded guarantee to specific forms of provision. With the passage of time, the delegation of funding to schools, weakened LEAs, a much more ruthless and competitive climate in the education system as a whole and a more prescriptive role for central government, the context and climate in which statements are planned and delivered has changed out of all recognition. Mary Warnock herself has expressed the wish that her committee had never conceived the idea in the first place and would like to see statements abolished. From an inclusion perspective, statements are divisive, since they draw a line between the small minority in each school who are funded through statements and other pupils on the SEN register, thus creating yet another set of categories.

Money, money, money

Decisions about the future of statements are inextricably bound up with much more fundamental decisions about how schools are to be funded and about finding better ways of ensuring that funding reflects the distinctive needs of each school.

Very recently, the government has conceded that the whole system of per capita funding in primary and secondary schools is deeply flawed and in need of review and that the variations in such funding between LEAs is inequitable. We can only hope that this review will produce a more rational and equitable system of funding for all pupils and that the funding available to schools will enable them to meet a much wider range of individual needs within their own resources.

There is general agreement that current methods of funding are unfair and ineffectual but little agreement on alternatives. For children not on statements, attempts are now being to develop proxy indicators of social deprivation that are less insensitive than free school meals, with the aim of developing funding formulas that would enable schools to take more responsibility for determining priorities. These include indices based on post code, child protection data, dental service data, crime statistics, casual admissions, number of pupils registered as needing support for English as an additional language and a composite 'z score' index (Moore 2000).

The issues are complex but hopefully not insoluble. In a symposium on resource allocation for inclusion, Moore (2000) pinpointed some fundamental principles and rightly identified the Code of Practice as the chief obstacle to inclusive funding.

> As local authorities move towards funding schools in partnership with other agencies, rather than individual pupils, in pursuance of a policy of inclusion, so schools will need to place less reliance on identifying individual pupils' needs and concentrate more on addressing whole school issues that arise out of planning for diversity. Further . . . the LEA will need to find alternative methods of funding to those which require a head count of individual pupils at each stage of the Code of Practice . . . which, with its accumulative stages of resource allocation does not easily support such a shift in emphasis.
>
> (Moore 2000)

Statements were originally intended to guarantee the specific resources needed by the individual child. But as time has gone on, it has become clear that 'tying money to individual children' is not necessarily the best way to promote inclusion. It may also lead to confrontation with parents who are naturally concerned that resources specified on their child's statement are spent on their child and on nothing else. For example, parents of a child funded by a statement are likely to protest if an LSA is used a resource for the class as a whole. The argument has come full circle. The 'flexible' use of the time of an LSA may do more to create an inclusive classroom than the same amount of time spent on an individual child. In practice, as we have seen in reviewing the research (Chapter 8), LSAs are increasingly used in this way. If they are funded from the school's own budget, this is not a problem.

The good news on funding for inclusion comes from the substantial increases to the Standards Fund (the most accessible summary is provided on the CSIE website (CSIE 1999)). The main source is likely to be Section 18 but other sections are also relevant.

Section 18 supports projects that:
- promote inclusion for pupils with SENs in mainstream schools and develop and extend links between special and mainstream settings – the projects may focus on: facilitating better or increased levels of inclusion with their peers in mainstream settings; devising and implementing reintegration programmes for specific pupils or boosting outreach links between special and mainstream settings;

- provide targeted support for children with, or at risk of developing emotional and behavioural difficulties – the project may focus on: costs of trialing or evaluating projects aimed at difficulties developed during the primary years; facilitating the return of children with difficulties to mainstream settings or identifying and providing for the learning needs of pupils with mental health problems.

Also included are support for SLT and parent partnership, including conciliation and training for SENCOs, teachers, LSAs and governors (CSIE 1999).

Before leaving the subject of funding, I would like to make an entirely outrageous suggestion, namely that the DfEE or the newly created regions assume responsibility for the payment of fees for pupils in residential special schools that are not run by the LEA, using a combination of top slicing and additional funding. This would cover all previously LEA funded placements in non-maintained and independent special schools, including those in other countries. An even more unthinkable next step would be for all special school placements to be funded on a regional basis, using the newly created DfEE regions for this purpose. This would be justified by the uneven distribution of special schools across LEAs that owes more to history, geography and politics than to rational planning. The advent of new unitary authorities, some with no special schools and some with more than they can handle, justifies 'thinking the unthinkable', or perhaps something approaching it.

My reason for making this suggestion is that it is totally inequitable for LEAs to have to fund such placements. Every £1,000 spent in this way is at the expense not only of the wider group of children with exceptional needs but of all other children. The cost of placing one child in some independent special schools is now approaching £100,000 a year: enough to pay for several SENCOs or support teachers and, at present rates of pay, perhaps a dozen LSAs. This argument is all the stronger if LEAs are forced into funding such placements against their own judgement by decisions of the SEN Tribunal or the courts. However, they also apply even if the LEA agrees that the child's needs are best met outside their own area.

What future for special schools?

The future of special schools in an inclusive educational system is a major policy tension not only for special schools but for all schools and for society as a whole. The question at issue is whether the continuation of a system of segregated special education is compatible with a commitment to inclusion, social justice and human rights. It is not about the closure of special schools in the short term or whether the needs of around 100,000 children now in special schools could be satisfactorily met in mainstream schools tomorrow. The issue is one of principle and policy that will affect children not yet in the system.

A policy review of the role of special schools is timely for a whole variety of reasons. Firstly, no national policy on inclusion would be complete without such a review. Secondly, the past decade has seen a vast increase in the number of pupils with statements in mainstream schools: some 60 per cent of all pupils with statements at the present time, the percentage rising every year. This means that many children who would previously have been sent to special schools are now attending mainstream schools full time, with appropriate levels of support deriving from a statement. This in itself provides justification for a review of the children in special schools as well as a reappraisal of the policy at the level of the LEA and of central government.

A commitment to encouraging many flowers to bloom is not some recent political aberration but rather a characteristic of English education. A country with a long tradition of coexistence of allegedly comprehensive primary and secondary schools alongside selective and independent schools will not find major inconsistencies in the continuation of segregated special schools for a minority of children with exceptional needs while all other schools are being encouraged to adopt inclusive policies and practices.

The government's silence on the fundamental principle is a matter of political expediency and reflects undertakings given to the present generation of parents and teachers. It is justified by reference to the need for a 'continuum of provision to match the continuum of need' and by promises made to parents that special schools, like grammar schools and independent schools, are safe with them and have a role to play in the future. This may also be intended to reassure those mainstream teachers who have legitimate doubts about the implications of inclusion and need to know that special schools will remain an option for children whose needs could not be met in mainstream education.

The government has set up a working party with rather limited terms of reference that seem to preclude any consideration of alternatives to the present system. Its remit is to 'identify and disseminate examples of good practice in establishing effective links between special and mainstream schools within the context of inclusive education'. A CD-ROM is being published in the summer of 2000 and every LEA will be offered a training day, which will be run in association with NASEN. There is already a good deal of research on links between special and mainstream schools but it will be useful to bring this up to date.

LEAs are required to produce a policy on inclusion and a support plan as part of their overall education development plans, but research commissioned by the DfEE reflected considerable 'confusion and uncertainty on the part of LEAs on what is meant by inclusion in relation to educational provision' (Ainscow *et al.* 1999), suggesting that the least the DfEE can do is to set out a series of alternative plans. LEAs could also be required to publish a long-term plan for the future of their special schools and how in the short and medium term such schools will contribute to the development of inclusive policy and practice.

In the meantime, LEAs could be asked to provide information on the number of pupils transferred from each special school to mainstream provision: less than 1,000 – or around 1 per cent – did so in 1998–99, whereas 3,000 children travelled in the other direction (DfEE 1999i). This contrasts with an earlier Audit Commission and HMI report (1992) based on 12 LEAs, which found that special schools transferred one child in 60 per year to mainstream schools.

Whatever view is taken of the role of special schools in a more inclusive system, the government seems unwilling to provide any clear leadership. The steps it has taken are useful but only skirt around the edge of a policy. In the meantime, the policy is essentially one of status quo, apart from welcome additional funding to promote links and good practice.

In the absence of more up-to-date information at national level, a number of questions suggest themselves:

- Are special schools routinely considering whether any of their pupils could be transferred to mainstream schools with appropriate levels of support?
- How often is this possibility considered at annual reviews of children in special schools?
- Would special schools lose income if funding follows the pupil and could this be a perverse incentive?
- How many annual reviews include a SENCO from an appropriate mainstream school who could contribute to discussion on how the child's needs could be met in the mainstream setting and what resources and adaptations might be necessary to enable this to happen?
- What support is given to parents who want at least to explore the possibility of their child moving to a mainstream school?

So what do we know about the work of special schools? According to DfEE statistics, the number of maintained special schools in England fell by 15 per cent in the period 1986–96, from 1,405 to 1,191, but the number of pupils in these schools has remained steady at just under 100,000. The average size of the schools has risen from 73 to 80 (DfEE 1999d). Some new schools for children with emotional and behavioural difficulties have been created in response to inexorable demands for alternatives to mainstream schools. This is also seen in the galloping increase in permanent exclusions discussed in Chapter 5 and also in the growth of pupil referral units since the early 1990s.

The available statistics (which are none too reliable) reflect enormous variations. For example, Wandsworth has 2.6 per cent of its pupils in special schools, compared with 0.32 for Newham (Male 1998). Newham is exceptional in having closed all but one if its special schools and having placed all other children in mainstream schools, but similar area-wide policies have been developed in other LEAs, including Nottinghamshire and Cornwall. Even a brief examination of the official statistics on the proportion of pupils in special schools does suggest that alternatives to special school placement are being considered in several places.

The most comprehensive information about the work of special schools comes from an analysis of inspections of some 1,300 special schools carried out between 1994 and 1998 (OFSTED 1999d). Although the report does not address any of the questions posed above, the overall evaluation reflects considerable improvements in the work of the schools.

- By the end of the period, pupils were making at least satisfactory progress in nine out of ten schools – this proportion is comparable with mainstream schools.
- The greatest improvement over time took place in EBD schools.
- The quality of teaching was satisfactory or better in nine out of ten schools but was lowest in EBD schools.
- Pupils' attitudes to their learning were satisfactory or good in almost all schools.
- Behaviour was satisfactory or good in the great majority of schools.
- Fewer than half the schools had satisfactory practice in the assessment and recording pupils' progress.

The OFSTED report also provides a brief LEA context, based partly on its early experience of LEA inspections. Their report suggests that LEAs are concentrating on improving facilities and practice rather than in reviewing the role of special schools within the broad spectrum of provision. This confirms the picture of LEA uncertainty about the implications of an inclusive policy reflected in recent research (Ainscow *et al.* 1999).

Conclusions

As we enter the 21st century, we have reason to be positive about the prospects for more inclusive schools and a more inclusive society. The foundations are beginning to be laid, the building blocks are ready to be put in place, the economic outlook is promising and the money is beginning to flow. Above all, government policies are underpinned by clear statements of values and principle – for example those included in the new curriculum.

Perhaps the most important challenge for the future is to enable children and young people to speak for themselves, even if they challenge the system and the views of their families and the professionals who work with them. This process must begin in schools, in partnership with parents. It moves into a new dimension when young people leave school. At this stage, the quality of their lives and, in extreme cases, their very survival, depend on their ability to exercise choice and self-determination.

Schools are society's agents for the socialisation of its young and have not traditionally seen it as part of their role to support their students in criticising the system or the decisions made on their behalf by others. But if we are concerned with promoting autonomy and personal growth, we have to prepare young people to confront the discrimination and underestimation that they are likely to encounter in a system still working towards inclusion.

Abbreviations

ACSET	Advisory Committee on the Supply and Education of Teachers	GEST	Grants for Educational Support and Training
APU	Assessment and Performance Unit	GNVQ	General National Vocational Qualification
AT	attainment target	GP	general practitioner
BCODP	British Council of Organisations of Disabled People	GTC	General Teaching Council
		HELIOS	Handicapped Europeans Living in an Open Society
BEd	Bachelor of Education	ICT	information and communications technology
CAME	Cognitive Acceleration through Maths Education		
CASE	Cognitive Acceleration through Science Education	IEP	individual education plan
		ILEA	Inner London Education Authority
		INSET	in-service education and training
CPD	continuing professional development	IPSEA	Independent Panel Supporting Special Education Advice
CSIE	Centre for Studies in Inclusive Education	IT	information technology
		ITE	initial teacher education
DES	Department of Education and Science	LEA	local education authority
		LSA	learning support assistant
DfE	Department for Education	MENCAP	Royal Society for Mentally Handicapped Children and Adults
DfEE	Department for Education and Employment		
		MP	member of parliament
DoH	Department of Health	NASEN	National Association for Special Educational Needs
DPI	Disabled Persons International		
DRC	Disability Rights Commission	NCC	National Curriculum Council
EAZ	education action zone	NCE	National Commission on Education
EFA	Education for All		
EPA	educational priority area	NCH	National Children's Homes
EU	European Union	NFER	National Foundation for Educational Research
EYDCP	Early Years Development and Childcare Partnership		
		NGO	non-governmental organisation
FEFC	Further Education Funding Council	NHS	National Health Service
		NLS	National Literacy Strategy
GCE	General Certificate of Education	NNS	National Numeracy Strategy
GCSE	General Certificate of Secondary Education	NPQHT	National Professional Qualification for Head Teachers

OECD	Organisation for Economic Cooperation and Development	SEN	special educational needs
OFSTED	Office for Standards in Education	SENCO	special educational needs coordinator
PGCE	Postgraduate Certificate in Education	SENTC	Special Educational Needs Training Consortium
PPO	parent partnership officer	SLT	speech and language therapy
PRU	pupil referral unit	TEC	Training and Enterprise Council
PSHE	personal, social and health education	TGAT	Task Group on Assessment and Testing
QCA	Qualifications and Curriculum Authority	TTA	Teacher Training Agency
		UN	United Nations
SCAA	School Curriculum and Assessment Authority	UNESCO	United Nations Educational, Scientific and Cultural Organisation
SEAC	Schools Examination and Assessment Council	WHO	World Health Organisation

References

Abbring, I. and Meijer, C. J. W. (1994) 'Italy', in Meijer, C. J. W. *et al.* (eds) *New Perspectives in Special Education: A Six Country Study of Integration*, 9–24. London: Routledge.

Acheson, D. (chair) (1999) *An Independent Enquiry into Inequalities in Health*, London: The Stationery Office.

Ainscow, M. (1994) *Special Needs in the Classroom: A Teacher Education Guide*. London: Jessica Kingsley and UNESCO.

Ainscow, M. (1999) *Understanding The Development of Inclusive Schools*. London: Falmer Press.

Ainscow, M. *et al.* (1998) *Effective Practice in Inclusion and in Special and Mainstream Schools Working Together*. London: DfEE (Research Report).

Alderson, P. (ed.) (1999) *Learning and Inclusion: The Cleves School Experience*. London: David Fulton Publishers.

Armstrong, D. (1995) *Power and Partnership in Education: Parents, Children and Special Educational Needs*. London: Routledge.

Armstrong, F. and Barton, L. (eds) (1999) *Disability, Human Rights and Education: Cross-Cultural Perspectives*. Milton Keynes: Open University Press.

Armstrong, F. *et al.* (eds) (2000) *Inclusive Education: Policy, Contexts and Comparative Perspectives*. London: David Fulton Publishers.

Atkins, H. (1999) 'The literacy strategy in schools for pupils with severe and profound learning difficulties', *SLD Experience* **24**, 7.

Audit Commission and HMI (1992) *Getting in on the Act*. London: HMSO.

Ball, C. (1994) *Start Right*. London: Royal Society of Arts.

Ball, C. (1999) 'Quality and professionalism in early childhood', in Abbott, L. and Moylett, H. (eds) *Early Education Transformed*, 41–7. London: Falmer Press.

Balshaw, M. (1999) *Help in the Classroom*, 2nd edn. London: David Fulton Publishers.

Barker-Lunn, J. (1970) *Streaming in the Primary School*. London: NFER.

Bastiani, J. (ed.) (1997) *Home–school Work in Multi-cultural Settings*. London: David Fulton Publishers.

Bastiani, J. and Beresford, E. (1995) *Home–school Policies: A Practical Guide*. London: JET Publications.

Bastiani, J. and Wyse, B. (1999) *Introducing Your Home–school Agreement*. London: Royal Society of Arts.

Bearne, E. (1996) *Differentiation and Diversity in the Primary Curriculum*. London: Routledge.

Berger, A. and Gross, J. (1999) *Teaching the Literacy Hour in an Inclusive Classroom*. London: David Fulton Publishers.

Berger, A. *et al.* (1999) *Implementing the Literacy Hour for Pupils with Learning Difficulties*. London: David Fulton Publishers.

Blamires, M. (1999) 'Universal design for learning: re-establishing differentiation as part of the inclusion agenda?' *Support for Learning* **14**(4), 158–63.

Blamires, M. *et al.* (1997) *Parent–teacher Partnership: Practical Approaches to Meet Special Educational Needs.* London: David Fulton Publishers.

Blunkett, D. (2000) *Raising Aspirations in the 21st Century.* London: DfEE.

Booth, T. (1999a) 'Inclusion and exclusion policy in England: who controls the agenda?' in Armstrong, D. *et al.* (eds) *Inclusive Education: Contexts and Comparative Perspectives,* 78–98. London: David Fulton Publishers.

Booth, T. (1999b) 'Viewing inclusion from a distance: gaining perspective from comparative study', *Support for Learning* **14**(4), 164–8.

Booth, T. and Ainscow, M. (eds) (1998) *From Them to Us: An International Study of Inclusion in Education.* London: Routledge.

Booth, T. *et al.* (1998) 'England: inclusion and exclusion in a competitive system', in Booth, T. and Ainscow, M. (eds) *From Them to Us: An International Study of Inclusion in Education,* 193–225. London: Routledge.

British Psychological Society (1999) *Professional Practice of Educational Psychologists.* Leicester: BPS, Division of Educational and Child Psychology.

Bronfenbrenner, U. (1974) *Is Early Identification Effective?* Washington, DC: US Department of Health and Welfare.

Burke, B. (1999) 'LEA support services: a Newham perspective', in Norwich, B. (ed.) *Rethinking Support for More Inclusive Schooling,* 18–24. Tamworth: NASEN.

Buzzi, I. (1995) 'Italy', in O'Hanlon, C. (ed.) *Inclusive Education in Europe,* 75–81. London: David Fulton Publishers.

Byers, R. (1998) 'Personal and social development for pupils with learning difficulties', in Tilstone, C. *et al.* (eds) *Promoting Inclusive Practice,* 39–61. London and New York: Routledge.

Cameron, S. and White, M. (eds) (1996) *The Portage Early Intervention Model: Making the Difference for Families Across the World.* Yeovil: National Portage Association.

Campaign for People with Mental Handicap (1987) *Begin at the Beginning: An Enquiry into Early Support for Families with a Handicapped Baby.* London: CMH (now Values in Action).

Campbell, J. and Oliver, M. (1996) *Disability Politics: Understanding Our Past, Changing Our Future.* London: Routledge.

Carpenter, B. (ed.) (1997) *Families in Context: Emerging Trends in Family Support and Early Intervention.* London: David Fulton Publishers.

Carr, J. (1995) *Down's Syndrome Children Growing Up.* Cambridge: Cambridge University Press.

Centre for Longitudinal Studies (1999) *Cohort Studies Newsletter,* no. 7.

Centre for Studies in Integrated Education (1986) *Caught in the Act?* Bristol: CSIE.

Centre for Studies in Inclusive Education (1999) *CSIE: Money for Inclusion.* http://inclusion.uwe.ac.uk/csie/moneyforinclusion.htm (accessed May 2000).

Centre for Studies in Inclusive Education (2000) *Index for Inclusion: Developing Learning and Participation in Schools.* Bristol: CSIE and London: DfEE.

Chalfant, J. C. *et al.* (1979) 'Teacher assistance teams: a model for within-building problem solving', *Learning Disability Quarterly* **2**(3), 85–96.

Charlton, T. (1998) 'Enhancing school effectiveness through using peer support strategies with pupils and teachers', *Support for Learning* **13**(2), 50–53.

Clarke, C. *et al.* (1997) *New Directions in Special Needs.* London: Cassell.

Cline, T. (ed.) (1992) *The Assessment of Special Educational Needs: International Perspectives.* London: Routledge.

Coard, B. (1971) *How the West Indian Child is Made Educationally Subnormal by the Education System.* London: New Beacon Books.

Commission on Social Justice (1994) *Social Justice: Strategies for National Renewal.* London: Vintage.

Corbett, J. (1996) *Bad-mouthing: The Language of Special Needs*. London: Falmer Press.

Cox, T. (ed.) (2000a) *Combating Educational Disadvantage: Meeting the Needs of Vulnerable Children*. London: Falmer Press.

Cox, T. (2000b) 'Introduction', in Cox, T. (ed.) *Combating Educational Disadvantage: Meeting the Needs of Vulnerable Children*, 1–14. London: Falmer Press.

Croll, P. and Moses, D. (1985) *One in Five*. London: Routledge and Kegan Paul.

Croll, P. and Moses, D. (2000) *Special Needs in the Primary School: One in Five?* London: Cassell.

Cunningham, C. C. (1994) 'Telling parents their child has a disability', in Mittler, P. and Mittler, H. (eds) *Innovations in Family Support for People with Learning Disabilities*, 85–104. Chorley: Lisieux Hall Publications.

Daniels, H. and Garner, P. (eds) (1999) *World Year Book of Education: Inclusive Education*. London: Kogan Page.

Danks, C. (1999) 'Some current policy issues', in Norwich, B. (ed.) *Rethinking Support for More Inclusive Schooling*, 13–17. Tamworth: NASEN.

Daunt, P. (1991) *Meeting Disability: A European Response*. London: Cassell.

Daunt, P. (1993a) 'Western Europe', in Mittler, P. *et al.* (eds) (1993) *World Year Book of Education: Special Needs Education*, 89–100. London: Kogan Page.

Daunt, P. (1993b) 'The "New Democracies" of Central and Eastern Europe', in Mittler, P. *et al.* (eds) *World Year Book of Education: Special Needs Education*, 101–7. London: Kogan Page.

Davie, R. *et al.* (1972) *From Birth to Seven: A Report of the National Child Development Study 1958*. London: National Children's Bureau.

Dearing, R. (1993) *Review of the National Curriculum and Its Assessment*. London: SCAA.

Department for Education (1994) *Code of Practice on the Identification and Assessment of Special Educational Needs*. London: DfE.

Department for Education (1995) *Our Children's Education: The Updated Parents' Charter*. London: HMSO.

Department for Education and Employment (1997a) *Excellence for All Children*. London: The Stationery Office.

Department for Education and Employment (1997b) *Excellence in Schools*. London: DfEE.

Department for Education and Employment (1998a) *Meeting Special Educational Needs: A Programme of Action*. London: DfEE.

Department for Education and Employment (1998b) *£75 Million Boosts Radical Education Action Zones to Raise Standards,* press release, 23 June 1998. http://www.dfee.gov.uk/eaz/intro.htm (accessed May 2000).

Department for Education and Employment (1999a) *Meeting the Childcare Challenge: A Framework and Consultation Document*. London: The Stationery Office.

Department for Education and Employment (1999b) *Early Years Development and Childcare Partnership: Planning Guidance 1999–2000*. London: DfEE.

Department for Education and Employment (1999c) *Sure Start: Making a Difference for Children and Families*. London: DfEE.

Department for Education and Employment (1999d) *DfEE Statistical First Release: Special Educational Needs in England: January 1999*. London: DfEE and Government Statistical Service.

Department for Education and Employment (1999e) *From Exclusion to Inclusion. Report of the Disability Rights Task Force*. London: DfEE.

Department for Education and Employment (1999f) Social inclusion: pupil support. Circular 10/99. London: DfEE.

Department for Education and Employment (1999g) *Meet the Challenge: Education Action Zones*. London: DfEE.

Department for Education and Employment (1999h) *Excellence in Cities*. London: DfEE.

Department for Education and Employment (1999i) *Statistics of Education: Special Educational*

Needs in England: January 1999, Issue 12/99 (October). London: The Stationery Office.

Department for Education and Employment (2000) *Professional Development: Support for Teaching and Learning*, consultation document. London: DfEE.

Department for Education and Employment and Qualifications and Curriculum Authority (1998) *Supporting the Target Setting Process: Guidance for Effective Target Setting for Pupils with Special Educational Needs*. London: DfEE.

Department for Education and Employment and Qualifications and Curriculum Authority (1999) *The National Curriculum: Handbooks for Primary and Secondary Teachers*. London: DfEE.

Department of Education and Science (1968) *Psychologists in Education Services* (Summerfield Report). London: HMSO.

Department of Education and Science (1972) *Education: A Framework for Expansion*. Cmnd. 5174. London: HMSO.

Department of Education and Science (1978) *Special Educational Needs: Report of the Enquiry into the Education of Handicapped Children and Young People*. London: HMSO.

Department of Education and Science (1987a) *Report of the Task Group on Assessment and Testing*. London: HMSO.

Department of Education and Science (1987b) *A Special Professionalism: Report of the Further Education Teacher Training Working Group*. London: HMSO.

Department of Education and Science (1989a) *Discipline in Schools* (Elton Report). London: HMSO.

Department of Education and Science (1989b) *The National Curriculum: From Policy to Practice*. London: DES.

Department of Education and Science (1991) *Standards in Education: Annual Report of HM Chief Inspector of Schools*. London: HMSO.

Department of Health (1995) *Child Protection: Messages from Research*. London: HMSO.

Dew-Hughes, D. and Brayton, H. (1997) 'Initial teacher training and pupils with special educational needs', *Support for Learning* 12(4), 175–9.

Diniz, F. (1999) 'Race and special educational needs in the 1990s', *British Journal of Special Education* 26(4), 213–17.

Douglas, J. W. B. (1964) *The Home and the School*. London: Mcgibbon and Kee.

Doyle, M. B. (1997) *The Paraprofessional's Guide to the Inclusive Classroom: Working as a Team*. Baltimore, MD: Paul H. Brookes.

Dyson, A. (1997) 'Social and educational disadvantage: reconnecting the system', *British Journal of Special Education* 24(4), 152–7.

Dyson, A. (1999) 'Inclusion and inclusions: theories and discourses in inclusive education', in Daniels, H. and Garner, P. (eds) *World Year Book of Education: Inclusive Education*, 36–53. London: Kogan Page.

Evans, J. *et al.* (1999) *Collaborating for Effectiveness: Empowering Schools to be Inclusive*. Buckingham: Open University Press.

Evans, P. (1999) 'Globalisation and cultural transmission: the role of international agencies in developing inclusive practice', in Daniels, H. and Garner, P. (eds) *World Year Book of Education: Inclusive Education*, 229–37. London: Kogan Page.

Fagg, S. *et al.* (1990) *Entitlement for All in Practice: A Broad, Balanced and Relevant Curriculum for Pupils with Severe Learning Difficulties*. London: David Fulton Publishers.

Farrell, P. (1995) 'Some reflections on the role of educational psychologists', in Lunt, I. *et al.* (eds) *Psychology and Special Educational Needs*. Aldershot: Arena.

Farrell, P. (1997) *Teaching Pupils with Learning Difficulties*. London: Cassell.

Farrell, P. *et al.* (1999) *The Management, Role and Training of Learning Support Assistants*, research report RR 161. London: DfEE.

Feinstein, L. and Symons, J. (1999) *Attainment in Secondary Schools*, Oxford Economic Papers 51(2).

Ferri, E. (ed.) (1993) *Life at 33: Fifth Follow Up of the National Child Development Study.* London: National Children's Bureau and City University.

Feuerstein, R. (1980) *Instrumental Enrichment.* Baltimore, MD: University Park Press.

Fletcher-Campbell, F. (1994) *Still Joining Forces? A Follow-Up Study of Links between Ordinary and Special Schools.* Slough: NFER.

Fletcher-Campbell, F. and Lee, B. (1995) *Small Steps of Progress in the National Curriculum,* final report. Slough: NFER.

Forlin, C. (1995) 'Educators' beliefs about inclusive practices in Western Australia', *British Journal of Special Education* **22**(4), 179–85.

Frankenberg, W. *et al.* (1971) 'The revised Denver developmental screening test', *Journal of Paediatrics* **79**, 988–95.

Fullan, M. (1991) *The Meaning of Educational Change,* 2nd edn. London: Cassell.

Further Education Funding Council (1996) *Inclusive Learning: Report of the Learning Difficulties and Disabilities Committee.* London: FEFC (see Tomlinson 1996).

Furze, T. and Conrad, A. (1997) 'A review of parent partnership schemes', in Wolfendale, S. (ed.) *Working with Parents of SEN Children after the Code of Practice,* 82–97. London: David Fulton Publishers.

Garner, P. *et al.* (1995) *What Teachers Do: Developments in Special Education.* London: Paul Chapman Publishing.

Gartner, A. and Lipsky, D. (1997) *Inclusion and School Reform: Transforming America's Classrooms.* Baltimore, MD: Paul H. Brookes.

Gascoigne, E. (1995) *Working with Parents as Partners in SEN.* London: David Fulton Publishers.

Giangreco, M. (1997) 'Key lessons learned about inclusive education', *International Journal of Disability, Development and Education* **44**(3), 193–206.

Gipps, C. and Murphy, P. (1994) *A Fair Test? Assessment, Achievement and Equity.* Buckingham: Open University Press.

Glass, N. (1999) 'Sure Start: the development of an early intervention programme for young children in the United Kingdom', *Children and Society* **13**, 257–64.

Graham, S. and Harris, K. (eds) (1999) *Teachers Working Together: Enhancing the Performance of Students with Special Needs.* Cambridge, MA: Brookline Books.

Grant, J. (1991) *State of the World's Children.* Oxford: Unicef and Oxford University Press.

Gray, P. (1999) 'Policy issues raised by rethinking support', in Norwich, B. (ed.) *Rethinking Support for More Inclusive Schooling,* 9–12. Tamworth: NASEN.

Gregory, E. (2000) 'Recognising differences: reinterpreting family involvement in literacy', in Cox, T. (ed.) *Combating Educational Disadvantage: Meeting the Needs of Vulnerable Children,* 103–20. London: Falmer Press.

Gulliford, R. (1971) *Special Educational Needs.* London: Routledge and Kegan Paul.

Guralnik, M. (1991) 'The next decade of research on the effectiveness of early intervention', *Exceptional Children* **58**, 174–83.

Hall, J. (1997) *Social Devaluation and Special Education: The Right to Full Mainstream Inclusion and an Honest Statement.* London: Jessica Kingsley.

Halsey, A. (1972) *Educational Disadvantage.* London: HMSO.

Hanko, G. (1995) *Special Needs in Ordinary Schools: From Staff Support to Staff Development,* 3rd edn. London: David Fulton Publishers.

Hannon, P. (1995) *Literacy, Home and School: Research and Practice in Teaching Literacy Skills with Parents.* London: Falmer Press.

Hargreaves, D. (1982) *Challenge for the Comprehensive School.* London: Routledge.

Hart, S. (1992) 'Differentiation: way forward or retreat?' *British Journal of Special Education* **19**(1), 10–12.

Hegarty, S. (1993a) 'Reviewing the literature on integration', *European Journal of Special Needs Education* **8**(3), 194–200.

Hegarty, S. (1993b) *Meeting Special Needs in Ordinary Schools,* 2nd edn. London: Cassell.

Hegarty, S. *et al.* (1981) *Educating Pupils with Special Needs in the Ordinary School.* Windsor: NFER-Nelson,

Hornby, G. (1995) *Working with Parents of Children with Special Needs.* London: Cassell.

Hornby, G. (1999) 'Inclusion or delusion: can one size fit all?' *Support for Learning* **14**(4), 152–7.

Hornby, G. *et al.* (1997) *Controversial Issues in Special Education.* London: David Fulton Publishers.

House of Commons (1989) *Children Act 1989.* London: HMSO.

House of Commons (1990) *Starting with Quality*, Committee of Enquiry into the Quality of Educational Experiences Offered to 3 and 4 year olds (Chair: A. Rumbold). London: HMSO.

House of Commons Select Committee on Education (1996) *Special Educational Needs: The Working of the Code of Practice and the Tribunal.* London: HMSO.

Inner London Education Authority (1984) *Improving Secondary Education* (Hargreaves Report). London: ILEA.

Inner London Education Authority (1985) *Equal Opportunities for All?* (Fish Report). London: ILEA.

Jackson, S. (2000) 'Promoting the educational achievement of looked after children', in Cox, T. (ed.) *Combating Educational Disadvantage: Meeting the Needs of Vulnerable Children*, 65–80. London: Falmer Press.

Jackson, S. (2003) *By Degrees: The First Year – From Care to University.* London: National Children's Bureau.

Jenkinson, J. (1997) *Mainstream or Special? Educating Students with Disabilities.* London: Routledge.

Jensen, A. R. (1969) 'How much can we boost IQ and scholastic achievement?' *Harvard Educational Review* **39**, 1–123.

Johnstone, D. (1995) *Further Opportunities: Learning Difficulties and Disabilities in Further Education.* London: Cassell.

Jordan, A. (1994) *Skills in Collaborative Consultation.* London and New York: Routledge.

Jowett, S. and Baginsky, M. (1991) *Building Bridges: Parental Involvement in Schools.* Slough: NFER-Nelson.

Khan, J. and Russell, P. (1999) *Quality Protects: First Analysis of Management Action Plans with Special Reference to Children with Disabilities or Special Educational Needs and Families.* London: National Children's Bureau and DoH.

Khatleli, P. *et al.* (1995) 'Schools for all: national planning in Lesotho', in O'Toole, B. and McConkey, R. (eds) *Innovations in Developing Countries for People with Disabilities*, 135–60. Chorley: Lisieux Hall Press.

Kinder, K. *et al.* (2000) *Working Out Well: Effective Provision for Excluded Pupils.* Slough: NFER.

Kirk, S. A. (1964) 'Research in education', in Stevens, H. and Heber, R. (eds) *Mental Retardation.* Chicago, IL: Chicago University Press.

Kolvin, I. *et al.* (1990) *Continuities of Deprivation: The Newcastle 1000 Families Study.* Aldershot: Avebury.

Kumar, V. (1993) *Poverty and Inequality in the UK: The Effects on Children.* London: National Children's Bureau.

Lacey, P. and Lomas, J. (1993) *Support Services and the Curriculum.* London: David Fulton Publishers.

Landy, M. and Gains, C. (1996) *Inspecting Special Needs Provision in Schools.* London: David Fulton Publishers.

Lazar, L. and Darlington, R. (1982) 'The lasting effects of early education: a report from the consortium on longitudinal studies', *Monographs of the Society for Research in Child Development* **47**(2–3), serial 195.

Lewis, A. (1995a) *Primary Special Needs and the National Curriculum*, 2nd edn. London:

Lewis, A. (1995b) *Children's Understanding of Disability*. London: Routledge.

Lewis, A. (1996) 'Summative National Curriculum assessments of primary aged children with special needs', *British Journal of Special Education* **23**(1), 9–14.

Lindsay, G. and Desforges, M. (1998) *Baseline Assessment: Practice, Problems and Possibilities*. London: David Fulton Publishers.

Little, M. and Mount, K. (1999) *Prevention and Early Intervention with Children in Need*. Aldershot: Ashgate.

Male, D. (1998) 'Special educational needs statistics and trends', *Tizard Learning Disability Review* **3**(3), 40–45.

Mallett, R. (1997) 'A parental perspective on partnership', in Wolfendale, S. (ed.) *Working with Parents of SEN Children after the Code of Practice*, 27–40. London: David Fulton Publishers.

McBrayer, K. F. and McBrayer, P. A. (1999) 'Preparing Hong Kong schools to establish school-based problem-solving teams: a pre-pilot investigation', *Journal of International Special Needs Education* **2**, 7–14 (US Council for Exceptional Children).

McCallum, I. (1996) 'The chosen ones?', *Education*, 19 January, 1, 2–13.

McCallum, I. (1997) report, *Times Educational Supplement*, 18 April, 2.

McConkey, R. (1994) 'Early intervention: planning futures, shaping years', *Mental Handicap Research* **7**, 4–15.

McNamara, S. and Moreton, G. (1997) *Understanding Differentiation: A Teachers' Guide*. London: David Fulton Publishers.

Meijer, C. W. *et al.* (eds) (1994) *New Perspectives in Special Education: A Six Country Study of Integration*. London: Routledge.

Mittler, P. (1970) 'Introduction', in Mittler, P. (ed.) *Psychological Assessment of Mental and Physical Handicaps*. London: Methuen.

Mittler, P. (1990) 'Collaboration in the new era', *Division of Educational and Child Psychology Newsletter* **7**(2), 5–14.

Mittler, P. (1993) *Teacher Education for Special Educational Needs*. Tamworth: NASEN.

Mittler, P. (1994) 'Early intervention: ways forward', in Carpenter, B. (ed.) *Early Intervention: Where are We Now?* Oxford: Westminster College.

Mittler, P. (1995a) 'Professional development for special needs education', in Lunt, I. *et al.* (eds) *Psychology and Education for Special Needs*, 211–28. Aldershot: Ashgate.

Mittler, P. (1995b) 'Rethinking partnerships between parents and professionals', *Children and Society* **9**(3), 22–40.

Mittler, P. (1996a) 'Portage: the next 25 years', in Cameron, R. J. and White, M. (eds) *The Portage Early Intervention Model: Making the Difference for Families Across the World*, 3–10. Yeovil: National Portage Association.

Mittler, P. (1996b) 'Preparing for self advocacy', in Carpenter, B. *et al.* (eds) *Enabling Access: Effective Teaching and Learning for Pupils with Learning Difficulties*, 279–91 (revised edn in press). London: David Fulton Publishers.

Mittler, P. (1999) 'Equal opportunities – for whom?' *British Journal of Special Education* **26**(1), 3–7.

Mittler, P. (2000) 'Time to stop being special', in Miller, C. *et al.* (eds) *Effecting Change for Pupils with Special Educational Needs: A Celebration of the Contribution of Professor Ronald Gulliford*. Tamworth: NASEN.

Mittler, P. and McConachie, H. (eds) (1983) *Parents, Professionals and Mentally Handicapped People*. London: Croom Helm.

Mittler, P. and Platt, P. (1995) *Evaluation of Integration Pilot Programme in Lesotho*. Report to Save the Children Fund (UK) and Ministry of Education, Lesotho.

Mittler, P. and Sinason, V. (eds) (1996) *Changing Policy and Practice for People with Learning Difficulties*. London: Cassell.

Mittler, P. and Ward, J. (1970) 'The use of the Illinois test of psycholinguistic abilities on British

Mittler, P. and Ward, J. (1970) 'The use of the Illinois test of psycholinguistic abilities on British four year old children: a normative and factorial study', *British Journal of Educational Psychology* **40**(1), 43–54.

Mittler, P. *et al.* (eds) (1993) *World Year Book of Education: Special Needs Education*. London: Kogan Page.

Mittler, P. A. (1998) 'Inclusive schools, effective schools: first findings from a Hong Kong project', *Hong Kong Special Education Forum* **1**(2), 10–20.

Mittler, P. J. and Mittler, P. A. (2000) 'Training for inclusion', *Canadian Exceptionality* **9**, 39–56.

Moore, J. (2000) *Developments in Additional Resource Allocation to Promote Greater Inclusion*. Tamworth: NASEN.

Mortimore, P. and Whitty G. (2000) 'Can school improvement overcome the effects of disadvantage?' in Cox, T. (ed.) *Combating Educational Disadvantage: Meeting the Needs of Vulnerable Children*, 156–76. London: Falmer Press.

Mortimore, P. *et al.* (1988) *School Matters: The Junior Years*. Salisbury: Open Books.

Moylett, H. and Abbott, L. (1999) 'A vision for the future – reforming or transforming?' in Abbott, L. and Moylett, H. (eds) *Early Education Transformed*, 1–9. London: Falmer Press.

National Association for Special Educational Needs (1998) *Baseline Assessment: Benefits and Pitfalls*. Stafford: NASEN.

National Children's Home (1995) *NCH Factfile 1995*. London: NCH.

National Children's Home (1998) *NCH Factfile 1998*. London: NCH.

National Children's Home (2000) *NCH Factfile 2000*. London: NCH.

National Children's Homes (1999) *Action for Children. Factfile 1998*. London: NCH.

National Commission on Education (1993) *Learning to Succeed: A Radical Look at Education Today and Strategy for the Future*. London: Heinemann.

National Curriculum Council (1989a) *Implementing the National Curriculum – Participation by Pupils with Special Educational Needs*, Circular No. 5. York: NCC.

National Curriculum Council (1989b) *A Curriculum for All: Special Educational Needs in the National Curriculum*, Curriculum Guidance 2. York: NCC.

National Curriculum Council (1992) *The National Curriculum for Pupils with Severe Learning Difficulties*, Curriculum Guidance 9 and 10. York: NCC.

Norwich, B. (1996) 'Special needs education or education for all: connective specialisation and ideological impurity', *British Journal of Special Education* **23**(3), 100–104.

Norwich, B. (ed.) (1999) *Rethinking Support for More Inclusive Schooling*, Policy Options Paper No 1, 3rd series. Tamworth: NASEN.

Office for Standards in Education (1993) *Access and Achievement in Urban Education*. London: OFSTED.

Office for Standards in Education (1995) *Guidance on the Inspection of Nursery and Primary Schools*. London: HMSO.

Office for Standards in Education (1996) *Exclusions from Secondary Schools 1995/6*. London: OFSTED.

Office for Standards in Education (1997) *The SEN Code of Practice Two Years On*. London: OFSTED.

Office for Standards in Education (1998a) *Quality of Provision for Funded Four Year Old Children in Portage*. London: OFSTED.

Office for Standards in Education (1998b) *The National Numeracy Project: An HMI Evaluation*. London: OFSTED.

Office for Standards in Education (1998c) *Teacher Assessment in the Core Subjects at Key Stage 2: Policy and Practice*. London: OFSTED.

Office for Standards in Education (1999a) *Annual Report of Her Majesty's Chief Inspector of Schools – Standards and Quality in Education, 1997/1998*. London: OFSTED.

Office for Standards in Education (1999b) *The National Literacy Strategy: An Interim Evalua-*

Office for Standards in Education (1999c) *The SEN Code of Practice Three Years On: The Contribution of Individual Education Plans to the Raising of Standards of Pupils with Special Educational Needs* (HMI 221). London: OFSTED.

Office for Standards in Education (1999d) *Special Education 1994–1998: A Review of Special Schools, Secure Units and Pupil Referral Units in England.* London: The Stationery Office.

Office for Standards in Education (2000a) *Improving City Schools.* London: OFSTED.

Office for Standards in Education (2000b) *Annual Report of HM Chief Inspector of Schools, 1998/1999.* London: OFSTED.

Office for Standards in Education (2000c) *Inspecting Schools: The Framework.* London: OFSTED.

O'Hanlon, C. (ed.) (1995) *Inclusive Education in Europe.* London: David Fulton Publishers.

Organisation for Economic Cooperation and Development (1997) *Parents as Partners in Schooling.* Paris: OECD.

Organisation for Economic Cooperation and Development (1999) *Inclusive Education at Work: Including Students with Disabilities in Mainstream Schools.* Paris: OECD.

Osborne, F. and Millbank, J. (1987) *The Effects of Early Education: A Report from the Child Health and Education Study.* Oxford: Oxford University Press.

O'Toole, B. and McConkey, R. (eds) (1995) *Innovations in Developing Countries for People with Disabilities.* Chorley: Lisieux Hall Publications.

Oxfam International (1999a) *Education Now: Break the Cycle of Poverty.* Oxford: Oxfam Publications.

Oxfam International (1999b) *Education Now: Break the Cycle of Poverty*, media report. Oxford: Oxfam Publications.

Paige-Smith, A. (1997) 'The rise and impact of the parental lobby: including voluntary groups and the education of children with learning difficulties or disabilities', in Wolfendale, S. (ed.) *Working with Parents of SEN Children After the Code of Practice*, 41–54. London: David Fulton Publishers.

Parsons, C. and Castle, F. (1998) 'The cost of social exclusion in England', *International Journal of Inclusive Education* 2(4), 277–94.

Peter, M. (1996) 'Lobbying for special education', in Lunt, I. *et al.* (eds) *Psychology and Special Educational Needs.* Aldershot: Arena.

Phillips, S. *et al.* (1999) *Management Skills for SEN Coordinators in the Primary School.* London: Falmer Press.

Pijl, S. J. *et al.* (eds) (1997) *Inclusive Education: A Global Agenda.* London: Routledge.

Pilling, D. (1990) *Escape from Disadvantage.* London: Falmer Press.

Platt, P. (1989) 'Consultancy in action', in Bowers, T. (ed.) *Managing Special Needs*, 54–73. Buckingham: Open University Press.

Posternak, Y. (1979) *Integration of Handicapped Children and Adolescents in Italy.* Paris: OECD.

Pumfrey, P. and Mittler, P. (1989) 'Peeling off the label', *Times Educational Supplement*, October 13.

Qualifications and Curriculum Authority (1997) *Assessment and Reporting Arrangements at Key Stage 2* (ref. QCA 97/002). London: QCA and DfEE

Qualifications and Curriculum Authority and DfEE (1999) *Early Learning Goals.* London: QCA.

Reynolds, D. (1995) 'Using school effectiveness knowledge for children with special needs – the problems and possibilities', in Clark, C. *et al.* (eds) *Towards Inclusive Schools?*, 109–26. London: David Fulton Publishers.

Rieser, R. and Mason, M. (1990) *Disability Equality in the Classroom: A Human Rights Issue.* London: ILEA.

Rioux, M. and Bach, M. (eds) (1994) *Disability is not Measles: New Research Paradigms in Disability.* Toronto: Alan Roeher Institute.

Rose, R. *et al.* (1996) *Implementing the Whole Curriculum for Pupils with Learning Difficulties*, 2nd edn. London: David Fulton Publishers.

Rosenthal, L. and Jacobson, D. (1968) *Pygmalion in the Classroom*. London and New York: Holt, Rhinheart and Wiston.

Russell, P. (1997) 'Parents as partners: some early impressions of the impact of the Code of Practice', in Wolfendale, S. (ed.) *Working with Parents after the Code of Practice*. London: David Fulton Publishers.

Russell, P. (2000) 'Developing a comprehensive and integrated approach to early years services for children with special educational needs – opportunities and challenges in current government initiative', Paper to SEN Policy Options Group seminar on Early Years, London, December 1999. Stafford: NASEN (in press).

Rutter, M. *et al.* (1979) *Fifteen Thousand Hours: Secondary Schools and their Effect on Children*. London: Open Books.

Rutter, S. and Seyman, S. (1999) *He'll Never Join the Army*. A report of the Down's Syndrome Association survey into attitudes to people with Down's syndrome amongst medical professionals. Mitcham: Down's Syndrome Association.

Sammons, P. *et al.* (1995) *Key Characteristics of Effective Schools: A Review of School Effectiveness Research*. London: Institute of Education for OFSTED.

Saunders, L. (1996) 'QUASE (quantitative analysis for self evaluation) and the special education sector', in Fletcher-Campbell, F. (ed.) *Value Added and Special Educational Needs*, 1–6. Slough: NFER.

School Curriculum and Assessment Authority (1996a) *Desirable Outcomes for Children's Learning on Entering Compulsory Education*. London: HMSO.

School Curriculum and Assessment Authority (1996b) *Planning the Curriculum for Pupils with Profound and Multiple Learning Difficulties*. London: SCAA.

School Curriculum and Assessment Authority (1996c) *Supporting Pupils with Special Educational Needs: Key Stage 3. Consistency in Teacher Assessment*. London: SCAA.

School Curriculum and Assessment Authority (1997) *Baseline Assessment Scales: Teachers' Guide*. London: SCAA.

Schweinhart, J. L. *et al.* (1993) *Significant Benefits of the High Scope Perry Preschool Study Through Age 2–7*, Ypsilanti, MI.: High Scope Press.

Sebba, J. (1994) *History for All*. London: David Fulton Publishers.

Sebba, J. (1995) *Geography for All*. London: David Fulton Publishers.

Sebba, J. with Sachdev, D. (1997) *What Works in Inclusive Education?* Barkingside: Barnardos.

Sebba, J. *et al.* (1995) *Redefining the Whole Curriculum for Pupils with Learning Difficulties*. London: David Fulton Publishers.

Sewell, G. (1996) *Special Needs Provision: Assessment, Concern and Action*. London: Cassell.

Shorrocks, D. (1993) *Implementing National Curriculum Assessment in the Primary School*. London: Hodder and Stoughton.

Silver, H. and Silver, P. (1991) *An Educational War on Poverty: American and British Policy Making 1960–1980*. Cambridge: Cambridge University Press.

Simmons, K. (1997) 'Supporting parents at the special educational needs tribunal', in Wolfendale, S. (ed.) *Working with Parents of SEN Children After the Code of Practice*, 114–26. London: David Fulton Publishers.

Slee, R. (1998) 'High reliability organisations and liability students', in Slee, R. *et al.* (eds) *School Effectiveness for Whom? Challenges to the School Effectiveness and Improvement Movements*, 101–14. London: Falmer Press.

Slee, R. and Weiner, G. (1998) 'Introduction: school effectiveness for whom?' in Slee, R. *et al.* (eds) *School Effectiveness for Whom? Challenges to the School Effectiveness and Improvement Movements*, 1–10. London: Falmer Press.

Smith, D. and Tomlinson, S. (1989) *The School Effect: A Study of Multi-Racial Comprehensives*. London: Policy Studies Institute.

Social Exclusion Unit (1998) *Truancy and School Exclusion*. London: The Cabinet Office.

Special Educational Needs Training Consortium (1996) *Professional Development to Meet Special Educational Needs*. Stafford: Flash Ley Centre.

Special Educational Needs Tribunal (1999) *Annual Report 1988–1999*. London: DfEE.

Sylva, K. (1999) 'The role of research in explaining the past and shaping the future', in Abbott, L. and Moylett, H. (eds) *Early Education Transformed*, 164–79. London: Falmer Press.

Teacher Training Agency (1998a) *National Standards for Special Educational Needs Coordinators*. London: TTA.

Teacher Training Agency (1998b) *National Standards for Qualified Teacher Status*. London: TTA.

Teacher Training Agency (1998c) *National Standards for Head Teachers*. London: TTA.

Teacher Training Agency (1998d) *National Standards for Subject Leaders*. London: TTA.

Teacher Training Agency (1999) *National Special Educational Needs Specialists Standards*. London: TTA.

Teacher Training Agency (2000) *Using the National Standards for Special Educational Needs Coordinators*. London: TTA.

Thomas, G. (1992) *Effective Classroom Teamwork: Support or Inclusion?* London: Routledge.

Thomas, G. *et al.* (1998) *The Making of the Inclusive School*. London: Routledge.

Tod, J. (1999) 'IEPs: "Inclusive educational practices?"', *Support for Learning* 14(4), 184–8.

Tomlinson, J. (1996) *Inclusive Learning: Principles and Recommendations: A Summary of the FEFC Report*. London: FEFC.

Tomlinson, S. (1981) *Educational Subnormality: A Study on Decision Making*. London: Routledge and Kegan Paul.

Tomlinson, S. (2000) 'Ethnic minorities and education: new disadvantages', in Cox, T. (ed.) *Combating Educational Disadvantage: Meeting the Needs of Vulnerable Children*, 17–36. London: Falmer Press.

Topping, K. (1986) *Parents as Educators: Training Parents to Teach their Children*. London: Croom Helm and Cambridge, MA: Brookline Books.

Topping, K. (1988) *The Peer Tutoring Handbook: Promoting Cooperative Learning*. London: Croom Helm and Cambridge, MA: Brookline Books.

Topping, K. and Wolfendale, S. (eds) (1985) *Parental Involvement in Children's Reading*. London: Croom Helm.

Townsend, P. and Whitehead, N. (1988) *Inequalities in Health*. London: Penguin Books.

United Nations (1983) *World Programme of Action Concerning Disabled Persons*. Vienna and New York: United Nations.

United Nations (1989) *Convention on the Rights of the Child*. New York: United Nations.

United Nations (1993) *Standard Rules on the Equalisation of Opportunities for Disabled Persons*. New York: UN.

UNESCO (1994) *World Conference on Special Needs Education: Access and Quality* (includes Salamanca Declaration and Framework for Action). Paris: UNESCO.

UNESCO (1996) *Learning: The Treasure Within: Report of the Delors Commission on Education for the 21st Century*. Paris: UNESCO.

Vernon, J. (1999) *Parent Partnership and Special Educational Needs: Perspectives on Good Practice*, Research Report 162. London: DfEE.

Visser, J. (1993) *Differentiation: Making it Work*. Tamworth: NASEN.

Wade, J. (1999) 'Including all learners: QCA's approach', *British Journal of Special Education* 26(2), 80–82.

Wedge, P. and Prosser, H. (1973) *Born to Fail?* London: National Children's Bureau.

Westwood, P. (1997) *Commonsense Methods for Children with Special Needs*, 3rd edn. London: Routledge.

White, M. (1997) 'A review of the influence and effects of portage', in Wolfendale, S. (ed.)

Working with Parents of SEN Children After the Code of Practice, 10–26. London: David Fulton Publishers.

Who Cares? Trust (1999) *Equal Chances Practice Guide*. London: Who Cares? Trust and DoH.

Widlake, P. (1985) *Reducing Educational Disadvantage*. London: Routledge and Kegan Paul.

Winter, S. (2000) 'Peer power as an instructional resource', paper presented to International Special Education Congress, Manchester, July 24–8.

Wolfendale, S. (ed.) (1997) *Working with Parents of Children with SEN After the Code of Practice*. London: David Fulton Publishers.

Wolfendale, S. and Bastiani, J. (eds) (2000) *The Contribution of Parents to School Effectiveness*. London: David Fulton Publishers.

Wolfendale, S. and Cook, G. (1997) *Evaluation of Special Educational Needs Parent Partnership Schemes*. Research Report 34. London: DfEE.

Wolfendale, S. and Topping, K. (eds) (1996) *Family Involvement in Literacy*. London: Cassell.

Index